CAST MATES

SAM TWYFORD-MOORE is a writer and cultural critic. His first book, *The Rapids: Ways of Looking at Mania*, was published by NewSouth Publishing and the University of Toronto Press in North America. He was formerly Festival Director and CEO of the Emerging Writers' Festival. As a writer he has contributed to a wide range of publications, including the *Monthly*, *Senses of Cinema*, the *Los Angeles Review of Books*, the *Sydney Morning Herald*, and many others.

'Wry, erudite, engrossing, *Cast Mates* is a
red-carpet ride from home to Hollywood.'
BRIOHNY DOYLE

'More than a story of colourful characters and famous faces,
and more than a history of the movies, *Cast Mates* is an
illuminating and entertaining portrait of the relationship
between Australia and the United States.'
DAN GOLDING

'Passionate, opinionated, political, this journey through
Australia's iconic stars is meticulously researched and
absolutely enthralling. For lovers of Australian cinema
this is a must-read!'
MARGARET POMERANZ

'*Cast Mates* feels like the best kind of conversation in the
cinema foyer: astute, sharp-witted, and deliciously dishy,
excavating the sordid and startling tales of film history in a
country which has long seemed embarrassed of its screen.'
MICHAEL SUN

CAST MATES

AUSTRALIAN ACTORS IN HOLLYWOOD AND AT HOME

SAM TWYFORD-MOORE

NEWSOUTH

Warning: First Nations readers should be made aware that this book contains words, phrases and descriptions written by non-Indigenous people in the past that may be confronting and would be considered highly inappropriate today. First Nations readers should be aware that this book also contains the names of deceased persons.

A NewSouth book
Published by
NewSouth Publishing
University of New South Wales Press Ltd
University of New South Wales
Sydney NSW 2052
AUSTRALIA
https://unsw.press/

© Sam Twyford-Moore 2023
First published 2023

10 9 8 7 6 5 4 3 2 1

This book is copyright. Apart from any fair dealing for the purpose of private study, research, criticism or review, as permitted under the *Copyright Act*, no part of this book may be reproduced by any process without written permission. Inquiries should be addressed to the publisher.

 A catalogue record for this book is available from the National Library of Australia

ISBN: 9781742237541 (paperback)
        9781742238760 (ebook)
        9781742239705 (ePDF)

Design Josephine Pajor-Markus
Cover design Reg Abos
Cover image shutterstock / designium
Printer Griffin Press

All reasonable efforts were taken to obtain permission to use copyright material reproduced in this book, but in some cases copyright could not be traced. The author welcomes information in this regard.

This book is printed on paper using fibre supplied from plantation or sustainably managed forests.

CONTENTS

PROLOGUE: SYDNEY TO LOS ANGELES
AND BACK AGAIN   1

1   **THE PERFECT SPECIMEN:** ERROL FLYNN   14

2   **THE FORGOTTEN ELITE:** PETER FINCH   76

3   **THE RIGHT STUFF:** DAVID GULPILIL AM   138

4   **THE INTERPRETER:** NICOLE KIDMAN   199

EPILOGUE: WESTWARD EXPANSION   261

ACKNOWLEDGMENTS   280

NOTES   284

SELECT FILMOGRAPHY   294

INDEX   298

PROLOGUE
SYDNEY TO LOS ANGELES
AND BACK AGAIN

United before the same vision, enthralled by a common illusion, a populace might well believe itself to be a nation.

J. Hoberman, *The Dream Life*[1]

In 1982 a young musician named Russ Le Roq released a 7-inch vinyl with the aspirational title 'I Just Wanna Be Like Marlon Brando'. The title track had all the cheap jangle of any novelty single, but beneath its surface was serious, burning ambition. After all, Russ Le Roq was the pseudonym of one Russell Crowe, and Crowe did end up coming remarkably close to being just 'like Marlon Brando'. Indeed, he inherited one of Brando's signature roles in 2013, appearing in *Man of Steel* as Jor-El, the father of Superman, the very same role Brando had played in the original 1978 superheroic caper.

Crowe was on my mind at the tail end of the 2010s, when he seemed to be readying himself for further flirtations with

Brando-like levels of public eccentricity. At Crowe's age, Brando was about to shave his head and walk onto the Philippines-based set of Francis Ford Coppola's *Apocalypse Now* (1979), not having learnt his dialogue despite his $1 million advance. An ever-disruptive Brando descended into an increasingly odd public persona in the years that followed (Brando would be in Australia terrorising the cast and crew of *The Island of Dr. Moreau* in Cairns in the mid-1990s). Crowe, charging through his own middle age, wasn't far from prompting a similar intensity of head-scratching from the public when he was found in the press promoting 'The Art of Divorce', a Sotheby's-orchestrated auction of his own private collection of Australian art, guitars, watches, sporting memorabilia and, most curiously, personal keepsakes from the sets of his 30-odd-year career on film. The cover of the print catalogue – sold for $40 as a keepsake itself – featured a photograph of a silver-bearded Crowe, decked out in a tux, cocktail in hand, head invitingly tilted, toasting the prospective buyer. The staging was a masterclass in high Australian camp, and it left no mistake that this sale was all about Crowe's image – the wife Crowe was divorcing, singer and actor Danielle Spencer, was nowhere to be seen in the chaotic marketing collateral and attendant publicity blitz.

Much of the collection had previously been housed in his oddball 'Museum of Interesting Things', opened in 2008 to help boost tourism in the tiny northern stopover town of Nymboida – population count 298 (a dinosaur skull, which had been traded, over vodka, during a late-night drinking session with Leonardo DiCaprio might have been the most extreme object). Crowe clearly enjoyed the showmanship of his venture in 'museum making' as much then as he did a decade later. He also seemed completely aware of the perversity in testing the market value of his own legacy and that of the films he had starred in. Wider cultural worth, however, is a risky metric to invest in an auction, conferring the power of retrospective appreciation to a limited few with the necessary capital – just as the quality of a film isn't wholly determined by its box office performance.

In the lead-up to the actual auction, the collection was on display in a small space carved out within Sydney's cavernous Carriageworks cultural precinct. I dragged a friend along who wasn't at all keen on the idea, and was even less sold afterwards, but I was transfixed by what I saw. Crowe's upmarket garage sale seemed to speak to the way that Australian actors play a critical role in the way the nation sees – and, indeed, sells – itself. It did not matter that our sales representative wasn't actually an Australian. Despite having lived consistently in Australia since boyhood, Crowe has remained a citizen of New Zealand. In 2015, Crowe told a journalist that he had twice made applications to become an Australian citizen and was rejected on both attempts, a claim denied by the Department of Immigration, who issued a public retort saying, 'According to departmental records, Mr Crowe has not submitted an application for a permanent visa or for Australian citizenship.'[2] If Crowe could act as such a figurehead for Australian culture, and yet not hold citizenship, did it not reveal how fragile the concept of nationhood can be?

The individual items under the hammer, one by one, built a biography not only of the actor known as Russell Crowe but of the film industries he worked and played in for more than four decades, both in Australia and America. Crowe's chronological approach to the listings helped here. The auction's starting items were, after all, sourced from his pre-Hollywood work. Despite their prominence in the catalogue, they tended to stay within the auctioneers' estimates. For sale: a pair of faded maroon Doc Martens from *Romper Stomper*, which, surprisingly, made their estimate of between $10 000 and $12 000. Who would want a memento from the set of a bleached-out neo-Nazi drama shot in a bleak-looking Melbourne?

The very first item to come under the hammer was from one of the softest starting entries in Crowe's filmography – a small collection of modest costumes from Jocelyn Moorhouse's *Proof*. Released in 1991, Crowe plays a sprightly dish-pig who falls in with a blind photographer portrayed by Hugo Weaving. The young actor is pure light in the film – his boyish giggle is effervescent, a playfulness he would use sparsely, but which suited him so well when he did. The film carries a sad edge today: It was reported in the press at the time that Crowe and Moorhouse had clashed on her proposed adaptation of Murray Bail's *Eucalyptus*, with Crowe demanding rewrites. The *Age* suggested that he was delivering '11th-hour script suggestions'. According to the *New York Times*, Nicole Kidman's agent had said it had become 'a very volatile situation'.[3] Fox Searchlight, which was providing funding, withdrew support five days before shooting was supposed to start. The production collapsed. Moorhouse lamented in a later memoir that she 'was devastated: all my work had come to nothing. And I was sad that I had lost my friendship with Russell'.[4]

It was undeniable that Crowe had let Hollywood go to his head, which was a shame because while it might have appeared otherwise, Crowe was no overnight success there. Indeed, a number of Crowe's films on his way to becoming a legitimate player in the modern star system were false starts, works his auction briefly served to revive. A pair of iceskates, which sold for $671, represented *Mystery, Alaska,* Crowe's forgotten 1999 ice hockey film. A garish double-breasted purple suit that Crowe donned in the 1995 Denzel Washington – starring VR dystopia *Virtuosity* scored over $1800. Late-night TV satirist John Oliver was revealed as the buyer of Crowe's leather jockstrap (a winning bid of $8540) from his boxing biopic *Cinderella Man* (2005), along with a number of other costume pieces (spending $79 788 all up). Oliver donated the items to the last Blockbuster video store in Alaska, hoping to entice customers and save a small piece of America's fading film history. The store closed just a few months later, but Oliver's effort – joke or not – was testament that Crowe's auction had something serious to say about the preservation of movie culture.

The sense of accounting for legacy would not have been lost on Crowe. One scene in *Proof* shows a character putting together a composite of his image from photographs taken of different parts of his face. Throughout his career Crowe has, in a similar way, pieced together an image of himself to sell – as most actors do. In media interviews, he said it took over 12 months to put 'The Art of Divorce' together, and he seemed determined to explain the auction in curatorial terms – saying he matched items in a considered way, thinking not of their sale but of how they might 'go together'. In constructing a retrospective-as-auction – and vice versa – Crowe created a rare look into what exactly constitutes the lifespan of an acting career, what the culture permits a lasting reprieve, and what it lets die.

It only takes one film to cut through, though. Curtis Hanson's razor-sharp 1997 crime epic *L.A. Confidential* showed up in the auction only via a 'collection of ephemera' – two flimsy signed promotional photographs, and a small selection of props lifted from the set, including a folded menu from The Formosa, a real-life LA restaurant that opened in 1939, which featured in the fictional film. The red-tinged interiors formed the backdrop to a scene in which a cop accosts a lookalike Lana Turner who turns out to actually be Lana Turner.[5] It was a little piece of Los Angeles lore that served as a reminder that Crowe and his Australian cast mate, Guy Pearce, had been introduced in a funhouse mirroring of Hollywood. Crowe had used the opportunity to make full use of his trademark antipodean reticence. His brutal portrayal of the hard-nosed, tight-lipped cop Wendell 'Bud' White – splintering a wooden chair with his bare hands – took the stock figure of the detective out of the shadows and into the Australian-like glare of LA light. Film critic J. Hoberman would use *L.A. Confidential* as the key to unlocking what he called 'Sunshine Noir'. In a piece for *Artforum*, Hoberman explained: 'Noir is its own place, but it belongs to Los Angeles; it is a dark shadow cast by the radiant City of Angels. A particular subset of film noir deals with local history – the city's or the movies.'[6]

The fact that *L.A. Confidential* was a movie particularly engaged with the city that gave it its punchy name was no surprise. What was surprising was that Crowe and Pearce were there to help tell Hollywood's hidden, cruel histories. Crowe would, in fact, go on to be an actor Hollywood would use effectively to revive its long-dead properties, excavating old genres, including Westerns (remaking *3.10 to Yuma*), another *Robin Hood*, and most famously pumping new blood into the 'sword-and-sandal' epic via Ridley Scott's 2000 *Gladiator* (though that particular genre originated in Italian silent cinema – Hollywood never stumbled onto an idea it wouldn't happily steal). He was rewarded for these efforts: in a rare feat for what is in essence an action film, *Gladiator* landed Crowe the Academy Award for Best Actor and cemented his status as 'A-list' talent.

How was Crowe so ready to make the crossover from one local industry to the other? Is there some kind of psychic gangway between Sydney and Los Angeles, between Australia and Hollywood? The critic-from-Kogarah Clive James once quipped of Los Angeles that you were 'already living in it before you get there'.[7] To misquote James then: Is an actor already working in LA before they've even stepped foot in the place?

Crowe understood the material back-and-forth between Australia and America. He had, after all, expended immense capital amassed in Los Angeles to loom large over Sydney. In 2003, he bought four apartments at the end of the historic Finger Wharf in Woolloomooloo, adjoining them to create a thousand-square-foot floating abode. The Finger Wharf had been built in the early 1910s atop Sydney's first fish markets. During the world wars, it became a drop-off point for troops for deployment, and from the mid-1950s it was a passenger terminal for new migrants coming into the country. Crowe's hold over the cultural imagination of the port city was then given its physical form, able to jut out over the harbour just by sitting at home.

There is another very Sydney edge to the story: one of sites of significant working-class history being remodelled as homes of the super-rich. Sydney and Los Angeles share an urge to push out the poor. The critic and novelist Delia Falconer suggested that the two cities are 'sometimes unfavourably compared'. In her short cultural history *Sydney*, Falconer wrote that her home city had 'been as ravaged by the car, as dazzled by its improbable location, as prone to boosterism and corruption as Los Angeles'.[8] Patrick White, Australia's cantankerous Nobel Laureate, might have agreed. He lived on in Sydney begrudgingly but held firm that Los Angeles was 'one of the three arseholes of the world'.[9] For his part, Crowe suggested he would only live in the City of Angels if New Zealand and Australia were both wiped out by tidal wave through some demonic intervention.

RUSSELL CROWE LOST THE MAJORITY OF HIS POST-*Gladiator* decade to a series of rote reunions with Ridley Scott (*A Good Year, Body of Lies, American Gangster, Robin Hood*). In the same period, he wrote off an inordinate amount of personal good will. He was arrested by New York police in 2005 and charged with second-degree assault of a 28-year-old hotel clerk, Nestor Estrada, after he threw a telephone at Estrada in a fit of rage, cutting him beneath his eye. He would radically transform that most American icon of all: The Outlaw. Photographs of Crowe, handcuffed and being led on a 'perp walk' out of a courthouse, were shared across the world. In the year of this dramatic arrest, author Helen Garner spent a week revisiting a significant swathe of Crowe's filmography, drawing her to the solemn conclusion that 'Crowe's public persona, noisy and humourless and strutting, is forever making rude gestures in the corner of my eye, demanding attention and cursing those who give it.'[10]

It was the little-known Sydney journalist named Jack Marx, however, who provided the definitive portrait of Crowe as an approval-driven sycophant, in a tell-all confessional called 'I Was Russell Crowe's Stooge', which ran novella-length in the pages of the *Sydney Morning Herald*. Crowe had solicited Marx's services to write a positive profile to plant within the

Australian press, admitting to Marx that he regularly swayed media coverage by tempting gossip pages with promises of exclusive access. Over months, Marx and Crowe met together in Sydney to discuss details and talk strategy. The picture Marx painted was one of Russell Crowe as a Brando-like Don, consorting in his office with his newly appointed consigliore. Marx understandably found it hard to turn down Crowe at first – in clichéd movie-speak, an offer too good to refuse – observing that 'next to the Prime Minister and the odd media magnate, there was nobody more powerful in Australia than Mr Russell Crowe, and any crumb that might spill from his table would tumble as a banquet to my world'.[11]

During the 2022 federal election, Crowe was photographed alongside prime ministerial hopeful Anthony Albanese at a Rabbitohs football game. Albanese had been a long-time supporter of the South Sydney team. More than a decade earlier, Crowe had become their co-owner, investing with Peter Holmes à Court – the son of Australia's first billionaire – in the hope of reviving the long-downtrodden club, buying into another important piece of Sydney in the process. For Crowe and Holmes à Court, the effort paid off. In 2014 the club won their first premiership in over 40 years and their hometown streets of Redfern broke into a celebratory reverie for days.

Crowe was no longer just an actor to Sydneysiders, but a bigger player, essential to the cultural fabric of the city. He would move on to provide a dramatic, gravel-voiced voice-over for one of Albanese's election pitch videos. There was something spectacularly American about the direct politicking – landing as something close to Warren Beatty throwing a benefit for George McGovern's 1972 presidential campaign – but the connection barely made an impression on the

Australian public, perhaps because Crowe's star power had waned in the years since but also Australians were politic-fatigued by the time the election rolled around after two years of a pandemic and environmental crises.

THE 60-SECOND SPOT WAS MET WITH TIMID YET PER-sistent complaints on Twitter that as a New Zealand citizen, Crowe couldn't even vote, so why was he stumping in the election? Movie stars are by their extreme public visibility deeply political figures. Pop culture is a partisan arena. In his 2003 book *The Dream Life* J. Hoberman argued that cinema exists 'as shared fantasy and social myth', building a survey of movies and politics – movies as political events, and political events experienced as movies – across the vast canvas of America. Reading a work like *The Dream Life* as an Australian is an envy-inducing experience, because drawing a map of the 20th century would be difficult in Australia if you were to rely on movies alone, given the film industry's long periods of dormancy. Despite its claim to being the first country to produce a feature-length film – *The Story of the Kelly Gang*, filmed in Melbourne and released in 1906, ran at a lean but landmark 60–70 minutes – Australia suffered incredibly long stretches of creative drought through the middle of the 20th century.

The problem wasn't one of a lack of energy or ideas on the part of working filmmakers. Nor did it necessarily relate to the appetites of local audiences. Australians were enthusiastic cinemagoers from the start. They fell in love hard and fast. Stories of early cinema attendances around the world usually cite the Lumière Brothers' *L'Arrivée d'un train en gare de La Ciotat* having such a strong effect on audience members that they fled their seats, bolting to the back of the room, thinking that the train shown steaming towards them really was an oncoming danger. Most historians have since deemed that story to be apocryphal. Australians, however, can proudly boast that when their first audience sat in a cinema – inside the Melbourne Opera House in 1896 – the crowd did not cower. As they watched a foamy wave wash towards them, the surf-loving crowd did not run, they burst into wild applause.

From there grew great appetites for cinema attendance in Australia. In 1928, the year talkies arrived in Australia, the population hovered at around just 6 million people, yet between them Australians went to the cinema a remarkable 187 million times, averaging about 30 visits a year per person. Since the early 2010s, in a life crowded with wall-mounted and pocket-size alternatives to the big screen, per capita cinema attendance in Australia has dropped to about three films a year. Still, Australians stood as proud cinephiles among the world's population throughout the 20th century, and they enthusiastically embraced what Hollywood had to offer above all else. In her history of Australian cinemas and culture, *Hollywood Down Under*, Diane Collins observed that in 1922, and then again from 1926 to 1929, the US Department of Commerce reported that Australia was the number one importer of American films.[12]

Production in Australia struggled in the years after, partly down to the sheer relentlessness of this exact American market domination. There were other factors: governmental indifference, adverse economic conditions, and the devastating disruptions of the Second World War. Those roadblocks meant Australian cinema went deathly quiet in the exact period J. Hoberman was writing about: the 1950s and 1960s. So it is incredibly difficult to mount a cultural history of Australian cinema – and its dependent relationship to Hollywood – going by the movies alone. If, however, you can isolate actors, and study them individually, you might have a chance. For Australian actors worked consistently throughout the 20th century. Indeed, their lives – and migratory patterns – can trace the story of how a nation's film industry was founded, then faltered and failed, before finding itself again.

It's a cultural history worth investigating, because the story of Australian film is one that is largely in lockstep with the making of the nation itself following federation. Both the country and its cinema embraced modernism in the 1920s and 1930s, succumbed to a creeping conservatism in the 1950s, found a growing confidence via social democratic investments in the 1970s, faced radical market deregulation in the 1980s, and, arguably, fell into a complacency from the 1990s to today. Alongside all of this was a continued fight to amplify First Nations stories in the face of inherent racism built into the very foundations of the settler state and, by association, its film industry.

The key players who feature in this book – Errol Flynn, Peter Finch, David Gulpilil AM and Nicole Kidman – form four distinct, yet overlapping, eras. They take the viewer from the early 1930s with one of Australia's first movies to use sound and the bust of the industry in the 1940s, through to Australian cinema's dramatic revival in the 1970s, and to the deregulated global economies of today's streaming 'content' and cinematic 'universes'.

Through his eccentric auction Crowe, unknowingly, provided a thorough model for writing about the life of an actor. His mix of personal history and chronological filmography through cultural artifacts showed me the framework I needed, and he gave me its very starting point: encased in glass, an olive-green outfit, with matching cape, and a waistband inscribed 'Mr Flynn #2'.

Throughout the sale costumes were a reliable item to best their estimates. The clear winner in terms of sheer sustained market interest was, unsurprisingly, *Gladiator*. A polyurethane breastplate from the film skyrocketed $100 000 over its reserve price. It was sad if somewhat unsurprising to find, then, that the green costume Flynn wore in 1948's *Adventures of Don Juan* failed to snare a single bid, perhaps pointing towards a steep depreciation of the stars of yesteryear. Flynn and Crowe intersected in as much as they both played Robin Hood (one near definitive, the other warmed-over) and it was hard not to wonder if Crowe watched that item with any particular interest. If he had paid it any mind, the ageing outfit might have presented a grim vision to Crowe: Flynn was dead by 50, having seriously over-indulged in all that life had to offer him, and so never got to play out a third act.

Flynn was, however, central to Australia's first act in cinema; its first symphonic dream of itself, born at the bottom of the world, before echoing high above the hills of Hollywood.

PART 1
THE PERFECT SPECIMEN: ERROL FLYNN

Skirting the outer edges of inner Sydney by car, pushing your way clear of Surry Hills, towards the city's beachside suburbs, a modest-looking side street flashes the name Errol Flynn Boulevard – its signage attached to a curved redbrick wall – though you would have to be really looking to find it. If you turn off, the sign will direct you to what was once the Fox Studios complex and to its multistorey car park. It is not much of a road, not much of a car park, but then the studio lot – now, quite suddenly, no longer Fox Studios but Disney Studios Australia – is not much of a cultural precinct for Sydney. Its café- and beer hall-lined strip is often empty at peak hour and its multiscreen cinema can feel ghostly at times. It could – and possibly should – mean more to the city. After all, Sydney was named a 'City of Film' by UNESCO (the United Nations Educational, Scientific and Cultural Organization) in 2010. The designation barely registers in a city that often doesn't seem interested in its own film history.

Located in the grounds of Moore Park, the Fox Studios site had long served as the home of the Royal Easter Show, but as the end of the second millennium approached, its new tenant Rupert Murdoch, having signed a 99-year lease, had ambitious plans for the space. Murdoch wanted a fully functional theme park, something in line with the Universal Studios 'entertainment complexes' in Universal City, Los Angeles and Orlando, Florida. Fox Studios launched The Backlot in 1999, opening as part of an overall $261 million development deal. The star attraction of The Backlot was *Titanic – The Experience*, an interactive ride designed to recreate the sinking of the *Titanic* as seen in James Cameron's 1997 romantic blockbuster. Guests were invited to tour the ocean liner's interiors as third-class passengers before experiencing the after-effects of an iceberg ripping through the ship's metal hull, with the surrounds flooding and catching fire. Understandably, restaging a real-life disaster – one in which 1500 people perished – was not everyone's idea of a fun day out. *Titanic – The Experience* and the entire Backlot theme park closed down just two years after first opening. To add to the uncanny nature of the entire project, as it was being demolished, the fake *Titanic* caught on fire for real, setting ablaze Moore Park's historic 1938 commemorative building.

The fake *Titanic* was threatening to take a living piece of Sydney's architectural history down with it. Before the simulacrum of disaster became a disaster in reality, Sydney was excited about the glamour Murdoch's new pet project might bring, the international film productions it might help secure and the local productions it might support. The studios had already given a sense of what was to come: Warner Bros brought 90s slacker icon Keanu Reeves to Sydney for *The Matrix*, and Paramount Pictures were working on the highly anticipated *Mission Impossible 2*, which would use the lot for part of its long and troubled shoot, pulling two of the world's biggest movie stars back into Sydney's orbit.

Party-hungry Sydneysiders were as keen as ever for any excuse to celebrate their city (and themselves). Murdoch was happy to help, enlisting his soon to be friend Hugh Jackman – then teetering on the edge of superhero stardom as the Marvel comic book character Wolverine for Fox – to host a 50-minute televised celebration. The show opened as a fever dream of the Golden Age of Hollywood: 16 Shirley Temples tap-danced aboard the deck of the *Titanic*, while multiple seasick Charlie Chaplins retched over the side of a life raft below. Kylie Minogue performed a chintzy rendition of 'Diamonds Are a Girl's Best Friend' in full Marilyn Monroe drag, before Jackman took to the stage to introduce a montage of classic films pulled from 20th Century Fox's film archives. There was little in the clip show that night to highlight Sydney, or Australia. It was once to have been otherwise. American studios had historically bought into cinema chains around the world, but 'nowhere was that ownership more concentrated than in Australasia.'[1] Fox Film Corporation, founded in 1915, had been the first American studio to truly sink its teeth into the Australian cinematic infrastructure, staking a controlling interest in the Hoyts Cinemas chain in 1930 (Paramount had attempted a similar takeover of the Union Theatres – later Greater Union – yet failed). In doing so, the studio had assured the public that it was interested in investing in local films, but showed no signs of following up on their word, angering Australia's first filmmakers and leading to calls for quotas to be introduced. No American studio would promise Australians so much, and leave so much undelivered. Decades later, there were no wholly Australian films from that era in the Fox library to unearth. Nor was there room in the show for an actor like Errol Flynn, despite the fact that Flynn was the biggest Australian star of the exact era that the show's

THE PERFECT SPECIMEN: ERROL FLYNN

producers were trying to evoke. It simply wasn't possible, however, for the ghost of Errol Flynn to front up to a Fox Studios bash. He had been a Warner Bros player, working steadily for them throughout the 1930s to 1940s, as part of their powerhouse stable of contracted players.*

Did it matter that Murdoch couldn't conjure up Flynn? By 1999, younger audience members tuning in to *Fox Studios Australia: The Grand Opening* might not have even known who he was. In 1981, a year before Russell Crowe was singing about wanting to be Marlon Brando, the band Australian Crawl were suggesting they would give anything to be just like Errol Flynn, but the Boomer members of that band were likely the last generation to see Flynn's films screened in cinemas or to catch them regularly repeated on TV.

What did he leave behind? There is a certain point where the fading memory of former idols reduces them to their basic signifiers. It's a strange disappearing act, driven by cultural forgetfulness, changing tastes, and the unforgiving carriage of time. The lingering collective memory of Flynn now might be the actor in his green tights in *The Adventures of Robin Hood* (1938) – perhaps pictured in the arms of his Maid Marian, the actress Olivia de Havilland, who starred in eight films with Flynn and died in 2020 at the age of 104. Some hardcore trivia heads might be able to recall the phrase 'In like Flynn' – popularised by goatish American GIs during the war and passed into popular culture with its semi-obvious explicitness.

If you are a reader of Truman Capote miscellanea, an essay detailing an outing with Marilyn Monroe might jog that

---

* Flynn might have found a home to haunt on the Gold Coast in 1991 when the Warner Bros Movie World theme park opened – Warner Bros becoming the other major studio to leave a tangible impression on Australia, via its gamification of cinema history.

memory. In 'A Beautiful Child', Capote produced a memorable Monroe quote, potentially fictitious – Capote always putting stress on the creative in creative non-fiction – about an otherwise 'half-ass party':

> Did I ever tell you about the time I saw Errol Flynn
> whip out his prick and play the piano with it? ...
> Thumped the keys.[2]

More reliably, David Niven continued the creation of Flynn marginalia in his own memoirs, reporting on his former co-star's energetic drug habits:

> He had, by then, used everything, including, as an
> aphrodisiac, just a pinch of cocaine on the end of
> his penis.[3]

At a certain point, however, Big Dick Energy becomes Big Dead Energy. The active lothario atrophies into lore. The lonely, unloved costume from *Adventures of Don Juan* that Russell Crowe tried – and failed – to hawk represents part of this decline (although *Don Juan*, despite being one of Flynn's better films, was considered something of a flop at the time). At a certain point, looking at Flynn's life, one has to ask: should efforts be made to remember him at all? The critic James Wolcott figured Flynn a 'sassy terror'.[4] Wolcott might have had some sense of the distance Flynn travelled to get from enfant terrible to adult terroriser. Credible charges of statutory rape that Flynn faced mid-career seem now largely forgotten. If they were still housed in our collective memory, why would the City of Sydney breezily name a boulevard after him? The question then becomes: how do you look back at the film roles of someone like Flynn without dropping the exercise because of his sordid history?

I blame my particular dogged persistence on Russell Crowe. If Crowe had taken me on a tour of the inter-connectedness between Los Angeles and Sydney, he was now sending me even further back to Flynn's catalogue, hungry to look at how an Australian first took a true stranglehold on Hollywood. What does it mean to work your way through Flynn's entire filmography – over 50 available films (a couple of early ones lost to time altogether) – in a time when we are coming up fast to a century since his screen-acting debut? Why subject yourself to it? The answer might lie in the fact that Flynn's excesses and entitlements tell part of a greater story of Australia in the 20th century and what we permitted ourselves to get away with – an emblem not necessarily of great classical acting, but the misdeeds of a young nation.

THE TALISMAN (1909–1933)

Flynn, born in Hobart in June 1909, was an unlikely prospect to ever make it to – let alone *in* – Hollywood. He was reared at the bottom of the world, in the same decade Australia became a federation. Tasmania joined the federation willingly – concerned about tariffs other states, New South Wales in particular, would impose if the government resisted – but as an island unto itself, it would always carry a sense of separateness. Later in life Flynn playfully corrected a biographer who described him as 'Australian'. No, he said, 'Tasmanian actually.'[5] Still, he abandoned the 'Apple Isle' while young, shipped out for schooling by his father, a biology professor at the University of Tasmania (his mother's family came from a long line of restless seafarers). He was sent first to an English boarding college, where he was expelled, before being brought to Sydney to another boarding school, where he was expelled yet again.

In Sydney he was enrolled at the Sydney Church of England Grammar School – better known as SCEGS or Shore – surrounded by old boys and likely admitted by trading off his father's standing and purse, rather than his own academic record. Washed ashore, Flynn was a classmate of a future prime minister, John Gorton, the man who would be central to initiating the Australian film revival decades later. Gorton, however, did not recall 'any close contact' with Flynn during their schooling together.[6] If he had lived long enough, Flynn might well have approved of Gorton's regenerative efforts within the industry that gave him his start.

Flynn was, after all, part of one of the first generations of screen actors to have grown up watching movies. In Hobart, as a hormonal teen, he had spent afternoons at the Strand cinema. There, on the other side of the world from Hollywood, he watched his predecessors – the stars of silent film – including Ramon Novarro, Adolphe Menjou and Rudolph Valentino. He was taking in exactly the kind of films in which he would later appear. He saw the barroom brawler *The Spoilers* (1923) – later remade with John Wayne – and Valentino's *The Sheik* (1921), which was the biggest hit in Australia at the time. Not far from Flynn, on the north coast of Tasmania, in the town of Burnie, queues for tickets were creating such chaos that police had to shut down sales. The film's success came down to repeat attendance, driven by Valentino's romantic hold over his audience. Flynn went to the movies on teen dates, and even then he brought his own devoted audience along to the cinema, as rows of girls would

THE PERFECT SPECIMEN: ERROL FLYNN

sit behind the young amorist, watching him and his partner on their date, knowing, perhaps, that a future idol was in their midst, and he was better than what was being offered on the screen.[7]

When he moved to Sydney, Flynn left Hobart's modest cinemas behind. Sydney in the 1920s and 1930s, through the interwar years, was finding its own identity, through urban expansion and attempts to embrace rampant modernity. It likely wasn't moving fast enough for Flynn. After his expulsion from SCEGS, he became a clerk at Miller's Point, and later handed out pamphlets for the Labor Party ('some radical political cause'), although without any personal party affiliation.[8] He wasn't satisfied with the work. Failing to find figurative mooring, he sailed for Papua New Guinea – then under Australian colonial administration – in the hope of prospecting for gold, drunk on stories of quick riches that had been running in the news. He had little success on the goldfields but charmed his way into a job as a cadet patrol officer, without the necessary qualifications, before quickly being found out. He stayed on for just over two years, later claiming to have returned to Sydney to recover from a bad case of gonorrhoea at the end of 1929. During his supposed convalescence, he would have his first exposure on the big screen, modelling suits for a local tailor in photographic advertisements run in the city's cinemas. It is unknown if he ever saw himself projected posing in those threads – unlike his teen years in Hobart, there is little trace of his cinema-going in Sydney in his early twenties. There is plenty of evidence of what he was doing instead: living it up with Sydney's social elite. He got his first taste of publicity via the city's social pages, where both his engagement to a socialite from the Southern Highlands and his renovations of a beloved yacht – the *Sirocco*

– made notices. In between the social climbing, he also found time to make his screen debut.

FLYNN WOULD ONLY EVER MAKE THE ONE FILM IN Australia: Charles Chauvel's strange, uneasy hybrid of documentary and drama, *In the Wake of the Bounty*. Released in 1933 as one of Australia's first films to capitalise on sound, Chauvel's 66-minute feature was a narrative retelling of the mutinous rebellion on the *Bounty*, which, simultaneously, served as a travelogue of the seas surrounding Tahiti. The non-fiction footage would later be purchased by Metro-Goldwyn-Mayer Studios (MGM) in America, who intended to cleave it into two short films, acknowledging Chauvel's imbalance in inelegantly mashing fact and fiction together. Original reports also suggested that the studio had an interest in keeping Chauvel's film off the market, but footage would eventually be spliced into trailers for MGM's own take on the story, *The Mutiny on the Bounty* (1935), starring Clark Gable as Fletcher Christian and Charles Laughton as a stroppy Captain Bligh. Any scenes of Flynn were excised, left on the cutting room floor.

Reports on exactly how Flynn came to be cast in the film varied wildly. Chauvel long held that he found his leading man in a newspaper article and sent a scout out to search the bars of Sydney. Another submitted that Chauvel had seen Flynn modelling those tailored suits in city cinemas and asked that the model be tracked down. Yet another reported that Chauvel had seen footage of Flynn as part of a documentary shot in Papua New Guinea. Flynn's most convincing biographer, John Hammond Moore, however, suggested it was a case of happenstance: Flynn was discovered by a casting director at Bondi Beach on a hazy Sunday afternoon. In the finished product, Flynn appears as rickety as the cheap floorboards he treads in his few scenes, and disappears from the film not long after it starts. He looks pale and uneasy. You can see his eyes darting over his dialogue in his mind, straining to reach for it before reciting it. There might have been expectations for him to be more naturally authentic in the role: Flynn had distant familial ties to the *Bounty* story. Lily Mary Young, Flynn's mother, was a descendant of Edward 'Ned' Young, the midshipman on the *Bounty* who had agitated for over-throwing Bligh.

The personal connection provided the young Flynn with no real advantage – certainly no added conviction – in playing the role of Fletcher Christian. Nor did it lead to any further screen work in Sydney. The other relatively well remembered Australian director of the era – Ken G Hall – was said to have turned him down for a role. Flynn would, instead, disappear from Australian cinema altogether and leave the city to return to Papua New Guinea. An article published after he arrived in America in the *Sydney Morning Herald* questioned whether Flynn's nomadic nature would mean he wouldn't stay in Hollywood for long, and whether he might eventually return to Sydney, 'especially if the film industry here has anything to offer him.'[9] Flynn never set foot in Australia again and the Australian film industry would certainly have had very little to offer him if he did. In 1935 – the year Flynn made his name in Hollywood – only three films were produced in the whole of Australia.

America was explicit about her intentions in exporting films to the world. In 1923, Will Hays, the president of the newly gathered Motion Picture Producers and Distributors of America, outlined in a speech delivered in London the lofty aims of his group and American cinema in general:

> Every film that goes from America abroad, wherever
> it shall be sent, shall correctly portray to the world
> the purposes, the ideals, the accomplishments, the
> opportunities, and the life of America. We are going
> to sell America to the world with American motion
> pictures.[10]

This was the exact form of rhetoric that had Australian politicians worried about the influence American cinema would have on their constituents. One naysaying senator expressed particular concern that the 'extravagance and luxury' shown in American movies would give way to Australians having feelings 'of discontent' and developing 'abnormal views of life'.[11] The leading independent film critic in Sydney, Beatrice Tildesley, warned that the Americanisation of Australia 'is a very real danger'.[12] Local film producers were also concerned about just how dominating American movies were fast becoming. These filmmakers lobbied for a government response, forming a strange coalition alongside nationalists who wanted quotas for Australian content, and wowsers who were calling for hardline censorship. The push was successful and the resultant Royal Commission on the Moving Picture Industry in Australia would run from 1926 until 1928. Only a few years before Hollywood made Flynn into a star, those behind the report were aware Australia would lose talent due to the competition in America:

> Australians have shown their adaptability in the moving
> picture world, and to-day there are many of them
> engaged in the industry in the United States of America
> who are capably filling posts as directors, actors,
> actresses, scenario writers, cameramen ...

> The unlimited scope afforded by the well-established
> industry in America has been responsible for their
> remaining in that country.[13]

The authors of the report conceded that it could not 'be expected that many of them would be prepared to sacrifice highly remunerative positions' to return to Australia to support the local industry 'unless every encouragement and assistance' were given to make local productions profitable and lasting employment viable. It was an early acknowledgement that human capital flight – the dreaded 'brain drain' – was a genuine concern for the industry and would partly aid in its death by quickening increments.

For many in the know, Flynn was the first truly big fish to escape the net. An article in the Tasmanian newspaper the *Mercury* stated simply that 'the Australian industry missed him'.[14] There was little to be done to retrieve him even with 'every encouragement and assistance'. The Royal Commission acknowledged that tempting players to return in the name of helping to reinforce the Australian film industry would be of little use. Patriotic grounds alone would not work, as Flynn was no patriot. He was an individualist with a strong libertarian streak. His future ghostwriter had him down as 'congenial democrat' only when he wasn't playing a 'confounded imperialist'. Democrat or imperialist, his personal politics were solely invested in the advancement of his own person. Pointedly questioning Flynn's sympathies during the Second World War, David Niven wrote in his bestselling memoir that Flynn felt 'no loyalty to Britain, and little to Australia'.

Cinema as a nation-building exercise would have meant next to nothing to him then. It certainly wouldn't have crossed his mind that movie-making could serve to symbolically bolster the Commonwealth's image and ideology. Australian filmmakers, however, were sometimes explicit in their intent to achieve such aims. The 'general consensus' for film historians was that Chauvel was the 'architect of the most avowedly nationalist filmmaking in Australia'.[15] Indeed, Chauvel's company carried with it a printed creed, which stated:

> It is our ambition to produce film attractions built upon
> industrial and pastoral backgrounds that will have
> both entertainment and advertising value to our great
> Commonwealth.[16]

Few would go so far as to question if Australia were a nation worth advertising to the world. Chauvel – despite being lauded for casting First Nations actors in his final film *Jedda* (1955) – appeared himself in blackface, playing an Indigenous stockman, in his first directorial effort, *The Moth of Moonbi* (1926). The Royal Commission, which Chauvel had actively participated in, was no better. The report has been cited in a number of histories of Australian cinema – and rightly so, as in many ways it is a prophetic accounting of a sector of the Australian arts under strain – but most have ignored the fact that it carries a rancid train of paternalistic racism that has long defined the country. In its shortest part, dashed off as if it was given no real thought at all, the writers, under a section titled 'The Film and Native Races', warned that First Nations audiences could be 'riotously aroused' by film and that cinema 'exerts a powerful influence over the natives and could by design instill into their minds dangerous and sinister motives'. The next sentence is bearly comprehensible on a grammatical level: 'The possibility of such a happening it is considered should not be allowed to remain'. The recommendation put forward was to censor all films for First Nations audiences. It was in keeping with the country's racist control mechanisms at the height of the White Australia policy.

The final report's overall political sway was questionable. Most of the recommendations put forward could not be acted upon constitutionally, due to powers to enact them resting with the states rather than the federal government. The US Vice Consul in Australia, anticipating the toothlessness of the Royal Commission, reported to the powers back home in America that the anti-Americanisation movement was simply the 'ranting of a few politicians and reform societies'. The Americans had little to worry about; Australia would not stand in their way for market and cultural dominance.

OBJECTIVE, HOLLYWOOD! (1934–1935)

In letters to his father published after his death, Flynn gave a sense of his direction in life before he made it to Hollywood. He had aspirations of being a writer, but as he admitted to his father 'in my present illiterate, almost un-intelligent, uneducated condition, my chances of very doing much worthwhile in literature are negligible'. Giving up Sydney again, Flynn returned to Papua New Guinea for a second attempt at making it rich, this time growing tobacco leaf for export, which had a higher chance for success than gold-mining, but he still struggled to make it work. He confessed that if he failed in his venture in tobacco he would head for England. 'New Guinea, with it's [sic] enormous variety of queer customers, has taught me more about men than I'd learn in 20 years in a city like London.' And yet London was calling.

Charles Chauvel knew Hollywood. He had been there in

both 1922 and 1928 to learn from the much larger industry, working for stints at United Artists and Universal City Studios, as well as under the influential comedy producer Hal Roach. He watched Raoul Walsh direct Douglas Fairbanks – two figures who would become important to Flynn – in *The Thief of Baghdad* (1924).[17] Despite this insider knowledge, he recommended Flynn go to England instead. It's unclear if Chauvel did this with the long game in mind for Flynn, but it was practical advice to suggest he continue to sharpen his skills outside the gaze of the global centre of film production.

Headed for England for the first time since his failed schooling, Flynn was reunited with his father and mother, who had relocated from Hobart to London. The aspiring actor signed on as a player in a small repertory company in Northampton, cutting his teeth on the stage. He had boisterously elbowed his way into the company, having padded out his CV with a variety of falsehoods, a habit that would be hard to break, right up until his death. He would falsely claim – one of the first of many lies – to have represented Australia in boxing at the 1928 Olympics. Thirsting for attention, he ran that lie in an advertisement he took out himself in a British theatre magazine, vainly spruiking his height (6 feet, 1 inch) alongside a headshot fitted out in a tuxedo, and another in which he went shirtless, posing as a boxer. Contrary to myths that Flynn was discovered out of nowhere, he was working hard to be seen. He would never admit it but it was his mother who drove him up to the doors of Teddington Studios, in Richmond on the Thames, which had been taken over by Warner Bros Pictures in 1931. It was as if she was driving him up to a school gate for an admission interview.

The gambit worked and Flynn was cast in the thriller *Murder at Monte Carlo* (1934) in the lead role of a Fleet

Street reporter.* *Murder at Monte Carlo* has no surviving print and it constituted what was known in Britain at the time as a 'quota quickie' – a fast and cheap production made primarily to appease the *Cinematograph Films Act of 1927*, which had introduced a fixed allocation for the number of Commonwealth films to be screened in British cinemas. Britain, like Australia, was combating an excess of American product and a quota was the exact approach that Australia's Royal Commission had recommended but failed to convince enacting. Even with an Act in place, America would still mount a resistance. Savvy studios, with the help of the British cinemas themselves, would conspire to invest in such films to keep their mutual businesses afloat. It was the reason Warner Bros took over Teddington.

Flynn's work in *Murder at Monte Carlo* impressed Teddington's head of productions – a company man named Irving Asher – who recommended him to the influential producer Hal Wallis and the head of the four Warner brothers and so the studio, Jack Warner. The commendation almost went nowhere. Warner could not be bothered to watch the print of Flynn sent to him. He replied to Asher, 'No, she stinks'. Wallis, however, overrode his boss and told Asher to ship Flynn on a transatlantic liner. It was a savvy investment. For years, however, it was assumed that Flynn was discovered by Warner Bros without any competition. In December 1934, a lone gossip column published in the *San Francisco Examiner*

---

* Flynn would co-star in the film with Eve Gray, who, though born in England, had spent her childhood in Sydney, and had once been deemed 'the most beautiful woman in Australia'. The *Bulletin* posited that Eve Gray's 'assistance makes [*Murder at Monte Carlo*] quite an Australian picture'. Like the film itself, no record of any exchange exists between Flynn and Gray about their shared origins.

suggested that MGM management were, in fact, searching high and low for Flynn – 'in England and Australia, to say nothing of New Zealand' – for their version of *Mutiny on the Bounty*, unaware that he was under contract with Warner Bros and already in Hollywood.[18] There were also traces of the fact that Universal Pictures had been contacting Chauvel, trying to track down Flynn's details to no avail.

It was while he was on the SS *Paris* sailing for America that Flynn fell for Lili Damita, a French-American actress who would become his first wife and introduction into Hollywood's social elite. The young actor felt listless in Hollywood upon arrival, spending his days waiting around for work, while playing tennis to keep fit and getting stoned by drinking a Coca-Cola spiked with two aspirins, a recipe recommended by a friend. (God knows how this worked to deliver a genuine buzz to the system; actual cocaine had been removed from the Coca-Cola recipe in 1903.) His mood changed when cheques started flowing from the studio and he realised he was getting paid basically to laze around and play sports.

Was it any surprise that a white Australian would find himself so at home in an industry that openly named itself a 'movie colony'? Flynn did his share of evoking colonial pastimes too, signing up to play for the Hollywood Cricket Club, where he fell in with a set of British emigrants – chief among them a dashing young David Niven, his fastest friend, with whom he would go on to share a Malibu beachside home, which they christened 'Cirrhosis by the Sea'. Flynn had his own expansionist approach to real estate too, helping define the urban footprint of the Los Angeles we now know: he was an early adopter of Mulholland Drive as an address – building his 11.5-acre (4.7-hectare) 'Mulholland Farm' in the now famed Hollywood Hills.

THE PERFECT SPECIMEN: ERROL FLYNN

When he eventually amassed his wealth, Flynn invested some of his obscene capital on art, including works by Manet and Van Gogh. But his favourite piece, by a great distance, was a Gauguin, whose Tahitian idylls surely reminded Flynn of his travels in Papua New Guinea. On a visit, his mother noticed that Flynn's 'handkerchiefs, the pockets of his dressing gown and his pyjamas were all embroidered with a question mark'. When she asked why, he explained it was his 'sign' and that he had stood before a 'picture of Gauguin of some Pacific natives sitting and looking at each other' at the Metropolitan Art Museum of New York. Underneath the painting was an inscription that Flynn thought summed up his entire attitude and path:

Where did we come from?
What are we?
Where are we going?

Flynn wasn't living in an idle lull in Los Angeles for long. He would marry Damita and their elopement to Yuma, Arizona would result in an explosion of press, with Flynn landing on the front page of the *Los Angeles Times* before he had made his name in film. Some speculated it was a marriage of convenience to generate profitable publicity for both stars. Indeed, the space between Flynn's marriage to Damita and his success in securing the starring role in one of Warner Bros' leading pictures of 1935 was only a matter of months. Flynn would replace the British actor Robert Donat – to whom he had a minor passing resemblance – in the seafaring epic *Captain Blood*. How Flynn turned around his stilted performance as Fletcher Christian two years earlier into the agile, fleet-footed Captain Blood would be beyond most scholars of acting.

That energetic performance properly marked the first of 12 collaborations with the Hungarian-born director Michael Curtiz – who would most famously direct *Casablanca* – after Flynn had briefly appeared in a non-speaking role, as the victim of a suspected murder, in Curtiz's Perry Mason crime caper *The Case of the Curious Bride* (Flynn lay still under a white sheet for one scene, and wordlessly recreated his fatal tussle in another). Those 12 collaborations were released between 1935 and 1941, an unimaginable production output today, which can be put down to the studio system of stars and directors making multiple films throughout the calendar year, but also to Curtiz's own hectic work ethic: before coming to Hollywood Curtiz had already made 64 films in Europe, and once in the US he directed, or co-directed, a further 102 films.[19]

Short-tempered Flynn and shorter-tempered Curtiz would have a productive if fraught relationship. There would be little choice in the creative partnerships forged within the studio system, or outside of it. They were arranged marriages devised by profit-driven studio heads. As his relationship with Curtiz frayed in the early 1940s, the studio would pair Flynn with eye-patched Raoul Walsh – a former assistant to DW Griffith – who would go on to be his other close directorial collaborator, working together on seven films all within that same decade. Flynn had apparently asked to work with Walsh, perhaps sensing that they shared a sensibility and would grow a genuine fraternal bond (to Flynn, Walsh was always 'Uncle'). But it was control freak Curtiz who would ultimately define Flynn's career.

From the start of the Curtiz run of films, Flynn was a charm-forward actor – the model of the matinee idol – and one of the reasons he works in many of those early action

THE PERFECT SPECIMEN: ERROL FLYNN

roles is that he is so clearly driven by speed, conviction and the sense of being on this earth to operate as a shit-stirrer. Cinema loves a contrarian (see: Bill Murray in basically anything). In Raoul Walsh's *Gentleman Jim* (1942), Flynn plays real-life heavyweight champion James J Corbett, and one scene tapers off with him purposefully walking against oncoming foot traffic, antagonising each individual in his path for no good reason. It is unsurprising, then, that *Gentleman Jim* feels like the role closest to Flynn's actual persona: an arrogant independent with charm enough to spare to go towards undercutting his worst, most selfish impulses. Manny Farber – one of the greatest and most idiosyncratic early film critics – agreed, noting that Flynn's:

> mocking overconfidence is cleverly employed in the role of a shameless social climber who maddeningly maintains poise and balance through endless rowdy Irish family bashes and heavyweight bouts.[20]

Flynn suggested that the reason *Gentleman Jim* worked so well – and had such a lightness of touch to it – was because it was made out from under the close eye of Jack Warner, who was away during its filming. In the same way that Flynn's experience as a keen sailor helped keep his seafaring pictures afloat, the fact that Flynn was a half-decent boxer gave *Gentleman Jim* grounding weight. Despite the fiction he had sold about representing Australia in the sport at the Olympics, Flynn did have practice at sparring. Fast on his feet, he looked the part, and it's a role that tells you everything about the actor's physicality and why he stands out. Flynn's build, from a distance, comes across as hard, but in close-up, his features soften – as if they had been drawn delicately with a fine paintbrush. The pencil-thin moustache he wore is outdated now, of course, but as a figure in the films of his time he stands out as something more modern. That might come down to his very Australian-ness and the fact that he just doesn't sound anything like any of the other actors of the era.

For many in middle America, Flynn might have served as their introduction to the Australian accent, although audiences at the time may not have known that was what they were listening to. A wave of Australian actors worked their way to Hollywood during the silent era, but few audiences, obviously, heard words coming out of their mouths. As the critic Isaac Butler noted, 'Actors of any nationality could be in a film because no one could hear their voices.'[21] Several young Australian women born in the 1880s and 1890s made it to America to make a string of appearances in early silent films – perhaps, most lastingly famous, the swimmer and vaudevillian Annette Kellerman (after whom a Sydney swimming pool was named in 2010). Indeed, vaudeville theatre in Australia proved a good training ground for the broad movements of the silent comedies.

Remarkably – and without much to explain it – a number of Melbourne-born women appeared in comedy shorts featuring the dumb and dumber duo of Laurel and Hardy, including Mae Busch, Daphne Pollard and Vera White. Both Busch and Pollard would play versions of Hardy's stern, disapproving wife on screen, but Brunswick-born Mae Dahlberg would become Laurel's actual de facto partner. Dahlberg would prove to be an early returning expatriate. Laurel's producing partner bought her a ticket back to Australia after he decided she was having a negative influence on Laurel's performances. She would return to America to sue Laurel for a share in his finances.

THE PERFECT SPECIMEN: ERROL FLYNN

Flynn didn't have quite as many predecessors when it came to male actors. The closest was likely Sydney Deane, a baritone singer and competitive cricketer turned actor, who made his debut in *Brewster's Millions* (1914), co-directed by Cecil B DeMille, an early effort which now sees him credited as the first Australian to star in a Hollywood film. The film itself, like Flynn's debut, is now considered lost. Deane would work with DeMille throughout the 1910s before signing a contract with Universal Pictures. His final film was DW Griffith's *America* with Lionel Barrymore. Like Flynn, Deane kept the sportsman alive within him, continuing to play cricket in America, in both New York (for the New York Veterans) and Los Angeles (for the Santa Monica Cricket Club). He died in New York after being hit by a motorcar in 1934.

Most Australian actors from this era – Deane included – didn't make it through the transition to sound. Their accents wouldn't have helped them as Americans grappled with hearing those they had only until now seen. This may well have been true of George Beranger, born in Enmore but a popular player in the Hollywood silent era. He was sometimes credited as André de Beranger, having crafted a fake backstory as a Frenchman, but was back to being George when he served as Flynn's first Australian cast mate in America. They appeared together in the extremely slight *Don't Bet on Blondes* (1935) just before Flynn stepped out as Captain Blood. Beranger had studied in Sydney at the College of Elocution and Dramatic Art, before going to America to star in a number of silent films, including, most significantly, for DW Griffith.[22] He appeared in Griffith's controversial *The Birth of a Nation* (1915) as the son of the Ku Klux Klan's founder in the fictional retelling. He was memorable, and incredibly expressive, in Ernst Lubitsch's *So This Is Paris*

(1926). Beranger continued to appear in films after sound was introduced, but he was often in un-credited roles, which, ironically, were non-speaking. In *Don't Bet on Blondes* he features only as a 'wedding dress fitter' with a single line calling a dress a 'symphony'. Closeted – and boyishly handsome – he entered into a marriage of convenience with a neighbouring widow. He died alone in Laguna Beach, in a modest shack beside the towering Spanish Mission mansion he had built in the 1920s with his movie money, having been forced to sell the beloved property during his lean years after the advent of sound – a melancholy scene to rival any in Billy Wilder's lament for the silent stars in *Sunset Boulevard* (1950).

PLAYING PETER BLOOD, FLYNN WAS PERMITTED TO KEEP his accent intact as the titular Irish doctor-cum-pirate – not even bothering to make a lazy stab at a brogue – a decision which can make your head gently spin. The film, after all, is set in 1685, more than 100 years before colonisers invaded Australia and well before the accent had had a chance to form in the mouth. Like most historical films from Hollywood, *Captain Blood* was already cluttered with anachronistic detail, leading Graham Greene, moonlighting as a film critic, to report that he liked it but it played as a 'spirited mix-up'. Curtiz wouldn't correct it, even if he had been able to hear it. Precise verisimilitude and exactitude in an actor's performance was not necessarily the prized feat it now is, but it is still remarkable that throughout the rest of his career, Flynn did very little to alter his accent to fit a role, no matter what the nationality of the character he was playing. He played a Norwegian spy (*Edge of Darkness*), a Canadian Mountie of German origin (*Northern Pursuit*), a French criminal (*Uncertain Glory*) and several well-known American historical figures, each with that same unflinching Australian twang.

Things got weird indeed when Flynn began showing up in that most popular of American genres, the Western, starting out in the 1939 technicolour *Dodge City*, directed by Curtiz, in which Flynn plays its hero cowboy. Despite his character being assigned Irish, Flynn's Australian accent in *Dodge City* sounds even broader and more misplaced than before. Even Flynn's unchanging pencil moustache seems lighter and more manicured in this film than elsewhere. He was deeply anxious about making his debut in the genre – 'Putting me in cowboy pictures seemed to me the most ridiculous miscasting' – and his agency passed on a note to Jack Warner saying Flynn seemed 'a little dubious about his ability to play a part that is so essentially American – or accentuated, as he puts it'.[23] Flynn was certainly right to be nervous but, ultimately, audiences of the time didn't mind a bit. They ate him up with his feet still in the stirrups.

In his notorious, posthumously published autobiography *My Wicked, Wicked Ways*, Flynn confessed that in the Westerns he starred in, 'I had to alibi my accent, which was still a bit too English for the American-ear'. For decades Australians would bend to make themselves palatable to the American ear: as late as 1980, George Miller's post-apocalyptic thriller *Mad Max* had its dialogue re-recorded with American accents for its US release – a rare instance of an English-language film being dubbed. This was likely due to the fact that many of the characters speak in a particularly broad accent and the film is littered with lingo. The dub is potently bad – amplified by its sound mixing, clashing with Miller's many revving cars – but *Mad Max* was a huge and unexpected international success, becoming the most profitable film of all time (as in making the most amount of money from the smallest possible budget), earning over $100 million worldwide on a budget of around $400 000, so maybe the decision wasn't an entirely bad one. Flynn's Westerns were profitable too, and their concessions to American audiences affected their quality. Flynn confessed that he gave up trying to act in the genre – 'my heart wasn't in it, only my limbs' – dispirited by the scripts that had him lamely explain away his accent. In his memoirs he conjured some hokey sample dialogue that he believed 'got to be a trademark in my American films':

HEAVY: Where you from, pardner?

FLYNN: I happen to come from Ireland, but I am as American as you are.[24]

It would sound as tinny on film as it read on the page, but it humorously encapsulated that for most of his time in Hollywood, confusion reigned about Flynn's nationality. Indeed, Warner Bros might have been responsible for muddying the Australian identity in the minds of movie-going Americans. In their publicity bible for Flynn – an origin myth – they decided to spin that he was Irish. As he made his way from New York to Los Angeles by train for the first time, a representative from Warner Bros met Flynn in Chicago. This studio lackey was, according to Flynn, the one who came up with the idea – which was quickly parlayed into a photoshoot of Flynn as a motorcycle cop, because, according to the actor, 'that fitted into the American conception of what an Irishman fresh in from Ireland should look like and be'. The studio clearly thought it was easier to say Flynn was Irish, given the obvious origins of his surname and the fact that his parents were now

THE PERFECT SPECIMEN: ERROL FLYNN

based in Belfast, his father having taken up a teaching post at the Queen's University. Perhaps, it was all far simpler than explaining what an Australian actually was and where one came from. Entertainment journalists were happy to relay the false information to the public. Indeed, the very first mention of the actor in the *Los Angeles Times* was a single-sentence notice in an industry column, which read:

> Errol Flynn, Irish Actor just signed to a long-term ticket by Warners, once was a gold prospector in the wilds of New Guinea.[25]

This origin story seemed to go largely unchallenged. A single line in the Washington *Evening Star* in 1939 read that 'The Australians say that Errol Flynn was born in that country'. The report, however, gave no source, though they may have picked up reporting from the *Sydney Morning Herald* the year prior, which had attempted to correct the record:

> One of the most astonishing pranks of the motion picture industry must be the attempts by American publicity writers to distort the real facts about the career of Tasmanian-born Errol Flynn.[26]

That article suggested the publicity team at Warner Bros had also sold a story that Flynn was born in Paris and spoke only French until he was seven years old.

If Australians – and Tasmanians in particular – were starting to clue on to Flynn, they were wildly misled with another lie for years. Flynn's lie infamously ran in reverse for Merle Oberon, a star of early British films who later made her way to Hollywood, and who falsely claimed to be

39

Tasmanian. Oberon emerged after her breakout performance in *The Private Life of Henry VIII* (1933), directed by her future husband Alexander Korda. She arrived in Hollywood in the same year as Flynn and was on the ship's log of the exact same liner as Flynn had taken with Damita. Oberon would go to work for Samuel Goldwyn of MGM, rather than Warner Bros. Reporters were informed she was born in Tasmania. The backstory, however, was a forgery and the reason for the lie itself was far more sinister than Flynn's. Korda, and his publicity team, had likely designed the fabrication, in order to sell Oberon to the British public, disguising the fact that she had been born in Mumbai to a white father and a mother with Sri Lankan and Māori heritage. In Korda's fiction, Oberon's father became an English army officer, who died in Tasmania while the family was visiting his sister, and her mother became a mix of Dutch and French.

In a long profile in the *Chicago Tribune*, intended to introduce her to American audiences, the journalist noted that 'she has the chic of her French blood, that certain knack for wearing clothes, and that dark, arresting something in her beauty that Dutch blood sometimes bestows ...'[27]

Why Tasmania? Indeed, why not France or Holland? There would be neatness to the narrative if Korda and company had been inspired by Flynn's own origins, but there is a newspaper report introducing Oberon as a 'newcomer from Tasmania' in 1932, a year before Flynn had even starred in *In the Wake of the Bounty*. For Oberon, there was a sense of randomness instead, as if someone had spun a globe and their finger landed on Tasmania. The small island state was likely chosen because, sitting at the bottom of the world, it was so little known that no one would have the knowledge

THE PERFECT SPECIMEN: ERROL FLYNN

to question the veracity of any details of the story, and its population so out of reach that it would be difficult to contact to locals to investigate the truth. A British actor recalled the publicity director laughing that Tasmania was 'so remote that most people had not the slightest idea where it was'.[28] Indeed, one American journalist, profiling Oberon, implored his readers to 'Look it up in your geography. I had to do so'.[29]

Tasmanians fell for it wholeheartedly. A 2002 documentary about Oberon's origins still featured locals clinging to their claims on her as one of their own, despite proof to the contrary having existed since the early 1980s. A refrain in the film claimed that if Flynn was Tasmania's son, then Oberon was her daughter. Potential family members pleaded their case without evidence. It was, however, a collective delusion and one with its own form of racism built in – rumours stubbornly persisted for decades that Oberon was the daughter of a local Chinese dynasty, despite no real proof.

It was a lie that Oberon lived inside for the rest of her life. In fact, Oberon travelled to Hobart in 1978, the year before her death. In the years since, it has been unclear exactly why she accepted the invitation. Once there, she was deeply uncomfortable, holing up in the casino hotel, evading locals and refusing to speak to reporters. At a reception at the Hobart Town Hall, it was said that she fainted and also revealed that she wasn't born in Tasmania at all. What was she doing there, and why was she putting herself through such torture?

And yet, despite the pain and desire to come clean, in signing a guest book on the night, she wrote her address down as 'Malibu and Tasmania'.[30]

UNCERTAIN GLORY (1936–1948)

Hollywood in the mid-1930s – despite being bashed about by the Great Depression – was in surprisingly sturdy shape. The changeover from silent films to 'talkies' was complete. Indeed, there had been a major uptick in profits due to the interest in sound and while figures had dropped in the years after the novelty wore off, box office takings remained strong. Despite touting itself as a 'Depression-proof' industry, the studios were hard hit in 1931–32, but by the time Flynn put on a pair of piratical tights for Curtiz, there were sure signs of recovery. Franklin D Roosevelt gaily observed: 'During this Depression, when the spirit of the people is lower than at any other time, it is a splendid thing that for just 15 cents an American can go to a movie and look at the smiling face of a baby and forget his troubles.'*

Flynn was a popular player from the outset. There was no slow burn. *Captain Blood* was one of the top box office earners of 1935 and was nominated for an Academy Award for Best Picture. The rewards for Flynn were fast to arrive and free flowing. He grew large appetites as a result. In one of his earliest pieces of American publicity, published in the *New York Times*, the actor was at the Ritz being accused by a teasing Damita of eating three dozen oysters to himself the night before.

---

*   Flynn might have had only fleeting contact with John Gorton in school, but he would become close with the Roosevelts. Flynn thought highly of the New Dealer, noting he 'had more charm and magnetism than I ever found in anyone in Hollywood'. Flynn was invited to dine with the Roosevelts at the White House in 1939, with an invitation to see a play the next night. Flynn repaid the favour to the family, entertaining FDR Jnr in LA – at Bing Crosby's club The Pirate's Den.

THE PERFECT SPECIMEN: ERROL FLYNN

Flynn became famous under a completely different system from the free-agent one we know now. The 'star system' – regimented and studio-run – acted essentially to build a stable of actors for each studio, locked in by binding, long-term contracts, to be used across multiple films. Flynn originally signed up to a six-month contract, with options for seven years' coverage, and he did, indeed, go on to sign successive multi-year contracts with Warner Bros, meaning that he would star exclusively in their films for the majority of his career. The opportunities for asserting autonomy during this time were far slimmer, as independent film productions, free from studio control, were rare and not what they would later become. So the studio had a vested interest in Flynn becoming the success he did. *The Adventures of Robin Hood* (1938) would arrive only three years into Flynn's Hollywood career and, with a budget of $2 million, was Warner Bros' most expensive production to date. The studio watched him closely as a result. The actor was dogged by stories of unprofessionalism throughout his career – showing up to set drunk, not knowing his lines and not taking things particularly seriously. Contrary to much of what has been written about Flynn, however, he longed to be a better actor. He was surrounded by extraordinary talent at Warner Bros as part of an impressive set of players. Indeed, in some of the less well known films Flynn starred in, he can be found playing opposite some of the most iconic actors in the history of cinema. They are, without doubt, performing in some of their least iconic roles. Humphrey Bogart, for instance, appears in a xenophobic part as a Mexican bandit in Flynn's second stab at a Western, the wildly uneven *Virginia City* (1940). Better on the Bogart front, however, was a late scene in the slapstick romance *Never Say Goodbye* (1946), in which Flynn's romantic lead attempts to scare off his ex-wife's interfering love interest by dressing up as a gangster and faking a Bogart-like tough-guy voice – except in this case Bogart *really* did provide the voice. It's a humorous super-imposing of Warner Bros talent in an otherwise forgotten film that proves to be an incredible layering of icon on icon. Why watch old studio films today, other than for that sense of discovery? Seeing a star from the past, who has been reduced to their most famed mannerisms by the slow passing of time, in a lesser-known film can make them feel more alive, making their career progression seem more human and immediate. A role in a defining film, in contrast, can suspend them in pickling liquid.

Pre-pickling, Flynn played romantic co-star to the big-eyed Bette Davis, who could be found (over)acting circles around him in *The Sisters* (1938) and, later, in *The Private Lives of Elizabeth and Essex* (1939). Davis was the strong-willed Warner Bros player who often found herself at war with Jack Warner (importantly landing herself in a courtroom arguing for her right to star in better quality projects). She was well suited then to take on the defiant Elizabeth I. Davis played the monarch for the back of the room, replete with sunken eye-sockets, pallid make-up and nervy twitches. The story told of an unhappy partnership between Elizabeth and Essex and this tension bled into Flynn's and Davis's behaviour behind the scenes. Flynn dedicates a considerable stretch of his autobiography – the longest devoted to any one film – recounting the ways Davis, while wearing heavy, ornate jewellery, kept insisting on hitting him across the face for real during multiple takes, sending him back to his dressing room to retch on more than one occasion.

Bette Davis is, in fact, central to the curly question of whether Flynn was a good actor or not. David O Selznick was

THE PERFECT SPECIMEN: ERROL FLYNN

trying to borrow Flynn and Davis from Warner Bros, as a package deal, to star in his ambitious adaptation of *Gone with the Wind* (1939). In her memoirs, Davis suggested that she turned down the coveted role of Scarlett O'Hara because 'The thought of Mr. Flynn as Rhett Butler appalled me. I refused. I was not going to be part of that parcel.'[31]

Davis had already been horrified when Flynn was cast beside her in *The Private Lives of Elizabeth and Essex*, believing he was nowhere near being up to the task and feeling doubtful about his ability as a screen partner (she lobbied for Laurence Olivier). Years later, re-watching the film with its co-star Olivia de Havilland, Davis is reported to have offered a reassessment: 'I was wrong, wrong, wrong. Flynn was brilliant!'

FLYNN WOULD FIND A MORE OBLIGING PARTNER WHEN he twice starred alongside a young Warner Bros recruit from Illinois. Ronald 'Dutch' Reagan would eventually, partly off the back of his pointed amiability, rise to the highest office of power in the country, becoming so-called 'leader of the Free World'. As a result of this unexpected rise, Reagan would later be photographed standing alongside a succession of Australian prime ministers, but he stood beside Flynn first. Flynn was not entirely happy with the situation – in one instance he deliberately made Reagan move away from him so the younger actor would be further downward from the camera and almost be out of shot for a scene (Reagan pulled together a pile of dirt under his feet to push himself up and into the frame). Flynn need not have been so worried. Reagan considered himself the 'Errol Flynn of the Bs' – as in the sub-par movies Warner Bros were making at the time – and didn't see himself as any kind of competition to the older star.

CAST MATES

When they finally appeared together they made for a middling 'odd couple'. Reagan's cinematic performances often teemed with a kind of blind optimism – which would help him sell American Exceptionalism later in political life – just at the point when Flynn's knowing persona was hardening into undisguised cynicism, clearly tiring of the bland heroic roles he was repeatedly asked to play.

The first film they shared on screen was one of the highest grossing films of 1940 but it is easily the nadir of Flynn's filmography, and not for aesthetic reasons alone. Michael Curtiz's *Santa Fe Trail*, a misguided historical Western, tips perilously close to serving as Confederacy apologia. Why make an uncritical film from this perspective 75 years after the Civil War was won? The answer was likely that it was chasing *Gone with the Wind*'s success, given that massively popular film had largely told its epic story from the Confederate states' position. Writing to *Gone with the Wind*'s producer David O Selznick, the secretary of the NAACP (National Association for the Advancement of Colored People), Walter White, warned that 'the writing of history of the Reconstruction period has been so completely confederatized during the last two or three generations that we naturally are somewhat anxious'.[32] White encouraged Selznick to hire an African-American fact-checker to serve as an advisor on the project (Selznick eventually went with two white consultants instead).

In *Santa Fe Trail*, Reagan took on the role of George Armstrong Custer to Flynn's Jeb Stewart.* In Curtiz's telling,

---

* Only a year later, Flynn would switch roles and play Custer in the far superior *They Died with Their Boots On* (1941). His first film working with Raoul Walsh was also a largely ahistorical affair. This production flirts with high camp, presenting Flynn growing a mullet hairpiece mid-film, while heroically munching on raw spring onions.

THE PERFECT SPECIMEN: ERROL FLYNN

Custer and Stewart start out at cadet school, ribbing each other, before a half-hearted romantic plot takes over. The flippancy of prioritising an inconsequential love triangle – between Flynn, Reagan and Olivia de Havilland – feels particularly cold and unfeeling given the stakes of the story. The banal horror of the film, however, resides in its portrayal of the abolition movement. Raymond Massey plays the evangelical John Brown as religious zealot. With darting paranoiac eyes, Brown comes off as an early prototype of a maniacal James Bond villain – with all the theatrics of a madman holding the world to ransom with nuclear weapons, rather than a preacher radically advocating for the end of slavery. Jack Warner, being told the story of John Brown, declared 'We'll make the son of the bitch the heavy'.[33] *New York Times* critic Bosley Crowther was damning in his review of the film – 'for any one who has the slightest regard for the spirit – not to mention the facts – of American history, it will prove exceedingly annoying' – singling out the extreme presentation of Brown and the dangerous misreading it set up: 'he was hardly the crack-pot villain that the Warners have broadly implied, and he deserves a better classification in the minds of impressionable movie-goers than that just one peg above a marauding cattle rustler from Bloody Gulch'.[34]

In a scene roughly halfway through the film, Flynn and Reagan escape a skirmish on horseback, having successfully captured John Brown's son. Feeling reflective, they discuss Brown's motives. In *Santa Fe Trail*, Reagan, as Custer, is partly the voice of reason. He suggests that behind Brown's supposed zealotry is an immovable purpose – an undeniable righting of an historic wrong. Flynn, as Stewart, interjects and sternly counters that it isn't the men's job to decide who was right and who was wrong about slavery, to which Reagan's Custer sheepishly apologises. Reagan's capitulation and, indeed, a film like *Santa Fe Trail* could easily set the conservative rot in your head if you were not careful. You have to question whether just voicing the dialogue of such exchanges as those between Flynn and Reagan – capturing the abdication of personal political responsibility in one of the most politically consequential moments in American history – helped birth some of Reagan's 'small government' principles. They certainly countered the ideals he grew up with and which his parents had tried to instil in him. Reagan, after all, came from a Democrat-voting family in a predominantly Republican area of Illinois. His father strictly forbade him from seeing *The Birth of a Nation* due to its Ku Klux Klan sympathies.[35] Such discouragement was not widespread in Australia, where the film was a huge success. The day after the film opened in Sydney, an advertisement ran, claiming the production to be 'A Tremendous Argument for a White Australia'.

There was little to no chance that Flynn would have even bothered to question the script for *Santa Fe Trail* when it first touched his hands. There cannot, after all, be too many actors in the history of Hollywood where you have to sincerely ask yourself if they ever directly engaged in slave trading. And yet, as soon as I began digging into the early biographical details of Flynn's life, and his time working in Papua New Guinea, there were deeply disturbing stories of him doing just that. Flynn cycled through a number of jobs in Papua New Guinea. One of them was certainly that of a 'labour recruiter' or 'blackbirder', tasked with sailing up rivers, scouting for workers for a plantation on the volcanic Umboi Island. Flynn remained in the role for longer than other jobs, so he clearly enjoyed the work and was not concerned about its ethics. A diary Flynn had left behind in Papua New Guinea before he

THE PERFECT SPECIMEN: ERROL FLYNN

fled was discovered by a hotelier, and a journalist working for the *Pacific Islands Monthly* later transcribed it. A loose-leafed typed copy resides inside the State Library of New South Wales and gives some hint of his approach and attitude to the work:

> First boy this morning – good stamp of native too.
> He'll look well leading an axe about although he doesn't suspect it yet. He thinks he's going to be my cook. This is a very good omen – to get a boy from the Chief's village means that I'll almost certainly get as many as I want from other villages.

Towards the final pages of the transcribed diary is a notation that Flynn had left a 'list of boys' by name 'with an amount of money next to it'. The list is said to have continued for three and a half pages. Some of Flynn's biographers have questioned whether the workers were being paid or not. The diary entry isn't clear if the moneys are for Flynn or for the workers, but even modest remuneration doesn't offset other considerations, including the methods by which they were recruited, the conditions under which they worked, and the fact that Flynn misled them about the kind of work they would be doing. It was a family affair: Flynn's mother would later tell his ghostwriter that it was likely Flynn's forebears had also engaged in blackbirding in the South Seas.

Flynn was happy to admit to the American press that he had worked as a slave trader. Indeed, according to a long profile by the hardened American journalist George Frazier, Flynn was still bragging about 'when I used to buy slaves in New Guinea' during his Hollywood years. One screenwriter who overheard such a story from him and who later found himself in Papua New Guinea during the war received confirmation from a 'sea captain', who complained not of Flynn trading slaves, but of not settling his debts to the sale of some men.[36]

Flynn was not content to stop at confessions of slave trading; he also wanted 'acquitted murderer' on his self-devised rap sheet. In his memoirs, he wrote of being accused and put on trial for murder. The story only ever appeared in his posthumous account and a sole reference in a letter written to his father. Flynn claimed that he had been charged with the murder of a Papuan man and that he represented himself in court, pleading self-defence. He suggested that the prosecution could not produce a body, let alone a body of evidence. Others were certain that both events – murder and trial – never occurred at all. Still, that wildly disputed story hardened into mythology, and was fictionalised in film, in the limp biopic *My Forgotten Man* (1993) – blandly retitled *Flynn* for the American market – which starred a pre–*L.A. Confidential* Guy Pearce, in training to become an agile leading man himself.

Flynn would be the subject of many attempts at fictionalised biography, with writers and directors seemingly falling in love with the mythology of his misdeeds – none game enough, however, to touch on his slave trading. The latest efforts, *The Last of Robin Hood* (2013) and *In Like Flynn* (2018) would take $288 545 and $11 255 at the American box office respectively, a staggering depreciation, which suggests audiences' love for – indeed, knowledge of – Flynn has well and truly reached its endpoint. This likely had less to do with Flynn's crimes in reality than his absence in the popular imagination.

THE PERFECT SPECIMEN: ERROL FLYNN

IN 1942, FLYNN WOULD ACT ALONGSIDE RONALD REAGAN again in *Desperate Journey*, the film in which he finally played an Australian character.* There was no special personal meaning in it, however, for in the exact same year, he renounced his Australian citizenship. It might have proved ominous. The year was an *annus horribilis* for Flynn, though everything that befell him was certainly of his own doing and the consequences were worse for those on the receiving end of his transgressions.

Indeed, 1942 might be the year that Flynn's legacy begins to fray from the films he made as he drifts into the court of public opinion. *Desperate Journey* certainly wouldn't stand up to a memory test compared to the events that surrounded it. The film was a slight wartime thriller about a ragtag group of air force fighters shot down by Germans and forced into increasingly creative forms of escape. It might have planted seeds from which *The Great Escape* (1963) and the TV sitcom *Hogan's Heroes* (first aired 1965) sprouted but there is little lasting fondness for it otherwise.

In some ways it was remarkable that Flynn was making movies at all during this period. He was watching scores of Hollywood talent being shipped out to the actual war, both as entertainers for the troops and as servicemen themselves. For Flynn, though, participation in the war would be all play

---

*   In 1950, Flynn would be permitted to play an Australian again, as the stubborn sheepherding cowboy going up against territorial cattlemen in his penultimate Western, *Montana*. In brief references to his character's antipodean background, the dialogue simply trails off when the fact is mentioned. After Alexis Smith, playing his love interest and eventual rival, asks if he comes from Australia, all Flynn can manage is a singsong, 'Say there's a lovely country'. That appears to be all the screenwriters could muster and Flynn didn't offer any improvisation to extend the measly dialogue with insider knowledge about his country of birth.

and plenty of make-believe. He failed to pass the medical exams required to enlist in the US army. The results showed a long list of medical problems: cardiac issues, chronic malaria, back problems and, most worryingly, tuberculosis. FBI director J Edgar Hoover picked up a news item critical of Flynn's deferment – 'Errol looks healthier to us than many men they take everyday' [sic] – and instructed a special agent to look into Flynn's case, believing the *Dodge City* star might be dodging the draft. Contrary to Hoover's cynical reading, Flynn was genuinely ill but he was also desperate to contribute to the war effort and wanted to make a personal case to FDR. He wrote his own letter to Colonel William Donovan – the founding father of the CIA – offering to work as a spy for the US government, suggesting he be shipped to Ireland, to trade off his father's standing at the University of Belfast and his own conspicuousness as a film star. He believed a spy could hide in plain sight as a movie star; his proposal sounded deranged:

> If I were to go there openly, as a Hollywood figure in an American Army uniform, I would be far less suspected of gathering information than the usual kind of agent. A Hollywood movie star, behaving innocuously, would not, I am sure, excite suspicion ...[37]

Donovan passed the far-fetched letter on to FDR but there is no record of reply. Unfit to serve and unwanted by the president, Flynn was instead deployed by Warner Bros as a wartime propaganda instead. Made the year before, *Dive Bomber* (1941) was his last role working for Curtiz and a curiously inert drama about the development of methods to combat altitude sickness. The film is dotted with spectacular aerial footage and had the hefty support of the US Navy on screen to make it appear much larger than its lean story. The effort, however, has all the narrative energy of a videoed instruction manual. *Objective, Burma!* (1945) on the other hand, directed by Raoul Walsh, was gripping, if overlong. It featured Flynn leading a ragtag troop through dangerous jungle warfare (these scenes were filmed in the Los Angeles Botanical Gardens and in 'scrubby swamp' down in Orange County).*

The film proved extremely controversial throughout the Commonwealth. British audiences – including Winston Churchill – were incensed that the script had overplayed America's role in the conflicts in Burma. The critic David Thomson, in his typically chatty history of Warner Bros, noted that *Objective, Burma!* was 'so blind to British and Australian efforts that the film had to be withdrawn in Britain for a year.'[38] Flynn had evidently thrown his former countrymen under the bus to promote American Exceptionalism and rewrite the history of the war. As the face of the film, he would bear the brunt of the criticism. Walsh later recalled that a newspaper had run an editorial cartoon of Flynn 'holding an American flag and standing on the grave of a British officer.'[39] Incensed

---

*   The birdcalls for the staged jungle in *Objective, Burma!* came from somewhere else altogether: A distinctive Kookaburra call can be heard throughout scenes of the troop marching through the Burmese jungle. It proves incredibly distracting for the Australian viewer. That famous 'laugh' would appear in *The Treasure of the Sierra Madre* (1948, set in Mexico), *Cape Fear* (1962, on a river in North Carolina) and in the fictional woodlands of *The Wizard of Oz* (1939). As late as 1981, Steven Spielberg was using the birdcall as aural shorthand for the exotic jungle in the first Indiana Jones movie, *Raiders of the Lost Ark*, and then again, exposing his own fondness for the sound, in the Jurassic Park sequel *The Lost World* (1997). In cinema, if a Kookaburra can find itself in the Burmese jungle, why not a twangy Australian leading his all-American brigade?

Britain attempted to extend the ban to territories where the film might have a negative impact. When the film did, finally, return to British cinemas, it ran with a written apology.

AT THE END OF *DESPERATE JOURNEY*, HAVING COMMAN-deered a bomber from the enemy, Flynn and Ronald Reagan fly over the English Channel, and, as romantic music swells, Flynn deadpans, 'Now for Australia and a crack at those Japs,' the dialogue suggesting a sequel where a fictional version of Flynn finally makes it home. The fantasia of repatriation was taking hold in Flynn's real life. In the same month as the film's release, Flynn wrote excitedly to a friend telling him that he had met with William Randolph Hearst for a job interview, and had happily landed a gig as a reporter for Hearst's International News Service. 'Don't know where I'm heading for yet but think it will be either France or Australia.'

The idea of Flynn returning to Australia to cover the war was an endearingly romantic one, but it would not come to be. Only a few days after sending the letter to his friend announcing his happy news, he was visited by the Los Angeles Police Department, who arrested him and charged him with statutory rape. Flynn faced multiple accusations brought against him together in the one prosecution. Two teenagers – Betty Hansen and Peggy Satterlee – gave credible accounts of having been coerced into sex with Flynn while underage. Hansen was a runaway working in a drug store, when a Warner Bros employee spied her and said he would introduce her to Flynn. He took her to the Bel-Air mansion of Flynn's friend, Freddie McEvoy, an Australian sportsman and socialite, and encouraged her to sidle up to the actor. In a progression that would eerily repeat in such stories across the history of Hollywood, Flynn supplied her with a drink, likely spiked, that soon made Hansen extremely ill. Indeed, Flynn's case was a precursor to the blockbuster celebrity trials of OJ Simpson and Michael Jackson decades later. In an echo of recent allegations made against Harvey Weinstein and Charlie Rose, a singer named Lynne Boyer testified that she had overheard Flynn instructing from a bedroom that 'we are taking a shower'. Boyer would be so overwhelmed by press presence at the trial that she threatened to throw herself from a window and later collapsed.

Reports of the prosecution – and its resulting court case – were drip-fed back to Australia, appearing in single-paragraph notices in the newspapers at home, typically run straight from the Associated Press. The story didn't make the front page of the *Sydney Morning Herald*, but was instead tucked away on page number six. *They Died with Their Boots On* was playing in Melbourne cinemas, unencumbered by the revelations. *Desperate Journey* was advertised in the *Los Angeles Times* as 'The Talk of the Town', implying the stories in fact boosted interest in his screen output. The then film critic James Agee wrote up a screening at the Fox Theater in San Francisco for *TIME*, slyly suggesting as much: 'the verdict of the cinemasses was warm, spontaneous and ribald'. When Flynn was on screen in a romantic reverie, Agee suggested that the audience gave in to animal urges, citing a collective wolf cry – 'a long-drawn woooo-woooo-ooo' – coming from within the cinema.

Agee reported that Warner Bros had gone to the trouble of editing out a line in the movie's trailer which could have negatively evoked the court case for audiences. The revised teaser can be found online, in which a chummy narrator announces that leading the film 'is Errol Flynn, as a fighter who knew but one command'. An awkward silence replaces what that one command was: '*Attack*'. Agee implied that it was unlikely that word would have audiences imagining a dangerous Flynn coming at them with grabbing hands. Based on the enthusiastic audience reaction to *Desperate Journey*, he was still their hero. Indeed, in both the American and Australian press, and the courtroom itself, Flynn was seen in a largely favourable light. The case seemed to be swinging definitively his way when his legal team began to question Satterlee and Hansen's credibility, bringing up separate charges they were on and digging up effective dirt. Flynn's celebrity lawyer grilled Satterlee about an 'illegal operation' she had had. For his part, Flynn tried to pass off the whole affair as a political stitch-up – an overzealous Los Angeles attorney office combing Hollywood for a case to prove. Flynn drolly titled the section of his memoir that dealt with the trial 'Head Hunters of California'.

A jury of nine women and three men ultimately found Flynn not guilty of the three charges – an initial ballot was revealed to show that two of the men held out, convinced only as deliberations continued. After the final charge was dismissed, the courtroom burst into applause and Flynn 'rushed' the forewoman and shook her hand in thanks.[40] She later spoke to journalists, telling them that 'the women discussed the testimony of the girls and we decided they were not testifying truthfully' and that they then proceeded to talk the men around. It was hard to deny that movie culture had swayed their decisions, despite assertions that they had treated Flynn like an anonymous 'John Doe'. Celebrity allure played its part. One regional Australian newspaper ran a report that the judge brought order to the court before reportedly noting, 'I have enjoyed this case and I think you have too'.[41]

The judgment in his favour restored Flynn's faith in America. In an interview on his acquittal, he declared: 'My confidence now has been justified in essential American justice. I really mean it. I didn't become an American citizen for nothing.'

Back in his shrugged-off Australia, Sydney's tabloid *Daily Telegraph* newspaper interviewed a number of young women around the city about the verdict. Most were, unsurprisingly, on Flynn's side, thinking Satterlee and Hansen were 'in it for what they could get out of it'. There were rare dissenting opinions, none really in favour of the victims. 'I don't give a hang what happens to Mr. Flynn' came one. Another: 'Errol Flynn's been acquitted? So what! Now if it had been someone handsome and dashing like Ray Milland'. The movies had clearly enacted their hypnotic sway over both the jury in America and the *vox populi* on the streets of Sydney. Laurel Alderman, an 18-year-old machinist from Hurlstone Park, voiced the confusion between the actor and his characters that would let many men get away with crimes in Hollywood for decades to come: 'I've always known he was innocent. He couldn't play the parts he does if he was a villain in real life'.

CAST MATE: JUDITH ANDERSON

Another reading of how the allegations against Flynn were handled has since emerged: that the trial and its attendant publicity were, for Flynn and Warner Bros, extremely good for business.[42] The studio rushed Flynn's new films through to capitalise on the attention associated with the trial. One of the films, released after his acquittal, saw Flynn billed alongside Adelaide-born Judith Anderson. Lewis Milestone's *Edge of*

Darkness (1943) was a rare convergence of Australian actors during the Golden Age of Hollywood. In the film both Flynn and Anderson play Norwegian Nazi-resistance fighters, residing in a small coastal fishing town overrun by the SS. The town is so small – and the cast such a proper ensemble – that it sounds like 20 per cent of its population had been transplanted from the antipodes. Flynn and Anderson play off each other with subtlety. In one scene, Anderson reprimands Flynn and co-star Ann Sheridan for embracing while on watch for Nazi troops, but then she turns reflective, and, in that moment, it feels as if they could be siblings; Anderson a stern elder sister to Flynn's bratty younger brother.

Flynn had featured opposite an Australian, in a familial role, before Anderson. In *The Perfect Specimen* (1937), where the actor proved he could make a serious play at fizzy screwball comedy, Flynn stars as a young man who has been trained by his aunt to be the 'perfect specimen' (the phrase is repeated at least three times too many throughout the film) and the plot is largely centred around his rebellion against his controlling aunt, played by May Robson, who was Australian by birth. Unlike Flynn and Anderson however, you couldn't tell immediately without an accompanying biographical note. Robson left Australia as a child, young enough to lose her Australian accent. I watched *The Perfect Specimen* without knowing she had one in the first place. Robson was, in fact, the first Australian to be nominated for an Academy Award – securing the place in 1934 for the film *Lady for a Day*, at the age of 75. The *Los Angeles Times* reported that Flynn, Robson and Merle Oberon – acting as patroness – were to attend an Australia Day celebration to support the Anzac War Relief Fund, featuring 'a real "Billy Tea"' lunch and a polo match between Australian and New Zealand teams.[43] (There is little trace of the event itself, but it seemed a precursor to the G'Day USA galas designed by the Australian government as soft diplomacy events in America.)

In acting prowess, Judith Anderson outmatched all of them. Like Flynn, she had appeared in Warner Bros films alongside Humphrey Bogart and Ronald Reagan – although she was very far in the background in those. In *Kings Row* (1942), she appeared only briefly, but it was notable as the film that gave Reagan the title of his autobiography, *Where's the Rest of Me?*, lifting the hammy, melodramatic line that Reagan delivers after his character has his legs amputated. Reagan wrote in his letters that it was 'probably the finest picture I ever made' (a sad assessment). Anderson certainly starred in her share of campy fodder too but she now reads as Flynn's opposite: serious about the job. Dedicated to the finer details of acting – she had a long and highly distinguished career in theatre – Anderson didn't come to her career via dumb luck, waiting around in a bar to be discovered.

If Flynn wanted to be acknowledged as typically Tasmanian, Anderson – born in Adelaide – practically screamed old-world South Australian. There is a commonplace, though disputed, view that the population of Adelaide and its surrounds have a 'posher' accent than the rest of Australia, but Anderson's strong and clear diction, and her eventual passion for acting, came from elocution lessons taken in her youth.

Travelling by ocean liner with her mother, Anderson was in Los Angeles attempting to break into Hollywood by 1918 – after a brief career in the travelling theatre in Australia – at the same time as the more conventionally attractive blondes from Sydney and Melbourne were arriving. Anderson might have thought she had a genuine shot: she was carrying a letter of recommendation addressed to Cecil B DeMille, and secured a meeting, but was rebuffed by both the famous director and the industry as a whole. The silent era would not have scope for Anderson to display one of her best talents – that calm, steady and commanding voice. She travelled on to the east coast instead, crossing the country by train, mother still in tow. In New York she established herself slowly on Broadway. Anderson would return to Hollywood to make her film debut in the early 1930s. *Blood Money* (1933) – a relatively fast-paced crime drama – was the third release of the newly formed 20th Century Pictures, a new venture from Joseph Schenck and Darryl F Zanuck. Two years later, their start-up would merge with Fox Film Corporation – itself fresh from its takeover of Hoyts in the Australian market – to form 20th Century-Fox.

Fox, of course, had blocked local production in Australia, stopping Anderson from potentially returning home to make a film or two. Work in the movies, however, was slow for her even in America. As historian Desley Deacon outlines in her comprehensive biography of the actor, Zanuck had suggested Anderson had the potential for a long career, but he 'procrastinated' on sending her a new contract, leaving her 'seething with impotent rage'.[44] It would be another seven long years before Anderson starred in a follow-up to *Blood Money*, but in 1940 she featured in two films in quick succession. *Forty Little Mothers*, a Busby Berkeley romp, focuses on a nervous schoolteacher hiding his adopted baby, in the confines of an all-girls school, from Anderson's stern headmistress. The slight comedy has almost no cultural trace now, but the other film released that year would be the defining role of Anderson's cinematic career. To this day, Anderson remains best known for her performance as the coldly composed, secretly delusional housekeeper Mrs Danvers in an adaptation of Daphne du Maurier's gothic melodrama *Rebecca*. Its director,

THE PERFECT SPECIMEN: ERROL FLYNN

Alfred Hitchcock, had reportedly seen *Blood Money* and kept an eye on the Australian actor. It was, however, still a competitive process to secure the role. After years in England, *Rebecca* was to be Hitchcock's first American production, having been lured across the Atlantic by mega-producer David O Selznick, who was looking to follow up his all-consuming hit *Gone with the Wind* with something of comparable import. Hitchcock later told François Truffaut that he didn't quite see it as an American production, given that most of the players were 'English'. Anderson certainly gave off Anglophone airs with her clear diction, and she stood toe-to-toe with Laurence Olivier in the lead role and with her director too. Notoriously hard on his stars, Hitchcock appeared, however, happy to humour Anderson. A gossip column published in the year before *Rebecca's* release suggested that Anderson had been on set sternly instructing her co-star Joan Fontaine – the younger sister of Olivia de Havilland – on how to play a scene. Hitchcock permitted the moment, effectively sharing the director's chair, waiting for her leave, before observing, 'Actresses! They think they know about acting!'[45]

Anderson knew more about acting than most actors, and she was consequently aware of her limitations in front of the camera, in part because she was so sure of her strengths on the stage. Hitchcock's tight close-ups of the trembling Danvers gave Anderson an opportunity to display what only the sharp-eyed sitting in the front row of the theatre had to that point been able to see. The measured performance locked Anderson into a nomination for Best Supporting Actress at the 13th Academy Awards (Anderson was bested by Jane Darwell in John Ford's *The Grapes of Wrath*, meaning big-hearted Ma Joad beat out the black-hearted Danvers). Hitchcock would try to secure Anderson for two of his later films, but her theatre contracts wouldn't permit a reunion. She would be made a Dame in 1960 and would continue to work on the stage – ultimately becoming best known for her definitive take on Medea – and only intermittently appearing in films, often as a character actor, up until her death in 1992 at age 94.[*]

ANDERSON'S MOST FAMOUS DIRECTORIAL COLLABORATOR would eventually make his own 'Australian' film, without her, when he came to lens *Under Capricorn* (1949) – a film set in Sydney in the early 19th century but shot entirely in Britain and the USA (a high school in Canoga Park in Los Angeles was used as the front of Government House in Sydney). It was a light reworking of *Rebecca*, with another scheming housekeeper ratcheting up the tension behind closed doors. There was no real reason for the film to be set in Australia other than that is where the book on which it was based had set its plot, with only the slightest references to the country's colonial history. Nor were there any Australian cast mates. The call sheet was populated by British talent and headed by the Swedish-born Ingrid Bergman.

A decade after *Under Capricorn*, Hitchcock would travel

---

[*] Anderson was central to the rise of the female character actor – often standing out in a smaller, more supporting role and given more interesting work to do than the lead. Desley Deacon quotes the *LA Times* film critic Edwin Schallert praising *Rebecca* as 'the most striking picture ever made in terms of women character players' and that Anderson would be 'responsible for increased respect by the producers in casting of character players'. A character actor, however, can still become as typecast as any lead. In *The Strange Love of Martha Ivers* (1946) Anderson plays the domineering evil aunt Mrs Ivers, a surname so close to Danvers, and the character so similarly stern and swathed in black dress that you wonder if Danvers survived the house fire in *Rebecca* and walked into this later film.

to Australia to promote his latest effort, *Psycho* (1962). He had made sure to pack with him his sense of theatricality and marketing genius. While in Sydney, he visited The Gap – the famous cliff-side spot known for its history of suicides – and posed for photographs in which he pretended to climb over the ledge. In his mind, the ominous site was the perfect spot for a suspense movie, and he teased journalists with the idea of shooting a scenario there. He even detailed the camera angles required to take advantage of the location: a tussle between hero and villain, close-ups of their feet, a trick shot following the villain as he falls over the edge. Acknowledging that the Sydney Harbour Bridge would be a 'natural' fit for one of his films, he dismissed the iconic fixture, saying he had already used the Golden Gate Bridge in *Vertigo* (1958). No, he insisted, it had to be The Gap.

Nothing was to come of the fantasy. It would prove Sydney's loss.[46]

SHOWDOWN (1949–1959)

At the end of the 1940s, Flynn signed a new contract with Warner Bros, one that would let him work on one project outside of studio control per year. He defected to MGM for a single movie – *That Forsyte Woman* (1949) – but the finished film's poor box office performance suggested his profitability was seriously sliding and he parted with Warner Bros in the early 1950s. Flynn had to get out of America to find his old footing, making a series of films in Italy and England, attempting to pay off a growing list of debtors. Chasing uncertain success, Flynn was stuck retreading earlier roles – pirates, swordsmen, historical figures – with diminishing returns. His run of down-and-out films in his last decade of life lacked the polish and steady studio hands of his earlier films. Many actors of his earlier era were similarly lost.

The stars of the Golden Age were ageing and few knew what to do with them. Some were losing their lustre faster than others. Flynn looked like an athlete played out. Unimaginative producers had him running around like a much younger man and it looked as if he might be written off entirely, until Darryl F Zanuck – that wily 20th Century Pictures founder – approached Flynn to appear in a literary adaptation, bringing him back into the fold of Hollywood prestige after his years in the European wilderness. It must have been like a shot of vitamin B for the lagging actor. Indeed, Flynn displayed a surge of energy in Zanuck's otherwise pulseless adaptation of Ernest Hemingway's *The Sun Also Rises* (1957). For journeyman director Henry King, Flynn took on the role of dipsomaniac Mike Campbell, rarely seen on screen not toting his signature bota wine bag. The rest of the film stifled the youthful verve of Hemingway's short novel by miscasting a number of the leads, Zanuck having gone with actors at least 10 years too old for their roles. Flynn certainly fell into that category; he was only 47 at the time, but looked a good decade and a half older. Yet, set free from typecasting, Flynn seemed to be the only cast member having any fun. Stern Ernest Hemingway was not so impressed. It was widely reported that he stormed out of the film just 25 minutes in, giving a reporter a concession that 'I guess the best thing in the film was Errol Flynn'. It was certainly no more than a guess because Flynn doesn't show up until an hour into the picture, long after Hemingway had already made for the exits.[47]

After a lifetime of heavy, sustained drinking, was it any wonder Flynn could play drunk? He openly acknowledged

THE PERFECT SPECIMEN: ERROL FLYNN

that earlier in his career he hadn't quite been able to step up in the role of the souse in the Bette Davis soapie *The Sisters* – 'I must have played the worst lush' – doing little more than the usual slurred speech routine.* That film was made nearly 20 years before *The Sun Also Rises* and, to adopt the standard 'critic-speak', you could say Flynn had 'grown into the role'. But would it not be more correct to suggest Flynn had 'degenerated' into playing Mike Campbell so effectively?

Australians are wont to big-note their own enthusiastic drinking culture, and alcohol consumption in the country was on a steady rise after the Second World War. Flynn's father had long struggled with alcohol abuse, and the actor's youngest daughter would die from alcohol and drug abuse in her mid-forties in the 1990s. Drinking in Australia was actually at historic lows during Flynn's young adulthood and it's likely his problems with alcohol didn't come to a head until he made it in Hollywood. He had a seemingly limitless supply of role models. Style and method were also contagious: he discovered his serial co-star Ann Sheridan would drink tomato juice with vodka on the lot to avoid detection. 'Nobody need know you have had it, that's the theory.' Skipping the juicing, Flynn took things a step further: injecting oranges with vodka and walking around the set eating them.

When it came to drinking, Flynn would long be 'under the influence' of John Barrymore – the star of the silent screen, who, due to his motor-mouth skills, sonorous voice and traditional stage training, transitioned easily into the sound era. Barrymore, unlike Flynn, was born into an acting

---

* You might also ask, should a drunk be a great study in playing a drunk? The state of being that they are well versed in is one that encourages forgetting. Who remembers how they behave after one too many drinks?

dynasty (one that persists decades later; John Barrymore was the grandfather of the 1990s screen icon Drew Barrymore). When Barrymore died in 1942, Raoul Walsh 'borrowed' his cold dead body from the morgue, where it was being stored, for one last wild night out – inspiring the 1980s comedies *Weekend at Bernie's* (1989) and Blake Edwards' madcap *S.O.B.* (1981) – installing him in Flynn's house. The body snatching did not sit well with Flynn, though; he freaked and ran from his house.*

Flynn idolised John Barrymore above everyone else and was given the chance to play his former friend in a 1958 adaptation of Barrymore's daughter Diana's tell-all memoir *Too Much, Too Soon*, about her tumultuous rekindled relationship with her father and her own battle with alcoholism. The film would reunite Flynn with Warner Bros, but those at the studio, including Jack Warner, were distraught at his state. In a case of art imitating life, Flynn was struggling with drink on set – he couldn't play Barrymore without putting away similar amounts of alcohol, which had killed his idol. Production notes from the film provided multiple variations on the logged:

'drinking – unsatisfactory performance'.[48]

By the time Flynn appeared as a colonial barfly in John Huston's *The Roots of Heaven* (1958) – shooting on location in Africa – it was as if he had been typecast in the kind of role that had initially broken him free. Flynn was given top

---

*   The anecdote – apocryphal or not – was revived by Drew Barrymore in 2020 in a viral YouTube series, *Hot Ones*, where she is interviewed while eating a set of increasingly hot chicken wings.

THE PERFECT SPECIMEN: ERROL FLYNN

billing but had little more than a supporting role, and was barely standing for most of the film. It made you wonder who else he could play at that stage. Any of these resurgent performances were the sort of late-career revivals that acting awards annually fall over themselves to honour, partly as a covert recognitions of lifetime achievement, making up for past snubs. Even more so, Flynn's work in *Too Much, Too Soon* fell into one of Oscar's favourite categories: the biopic, and better still, the 'Hollywood' biopic, which often entrance the industry with stories of itself. In fact, his earlier appearance in *The Sun Also Rises* may, in fact, have been nominated for an Academy Award; an audio recording exists of a journalist congratulating Flynn on breaking news that he had been nominated, and Flynn acknowledging the news, 'Yes, isn't that something? I never thought it would happen to me.' Except for the fact that it didn't – the official list of nominations would not carry Flynn's name.

Longstanding rumours implied that Flynn's supposed political involvement in Cuba was the reason news of the nomination was muted and then hastily withdrawn. Flynn had happily holidayed in Cuba early in his career and in 1956 he went to work on a film there, starring in a bouncy Havana noir (Havanoir?), cutely titled *The Big Boodle*. It sounded more like a children's book than the modest crime caper it was. The unseriousness of the films he was being offered might have been what got Flynn thinking about covering revolutionary activity instead of acting. But he pitched himself to William Randolph Hearst's New York Journal-American to write about the political movements of a radical named Fidel Castro. Flynn spent five days with Castro, as the young revolutionary prepared to overthrow the populist, military-backed Batista, writing up their interactions like a Boys Own

Adventure, rarely speaking to Castro on his political ideology – nor grounding the overall dissatisfaction with Batista.

He was partly reliving his past. For ten days in 1937, Flynn had taken a break from his heavy filming schedule for Warner Bros and travelled to Europe to cover the Spanish Civil War, following the Loyalist cause. The war had been the *cause célèbre* of Hollywood celebrities and Flynn had simply taken it a step further by flying to the front rather than throw a fundraiser. Flynn's personal politics in such skirmishes were always a muddled mess. It was impossible to discern how much he believed in any individual cause above how it could aid his own heroic image. His most caring biographer, Tony Thomas, stressed that Flynn's 'interest in politics never went beyond idealism', tending towards the left (if writing for a right-leaning publication). Thomas figured Flynn was purely 'fascinated with revolutionaries'. He was only interested in Castro as an image and could only see the struggle of the Cuban people in cinematic terms:

> Maybe the making of the motion picture *Robin Hood* rubbed off on me – and when I see a poor land that wants its due, why then, I am willing to lend a hand ...[49]

Flynn was more Prince John than Robin Hood. He was barely interested in the everlastingly popular Hollywood model of philanthropy. You could hardly count him as a social democrat, much less a sympathiser to the Communist cause. In fact, he actively dodged contributing to the common good, provably making efforts to avoid paying his share of tax. In 1942, he formed Thomson Productions, Inc, following the lead of other actors who created shell companies designed to turn 'personal income into less heavily taxed corporate

THE PERFECT SPECIMEN: ERROL FLYNN

income.'[50] A late-in-life purchase of a heavily romanticised Jamaican property was an investment in an idyll for certain, Flynn eyeing retirement, but it also served as a tax haven for his estate. At one point, earlier in his career, he fled America owing hundreds of thousands of dollars in back taxes.

Flynn's reputation, at least, was genuinely at stake. When he was in Cuba, the House Committee on Un-American Activities was still at work in America – and the Hollywood blacklist were still *personas non grata* – so Flynn was careful to distance himself from the Communist movement, straining to make the point to his Red-scared American audience that Castro himself was 'definitely not a Communist' though admitting some in his organisation might be. Flynn wasn't interested in political realities or even reality itself: ever the entertainer, he was out in the press claiming to have 'fought for Castro' a fact disputed by some of Castro's own troops. Castro countered, perhaps seeing the potential for publicity in America. He said that Flynn was at least present, if not exactly taking up arms for the cause, vaguely pointing out to the *LA Times*: 'He was in the fighting zone as a kind of war correspondent'. The media were happy to act as accomplices in stretching the truth. Newspapers reported he had been shot in both Cuba (in the leg) and Spain (in the head). The *New York Times* retracted their story of Flynn's 'bullet to the face' story the day after running it. It seemed certain that Flynn was stoking the flame of these stories himself. When Castro was told that Flynn had claimed to have been wounded in the fighting, the revolutionary laughed, 'Why is everyone asking me about Errol Flynn?'

Flynn's proximity to Castro barely rated a mention in Australia, yet his final film, *Cuban Rebel Girls* (1959) would bring him full circle back around to his first role in Chauvel's

In the Wake of the Bounty. Both films existed as an uneasy mix of documentary and narrative fiction, both running slightly over an hour, and both include unnecessary scenes, there only to titillate prospective viewers. On *Cuban Rebel Girls* Flynn had a screenwriting credit, but he appears as an actor in just a handful of opening scenes, mostly there to provide a lengthy voice-over. It was widely agreed that the picture existed to serve as a starring vehicle for Flynn's new girlfriend, the teenaged Beverly Aadland, in a clumsy attempt to launch her career in Hollywood.

With three marriages already behind him – to Lili Damita, Nora Eddington and Patrice Wymore – Flynn was 48 when he met the 15-year-old Aadland. It was very clear he was shrugging off any concerns that his prior statutory rape trial would put his reputation at risk. If there was doubt seeded about his guilt in that earlier case, there was none whatsoever when it came to his relationship with Aadland. If not a paedophile, he was most certainly an ephebophile, fixated on mid to late adolescents. Indeed, when Flynn read Nabokov's *Lolita*, he was said to have identified with Clare Quilty – skipping straight past Humbert Humbert and zeroing in on the narrator's more sinister double.

In fact, he offered himself up to play Humbert in a package deal, only if Beverly Aadland was cast as Lolita. It is unclear how seriously the film's eventual director, Stanley Kubrick, entertained the offer, but Flynn would be out of commission by the time it went into production. He died three months shy of 1960 and the dawning of the new decade. He was up in Vancouver, trying to offload his beloved *Zaca* for a quick cash injection, before succumbing to a fatal heart attack with his Lolita by his side. His body was flown back to Los Angeles where he was buried in the Forest Lawn Memorial Park in

THE PERFECT SPECIMEN: ERROL FLYNN

Glendale, wearing a simple grey suit, drained of the colour of his life.

THERE IS AN ALTERNATIVE HISTORY WHERE ERROL Flynn is remembered – or, more accurately, forgotten – as an Australian writer of small note rather than an outsized Hollywood film star. His journalism efforts in Cuba and Spain were only late attempts. The long-held ambition took root during his second stay in Papua New Guinea, when Flynn, frustrated by the obstructions steep tariffs were putting on Australian tobacco growers in the region, knocked out a fiery letter of complaint, which was published in full by the Sydney-based *Bulletin* magazine. Off the back of the letter, Flynn campaigned to become a correspondent for the magazine. The publishers accepted his suggestion and he made small contributions, sending missives back attempting to capture the local colour.

Flynn would later capitalise on his newfound fame in Hollywood to secure a book deal to write a novel about his sailing adventures to and around Papua New Guinea, *Beam Ends*. The short novel appeared just two years after *Captain Blood*, after Flynn travelled to New York to negotiate a book contract and an agreement that it would be serialised in *Cosmopolitan* magazine. The book is little more than a fleshed-out ship's log, sticking to the chronology of events like an unseaworthy boat hugs the shore. On Flynn's behalf, was it a vanity project or canny business diversification? It remains uncertain whether *Beam Ends* is a novel or a memoir (a second novel, *Showdown*, appeared nine years later but was not as successful and a promised third novel about his years in Hollywood never appeared). *Beam Ends* certainly mixes fact with fiction, which led Flynn's old masthead the *Bulletin* to run a damning article titled 'The Debunking of Errol Flynn', by travel writer and tax consultant Frank Clune, taking the book to task for its factual inaccuracies and Flynn's habitual lying. Clune applauded Flynn for putting it over the 'simple sooks of Hollywood' but questioned the need to invent details of his time in his home country: 'Surely he is not ashamed of Australia?'[51]

Flynn's death itself would prompt a period of intense publishing output, much of it concerned with his personal legacy. Free of the threat of defamation proceedings, these publications would bring to light transgressions not yet on the record. Having died at just 50, it was unsurprising that both his parents survived him. His father, in grief, wrote a self-pitying pair of articles, attempting to gain the sympathies of female readers in Flynn's country of birth by publishing them in the *Australian Women's Weekly*. They amounted to a half-hearted defence of his dead son. 'More Sinned Against Than Sinning' ran the headline and in it Thomas Flynn was found re-prosecuting old ideas from the 1942 rape trial – that Flynn had been pursued by lustful women, and simply had no choice but to give in to their desires.

Beverly Aadland's mother, Florence, in turn, published *The Big Love* – a pulpy memoir about Flynn's romance with her daughter, in which she claimed Flynn had violently raped Beverly on their first night together. The most devastating and sustained corroboration of Aadland's account could be found in the testimony of Flynn's second wife Nora Eddington, in her stark, transfixing memoir *Errol and Me*. Flynn had first spied Eddington at her workplace – selling cigars outside of the courtroom of his 1942 trial. She was 18. In what appeared to be his MO, Flynn sent an employee to scout the young woman's availability and bring her up to his Mulholland Drive estate. Eddington and Flynn were chaste during their courtship – Eddington aware Flynn was seeing other women and wanting to see proof of that being put to an end before committing – and Flynn employed her as his secretary to keep her around. Their initial bond was barely romantic in tenor. Eddington's mother, also Nora, had Mexican heritage and Flynn would continuously call Nora the racist slur 'wetback'. There was no real physical contact between the couple until Flynn took Eddington home one night and drunkenly raped her. He declared his love for her only after this night, to save face – 'his declaration meant less than nothing to me'.[52]

After their marriage in 1944, Flynn's drug use worsened and he became erratically violent with Eddington, kneeing her in the stomach during her second pregnancy and, in a final indignity, punching her without warning while they were walking together one night. The end of the line came for Eddington when Flynn terrorised her in their Mulholland Drive bathroom, attempting to forcibly inject her with heroin so that she would understand his own addictions.

Eddington's candid memoir was part of a long, post-humous period of back and forth when it came to Flynn's reputation, but if anyone should have had the final word it was her. The gossipy biographer Charles Higham, however, overegged it when he released his bestseller *Errol Flynn: The Untold Story* in 1980. The director and film historian Peter Bogdanovich had clocked Higham as a 'gutter' journalist a decade before, when he caught him out fabricating quotes from Orson Welles for a biography. Using unsealed FBI documents relating to Flynn, Higham mounted a shaky case that Flynn had been a Nazi spy all along.[53] Higham had spent his early journalistic career in Sydney, working as a critic for the *Sydney Morning Herald* before becoming literary editor of the *Bulletin*, then seeking favour in Hollywood and writing the biographies of many actresses (including the bestselling and authorised life of Katharine Hepburn, simply called *Kate*). Australian readers were scandalised by the book but Flynn didn't need false claims of treason added to his list of misdemeanours to help damn him. Nora Eddington publicly admonished Higham, calling in to a popular Australian radio show to express her dismay over the book. Eddington told listeners that she wished Higham had 'stayed in your country, that's where he came from didn't he?'. The book would still be quoted as a reliable source for decades to come.

AS THE CENTENARY OF FLYNN'S BIRTH APPROACHED, locals in Hobart clashed over such questions, equivocating as to whether to honour Flynn or not. Debates raged and compromises were made. A longed-for statue was downgraded to a star outside the State Theatre. Petitioning to name a beach after the actor failed and a dog park was offered instead. The Tasmanian Errol Flynn Society President was not amused: 'It's really crazy when you think about it ... Any other city would have gone out of its way to acknowledge him. It makes Hobart a laughing stock on the international stage'. The stern, plainspoken reply arrived as: 'Things should be named after people that can be looked up to'.[54]

Frank Clune's question about whether Flynn was ashamed of Australia lingered during such debates. Flynn held some answers himself. He ultimately saw his Australian identity as being a sort of elemental being residing somewhere beneath the surface. True to this reading, this part of his character geysered from within whenever he reached boiling

THE PERFECT SPECIMEN: ERROL FLYNN

point. Throughout his *Wicked Ways* Flynn repeatedly states that the result of being provoked was that 'the Aussie was up in me' or that 'the Australian came up'. He physically assaulted a cameraman by pulling an 'Aussie trick' on him: stepping on his feet while simultaneously pushing him over. When this 'Australian' appears, violence typically ensues (Jack Warner is threatened with a beating over the phone; a New York cop gets his foot stomped on; in hasty anger, when leaving his house, Flynn recklessly reverses over his own dog). So, in Flynn's mind, the Australian character represented the very worst in him – irrepressible rage and violence. In turn, much of Flynn and the details of his life represented the worst in us too.

PART 2
THE FORGOTTEN ELITE:
PETER FINCH

The 49th Academy Awards were held in late March of 1977 in downtown Los Angeles. The nominations that night were dominated, with ten apiece, by two films: Sylvester Stallone's breakout boxing hit *Rocky*, and Sidney Lumet's *Network*, an acidic comedy about television's war for ratings. Martin Scorsese's *Taxi Driver* set a far bleaker, more directly nihilistic tone, but was happily nominated nonetheless. Movies set on the east coast had been catapulted to the top tier – New York, of course, but *Rocky* was there putting Philadelphia on the map too. The Best Actor race came largely down to the stars of those films. The eventual winner, announced by Liv Ullmann, was the Australian actor Peter Finch, Ullmann's recent co-star on two films. Finch's turn in *Network* as Howard Beale – the manic-depressive news anchor turned heretic on-air preacher – had captured a nervy zeitgeist within American populism, one in which televised media and corporate politics crashed violently into one another.

Finch was not there to accept the award that night. Two months earlier, he had been struck down by a fatal heart attack

THE FORGOTTEN ELITE: PETER FINCH

in a stairwell at the Beverly Hills Hotel. Paramedics arriving on the scene were unable to resuscitate him. The heart attack had hit him the morning after he had taped an appearance for the ever-popular *Tonight Show Starring Johnny Carson* to promote his new film. Few watching the taping that afternoon would have imagined that Finch would be dead by the next morning, nor that he would go on to become the first actor to win an Oscar posthumously. Finch would later, tragically, be joined in that narrow company by another Australian, the 28-year-old Heath Ledger.

The silver-haired star had only recently committed to living in Hollywood. With his third wife, Eletha, he was renovating a modest home in Beverly Hills. Fred Astaire lived across the road. Finch would live in the completed renovation for just 13 days, but it was significant that he was settling in a place he had once admitted to reviling. He simply wasn't made for Hollywood. The first big sign of that might have been that he would walk to meetings, an outlandish prospect to most locals. The solitary walker in car-mad Los Angeles is the ultimate outsider. In Noah Baumbach's *Greenberg* (2010), the underlying psychological instability of Ben Stiller's lead character is heightened by his taking to Los Angeles streets, in hazy wide shots as he mutters misanthropically to himself. Finch, like Greenberg, occasionally ran into trouble on his walks – he was pulled up by police and questioned – but he persisted on his individualist path.

On the last morning of his life, he walked the two kilometres from his new home down to his favourite spot, the Polo Lounge at the Beverly Hills Hotel. It was, at least, a matter of following a straight line. The same could not be said for his career. His whole life had been one of haphazard zigzagging. To start with, it was an about-face that meant he even reached

A SON IS BORN (1916–1938)

Finch was born in London to an English mother and an Australian father, a rather well-known Australian at the time – George Ingle Finch. George was a chemist with a talent for mountaineering, pioneering the use of oxygen for climbs. His book *The Making of a Mountaineer* made him famous; Peter Finch would carry a copy with him for years. The father's adventurous, roaming spirit, however, didn't leave much room for a son. Not that he didn't fight for him when it came time. George Finch filed for divorce from Peter's mother on the grounds of adultery, wresting custody of their son from her. It was an empty gesture. He didn't want anything to do with Peter. George, instead, immediately handed him over to the boy's aunt and his paternal grandmother, Laura Finch.

From there, Peter had a wild, eccentric childhood, largely indebted to the esoteric passions – 'advanced ideas', Finch called them – of his paternal grandmother. The itinerant spirit that ran through Peter started with Laura. She had set the whole family on that path; having been inspired after seeing Annie Besant speak in Sydney in 1894. Besant was a British feminist and socialist, and a leading proponent of Theosophy, a new religion founded in America in the late 19th century, which drew heavily on Hinduism and, in particular, Buddhism. Years later, still intoxicated by the ideas contained within Besant's lecture, Laura travelled to Europe with her three children and her much older husband, Charles Finch, ultimately settling in Paris in 1902. Charles Finch was the chairman of the Land Court of New South Wales, and was more conservative in his ways than his wife. He was concerned about leaving behind his considerable estate in the regional town of Orange. A year later, Charles wanted the family to return home to Australia, but Laura fiercely resisted, not wishing to disrupt her children's world-class education. She suggested her husband set sail on his own. They would never see each other again, although Charles continued to support his wife and children financially for the rest of his life, sending money from Australia.

Using these funds, Laura continued her own studies in Theosophy, eventually writing on the subject for a magazine called *Annals of Psychical Research*. She had set herself up in Vaucresson, a bohemian commune by the Seine. Peter couldn't remember when he went to live with her – some reports say at age three, some at six – but he did recall the oddity of his surrounds. It would turn out to be an extremely isolating early childhood, but one that would have profound influences on his future professional direction. To counteract this boyhood loneliness, Peter began to imitate the people who came and went in his life, in the hope of keeping some part of them with him. He had an immense, precocious gift for mimicry, and was often found practising the voices of family friends while lying in bed at night. His grandmother overheard these mutterings and mistook her grandson for a spiritual medium. The boy egged her on, pretending to be able to see spirits while playing in the garden. He would run back into the house and report that he had seen a grey figure standing under the trees, sometimes giving more specific character details, such as that he saw a 'French soldier I'd seen in a book in the uniform of Napoleon's time; or a cowled monk; or some beautiful, mediaeval French lady in a wimple'.[1]

Laura Finch thus became convinced that they needed to pursue his education in clairvoyance in India. Grandmother and grandson together departed Paris in 1925, arriving in India in time for the Golden Jubilee of the Theosophical Society. They settled in Chennai – then Madras – and Peter, at nine years old, was mainly left to his own devices, unsupervised. He found more friends in Chennai than he had in Paris, building rapport with a visiting Buddhist monk. They walked the streets together begging for food. Peter disappeared for three whole days, and when he was found, his head was freshly shorn and he too was wearing orange robes. He said to those who discovered him: 'I'm a Chela now.'

It was a step too far, even for the Theosophists. They didn't want to be party to a scandal. The religion was already vulnerable to international press paying attention to their unusual activities – stories of child sexual abuse surrounded them – and the idea of a young boy befriending a guru, while running around with a begging bowl, seemed too much of a risk. Laura's former idol, Annie Besant, scolded her, saying 'she wasn't fit to be trusted with that child.' For her part, Laura agreed that she could no longer control the boy, so it was decided that they would part ways and Peter would be shipped to Australia.

There was a simple solution to his housing. The Theosophical Society, through its Australian arm, had recently taken over the lease of a mansion in the suburbs to Sydney's north. The Manor in Mosman was a sprawling estate overlooking the harbour, and came with a bountiful surplus of 55 rooms. Finch was put in the care of two men and boarded the *Otranto* in Colombo, headed for Sydney. Finch wouldn't, however, stay at The Manor for long. His grandfather soon came calling for the boy, wishing to put an end to his wife's influence on any of his progeny. Charles Finch was too elderly to look after Peter himself, so he was placed under the care of extended family who lived nearby.

His life was straightened out, his hair was cut short and he was outfitted in small, smart suits. He lived with his family in Greenwich Point, slightly west of the Sydney Harbour Bridge, in a California bungalow. The Finches, like most Australians, struggled through the Depression, and Finch left school at 15, hired by a neighbour to work as a copy boy at the *Sun* newspaper. Even as junior staff, he carried sway, convincing the paper to hire his childhood friend Paul Brickhill. (Finch's young friend would find surprising success when his book *The Great Escape* was adapted as a Steve McQueen blockbuster of the same name.) Finch might well have made a decent newspaperman, but the hothead within, however, couldn't conform. He was fired after he dumped a pitcher of water over his editor.

Instead, he would go on to make his stage debut at 16. 'Sheer economic necessity' was how Finch would later explain his turn to acting during the Depression.[2] This wasn't entirely true; he was following a passion too: he later confessed, in a bastardised premonition of his most famous line, 'I was mad on acting'.[3] He had been skipping work at the newspaper to attend acting classes at Mosman and later with the New Sydney Repertory Company. To fully commit to the life, however, he needed to leave home and find his own way. Finch would hang in the inner east of Sydney, sleeping rough in Hyde Park (a ghostly echo: Errol Flynn had been sleeping rough in the nearby Domain park a decade earlier).

For Finch, despite living in destitution, Kings Cross was a paradise. He later told a reporter that nowhere – not 'London, Paris, Hollywood or New York'[4] – had been able to compare.

He found a sympathetic community of poets, artists, writers and conmen. Finch would front up to 'Poverty Point' – on the corner of Pitt and Park streets – where the city's young actors would come together to vie for work. There were four theatres in the area – the Royal, the Palace, the National and the Criterion – and, importantly, the offices of a number of booking agents.

Finch got his first breaks with walk-on parts in vaudeville revues, playing the straight man to visiting American comic actors.* He was recommended to seek them out after standing in the dole queue, where a fellow welfare seeker thought his 'toffee bloody voice' would be a good fit. The advice would point towards a future direction. Radio acting was the only regular acting work going around Sydney at the time. Finch didn't particularly care for the form, but he first became truly famous at home through his work at the Australian Broadcasting Commission (later Corporation). He was contracted to the ABC in 1939 and given six-monthly renewal options until he finally left in 1941. Even in early adulthood, Finch had a commanding, sonorous voice – 'toffee' – but that didn't stop producers at the ABC from finding a way to deepen it further for listeners, artificially lowering the frequency. The trickery worked, and in combination with his natural acting talents, he developed a cult-like following among his listeners.

The powers-that-be at the ABC, however, would constantly fret about what to do with the bohemian young actor

---

* One of those émigré stars – Bobby Capron – took Finch down to Melbourne to co-star in a popular comedy called *So This Is Hollywood*, playing at the Apollo Theatre. The season wouldn't last long though, as during a picnic by the Yarra River, Capron drowned while attempting to save his dog, who was being swept away by the waters. Finch dived in and attempted to save Capron, but ended up saving the dog instead.

on their hands. Finch was an erratic character. One morning, he woke with a violent hangover and shook it off by swimming across the width of Sydney Harbour, washing ashore at the Botanic Gardens, before walking to the ABC and arriving soaking wet. He was too popular, and too good a performer, to fire. He was their star, but it wasn't an exclusive contract. Branching out, Finch began to secure work in local films. His first, *The Magic Shoes*, was never released theatrically and was only ever intended to test the studios' shooting capacity.* He was cast in small roles in two early Australian comedies, both directed by Ken G Hall. The pioneering Hall was a former film publicist who made a staggering 15 features throughout the 1930s, including his extremely popular adaptation of Steele Rudd's *On Our Selection* (1932).

Like Charles Chauvel, Hall had travelled to Hollywood in the 1920s, as the silent era was fading, hoping to broaden his industry knowledge. The strategic young professional was aware that even in that early era of the artform, to leave Australia and 'come back with American experience ... greatly enhanced your stocks and market value.'[5] He returned home to establish Cinesound, an early and inspired attempt at a local Hollywood-style production studio. Working under the auspices of the Greater Union Theatre group – now known as Event Cinemas – Cinesound began at Bondi Junction,

---

* His co-star in *The Magic Shoes* was Helen Hughes, daughter of the prime minister, Billy Hughes. According to one of Finch's biographers, Elaine Dundy, Finch had, as a boy in Greenwich Point, imitated Billy Hughes for a small audience, writing: 'His expression, we are told, changed in tune with that of Hughes', while his childish hand waved, no drawing circles in the air, in unconscious emulation of Hughes' gestures.' Given this was before television, Finch must have seen Hughes either on a newsreel, or else in person while courting his daughter.

in a rollerskating rink which needed to remain operational throughout the day. The company erected a 'dog box', a twelve by twelve metre stage in the centre of the rink. Preparations for shooting at night were done during the day 'while hundreds of skaters whizzed by'. Hall and Cinesound would eventually run three studios in total: in addition to the Bondi studio, a site at Rushcutters Bay was built before the expansion of a third location in St Kilda down in Victoria.* Finch was broke when he went to work for Hall. His first role was in *Dad and Dave Come to Town* (1938), a sequel to *On Our Selection*. He only spent two days working on that film, but he had a larger role in *Mr Chedworth Steps Out* (1939) as the dandy son of a keep-to-himself clerk, who asks his father to pay off his gambling debts. Mr Chedworth was played by Cecil Kellaway, a South African–born actor, who had made a name for himself on the Australian stage before transitioning to film. Kellaway went from *It Isn't Done* (1938) for Ken G Hall in Australia to *Everybody's Doing It* (1938) for RKO Pictures in America. He returned to Australia from Hollywood to take up the role of Chedworth for Hall.

Kellaway was a cheery character actor with a singsong voice and an invitingly round face. In comparison, Finch was gaunt-looking, with sunken cheeks and big expressive eyes. It was all gravy for the screen though; Hall's camera soaked him up. The Sydney-based novelist Ruth Park, who collaborated with Finch on radio plays she wrote around this time, colourfully described him as 'yellow as a smoked fish with atabrin, the anti-malarial drug'.[6] Park also recalled Finch

---

* Ever the entrepreneur, during the Depression, Hall set up a mini-golf course in the basement of Sydney's State Theatre, where patrons could play a game for a shilling, with the operation taking in up to £800 a week, more than any theatre at the time for a theatrical production.

as a 'complex, sensitive character with whom one had to be careful'. Finch would invite Park to lunch and then leave her to pay for their meals. But he was generous when he did have money, giving most of it away. He had the same cash flow problems as the studios in Australia – the profit all went out the door.

SONS OF THE ANZACS (1939–1947)

Despite Hall's legendary productivity, Cinesound eventually found the economic risks of feature film production too great to continue making them. Greater Union backed down from further investments. The greatest obstruction, however, was the start of the Second World War. There were material challenges as a result: raw film stock was in short supply as it used some of the same components – namely nitrate – as explosives. The industry was short-staffed too, with many technicians and performers having been enlisted. Cinesound instead moved into producing newsreels, increasingly important as public information services during the Second World War, with footage provided by the Commonwealth Department of Information. Ken G Hall thrived under such conditions – the old publicist in him particularly suited to issuing propaganda. Indeed, Cinesound was behind the short documentary *Kokoda Front Line!* (1942) which detailed the movement of Australian troops in New Guinea, addressed to their 'wives and sweethearts', becoming the first Australian film to win an Academy Award. A small placeholder statue was sent to Hall as war regulations prohibited the Academy from casting their Oscars in gold.

Hollywood was certainly doing its part during the war.

In a similar spirit, Australian actors serving in the military across the world would put on shows for their fellow soldiers. Finch was among them. He had been uncharacteristically enthusiastic in signing up to serve in the war. Finch was assigned as an anti-aircraft gunner and was first stationed in Gaza, before his unit moved to Sri Lanka – then Ceylon – to fight the Japanese. He was moved again to Singapore and then Sumatra, before settling in Darwin as the war came closer to home. It was in Darwin that the actor began performing 'Finch's Follies' – featuring a grab bag of sketches, dances, songs and blue humour – for both Australian and Allied servicemen. The shows he put on were wildly popular.

The Australian government was getting in on the act too. The Department of Information established a National Films Council to advise their efforts in June 1940. In an echo of Allied powers at large, the council's membership included Australian representatives from the American companies MGM and 20th Century-Fox. Finch was placed on leave so he could narrate a number of their propaganda efforts. In the government-made *Jungle Patrol* (1944), Finch – credited as Gnr Finch – narrates the 19-minute documentary in second person, intending to give the viewer a direct sense of their orders if they were deployed in New Guinea.*

---

* One of Finch's most important narration jobs can be heard in *Indonesia Calling*, made just after the war in 1946 and produced by the Waterside Workers' Federation. It was directed by the Dutch documentarian Joris Ivens, working in Sydney, to document union blockades against Dutch shipments of arms to be used against the Indonesian independence movement. Decades later, the short film remains a remarkable record of a politically active, culturally diverse Sydney workforce coming together to support some of their nearest neighbours. It was only one hour of work in a soundbooth for Finch to record his reading of the script, but its qualities are incredibly lasting.

Finch was also loaned out by the army to appear in the rumpty *The Rats of Tobruk* (1944), Charles Chauvel's early attempt at telling the story of Australians fighting during the Second World War, made while it was still being fought. Chauvel's nationalistic style found a natural home within Anzac myth making, showing Australian troops fighting in Libya and later in New Guinea. He wanted to project the war back to Australians and give a sense of its scale, but it was a lean wartime production. Sand dunes at Cronulla stood in for the deserts of Libya. *The Rats of Tobruk* – partly funded by Hoyts, and so, by association, 20th Century-Fox – was significantly cut down for a delayed American release, a long seven years after it had come out in Australia. Bosley Crowther damned the film in the pages of the *New York Times*, writing that it was 'one of the most harrowing bores in years from anywhere – the Bush or the bushes at the bottom of the garden'.[7]

Trade was, as ever, far better in the other direction, but still presented a set of problems in need of creative solutions. The American studios operating in Australia during the war couldn't send profits they had made from film rentals back to the US due to wartime restrictions on the transfer of moneys. The managing director of Columbia Pictures' Australian outpost decided that the studio could funnel the money back into local investments instead, delivering a finished film to the US market and unfreezing their capital in the process. The Australian head of Columbia Pictures contracted Ken G Hall – and so Cinesound – to deliver the picture. Hall, as director, drew the conclusion that Columbia's best bet would be to make a biopic of a local famous identity, who also had international name recognition. Don Bradman, despite being a 'Supergod' according to Hall, was knocked out of contention early on. What market would there be for a film about a cricketer in

America? Ned Kelly was briefly considered, but the producing team decided that previous film adaptations had oversaturated the market for his story. Eventually, Columbia whittled down their shortlist to the opera-singing powerhouse Dame Nellie Melba and the aviation pioneer Sir Charles Kingsford Smith, the namesake of Sydney's international airport. The producers deemed the European opera house sets needed to tell Melba's story too expensive, so Kingsford Smith was decided as the more economical model.

Hall had also known Kingsford Smith from parties and nightclubs in Sydney before the pilot's disappearance over the Andaman Sea, and felt he had a good understanding of the man. The poet and occasional film critic Kenneth Slessor took a pass at the script, as did another critic, Josephine O'Neill. Hall ended up co-writing the film himself, working with Alec Coppel (who would most famously go on to co-write *Vertigo* with Alfred Hitchcock), and their completed work for *Smithy* – retitled *Southern Cross* for the UK market and *Pacific Adventure* for the US – would focus on Kingsford Smith's 1928 flight across the Pacific Ocean from San Francisco to Brisbane (with stopovers in Hawai'i and Fiji). The groundbreaking crossing, in a rickety three-engined Dutch airliner, had opened the possibilities for eventual commercial flights between the two countries.

The heroic role of Kingsford Smith was highly sought after by local actors, perhaps aware that the film had US backing and what that might mean for future career prospects. Finch was in the running for the lead role against a relative newcomer, Ron Randell. Finch and Randell had recently co-starred in Eric Porter's 1946 melodrama *A Son Is Born* (Finch played Randell's father in the first act of the film). *A Son Is Born* was shot before *Smithy*, but held over to capitalise on the larger film's marketing. Randell – younger and more conventionally handsome than Finch – had already appeared in a couple of Australian wartime propaganda films for Hall, and had spent time in the US, where he had sought treatment for tuberculosis at the Mayo Clinic. He ultimately beat Finch to the role. Hall later stated that his preference had always been to cast Finch as Smithy. The studio heads in America, however, were given access to screen tests Hall had shot with both Finch and Randell. The message came through loud and clear from Hollywood that Randell should be cast, as he had more potential as a romantic lead and had more 'woman appeal'. Hall conceded that Finch was still extremely thin after his three-year stint in the war and wasn't coming across well on camera. The director said the actor never forgave him.

Finch was right to be sore. The role delivered on the international attention it promised: on seeing the completed film, the head of Columbia Pictures, Harry Cohn – a proto-Weinstein of the casting couch era – bought Randell a ticket to America and put him on a contract with the studio.* Columbia failed to live up to previous promises that this might be a rolling model of investment in the local industry.

---

* In 1948, Randell published a small 48-page pamphlet called *In Hollywood*, emblazoned with a cartoon-character version of its author and intended as a letter home to his fellow countrymen, providing an insight into the bright lights of his new home city. Randell explained American culture, food, drink and, in crude terms, gender relations for the local audience. He was on to the importance of car culture in California. To be without a car in Los Angeles, for Randell, was like 'turning up to a Government House ball in Canberra in a dirty cricket shirt'. First impressions were important to Randell, knowing his place in history: 'I would be the first Australian that many of these people in the studio had met and they would judge Australia accordingly. I must put up a good show'. There is little doubt he made the effort, but Randell is barely remembered now by either country.

Cinesound didn't share in the profits and Cohn didn't want to create productions that were so far flung and out of his control. Hall believed that the reason Cohn so brutally edited the film for the American market was to hide the fact that it was made by Australians in the first place (music credits for the Sydney Symphony Orchestra were cut for instance).*

The production history of *Smithy* provided a potential map to how the Australian film industry could have sustained itself in the late 1940s and into the 1950s; the Australian government, through strategic legislation, should have required American film companies to direct part of their profits into local productions. It is a battle in Australia that seemingly has no end, with the federal Labor government announcing in January 2023 – as part of its sweeping new cultural policy – that it would attempt to pass legislation to introduce quotas for the streaming giants to support local content.

IF FINCH FELT WOUNDED BY HIS PERSONAL REJECTION from the film, and Randell's subsequent success, he reportedly didn't show it. It may have, however, made him drift from cinema, as he redoubled his efforts and enthusiasm for the theatre.

In 1946, the same year *Smithy* was released, Finch co-founded the Mercury Theatre, with a group of friends, lifting

---

* *Smithy* remains uniquely of note because it features the former prime minister Billy Hughes playing himself (perhaps encouraged to take up acting by his thespian daughter). Hughes, by then in his eighties, but playing himself in his sixties, was profoundly deaf and refused to take directions from Hall, adlibbing much of his dialogue and dragging out takes interminably.

the name of their company from Orson Welles' independent repertory launched in New York City less than a decade earlier. Welles' Mercury was famed for its modern-dress production of *Julius Caesar*, and news had clearly filtered through to Finch and his company about the Kenosha-born director's various successes, even if they weren't able to attend the actual productions. They were already looking towards America, scouting for big ideas.

One of Finch's co-founders at the Mercury, Sydney John Kay, was a composer, and provided the score to the Finch-starring *A Son Is Born* and the popular children's movie *Bush Christmas* (1947). Born Kurt Kaiser, Kay would change his first name to Sydney to signal his love for his adopted city. Finch and Kay met in cafes in the inner city, sketching out ideas for their fledgling theatre company, and in doing so they came up with a list of lofty goals to be delivered within an ambitious timeframe. They wanted to purchase or rent a building within two months of launching a series of short plays at the NSW State Conservatorium of Music. They outlined that the main company would open with five different plays, with 14 performances weekly. The productions would be English, American, Australian and 'Continental' with the hope to establish a touring revue. Beyond this, they wanted to add a children's theatre, launch a monthly critical review publication, set up a club of actors, and extend their activities to 'larger premises, country tours' and the 'foundation of companies interstate'.

If it sounds overly ambitious – not to mention exhausting – the Mercury Theatre was in keeping with the ambitions of independent arts organisations around Australia, where modernist influences were taking serious hold. Patrick White was willing his early, troubled novels into existence. Harry

Seidler had arrived in Australia to build his mother's house, before deciding to stay on, shaping modernist architecture across the country. William Dobell was challenging pre-conceived ideas about painting, causing controversy and panic along the way.

Indeed, one of Dobell's famous subjects, Margaret Olley, painted the sets for opening night when the Mercury presented three one-act plays at the NSW State Conservatorium of Music, just as they had hoped. The Mercury didn't go on to achieve all its goals – there was no children's theatre, no critical review – but it did manage to come good on establishing an acting school. Finch was out the front, teaching a handful of young hopefuls, using the Stanislavski system. Developed by the Russian theatre actor Konstantin Stanislavski, the system was a series of techniques designed to create more naturalistic performances through evoking actual emotions, conscious or subconscious, within the actor. Stanislavski's ideas were to rip through American cinema, motivating Marlon Brando, James Dean and their nearest contemporaries to strive for realism. In Sydney, Finch had been carrying with him a dog-eared copy of Stanislavski's *An Actor Prepares* since it was first published in Australia.

Finch was serious about his studies. After the war, he spent time in Tasmania convalescing, but he wasn't quite resting. While his first wife, the glamorous ballerina Tamara Tchinarova, who he had married in 1943, was touring with an Australian dance company on the small island state, Finch had holed up in a library in Hobart, where he hoped to write a book on the history of Australian theatre. Upon his return home, he gave lectures based on his research to the dramatic society of the University of Sydney. Finch extended these ambitions when he wrote and recorded a lecture for the

ABC titled 'The Case for a National Theatre in Australia'. For Finch, accessibility to this theatre was key. He was driven by social democratic ideals, arguing persuasively for a 'national theatre that will inspire our young local painters, actors, singers, dancers and producers to greater theatrical heights, the presentation of which may see at a price which the lowest-paid man in the community can afford'.

The Mercury might well have been the working model. Ultimately, however, not even a fixed space in Sydney could be locked down. Having a home base was an essential step towards any further-reaching national ambitions. This restriction did, however, lead to one of the company's most innovative programs: the Mobile Mercury Players, a roaming, decidedly unfixed theatre. Finch and the young company planned a touring program, with abridged plays that could be staged within the space of an hour-long lunchbreak for working-class theatregoers. Sydney John Kay designed a folding stage that could be packed up and moved around with relative ease and so the Mercury became a properly proletariat theatre. The company performed in school halls, surf clubs and factories.

It was on one of the floors of the latter – an industrial glass factory down by the water in Waterloo – that the key inflection point in Finch's career would take place. Sitting among the 450 workers that day were two of the most famous actors in the world, and they were both seriously impressed with the young Australian performing in front of them.

ENGLAND MADE ME (1948–1954)

Vivien Leigh and her husband, the recently knighted Sir Laurence Olivier, arrived in Australia in 1948, having agreed to tour the storied Old Vic Theatre, which Olivier had taken over as co-director at the end of the war. The Old Vic had taken on significant damage during the Blitz, and while reconstructions were underway it was clear that programming needed to be, quite literally, out of the box. The British Council had proposed the year-long junket to Australia, intending it as a thank you to the Anzacs for their war efforts. No one expected that Olivier would actually accept the invitation, but he saw it as a chance to develop and strengthen the troupe's touring capacity and work towards his ambitions – in step with Finch's own – for the establishment of a National Theatre.

The small group rehearsed at sea on the four-week journey before arriving in Western Australia. They would then move on to Adelaide, Melbourne and Hobart before finishing the Australian leg of the tour in Sydney and, briefly, in Brisbane. The Australian public was abuzz with their arrival: it was Beatlemania before Beatlemania. Leigh was immeasurably famous after playing Scarlett O'Hara in *Gone with the Wind*, widely considered, with inflation adjusted, to be the biggest box office success of all time. As O'Hara, Leigh had won the Academy Award for Best Actress. The year before their tour, Olivier had finished work on his filmed version *Hamlet* – featuring his iconic and shocking blond dye job – which would be released in cinemas the same year as their Australian tour, and would win him Best Actor and Best Picture at the Oscars ceremony held in 1949. Olivier and Leigh went to see it at a premiere while they were in Melbourne, and at a charity matinee in Sydney.[8]

It was remarkable that they found the time. The couple's schedule was crowded with public duties. They were expected to give speeches across the country, in any city in which they arrived, which added to an already significant workload. They did the best they could to acknowledge the local industry. Olivier and Leigh were still theatre royalty and they acted like proper emissaries, steeped in the etiquette of theatregoing, and reverent to it above all else. If they did want to take in the local scene, the local scene very much wanted to let them in. The chance to have genuine stars in the audience was too much to simply let slide. Sydney John Kay wrote to Olivier, inviting him to see the Mercury's staging of Molière's *The Imaginary Invalid*. Given the name of the company, Olivier might well have thought he was getting an invite from Orson Welles. Olivier wrote back that their schedule was incredibly tight and he couldn't make the proposed date, but if the Mercury could suggest alternatives, they would try to fit the play in.

Finch was furious. He didn't want Olivier to attend at all. Behind his fury was an intense, and understandable, set of nerves. Finch would naturally struggle to think of a more intimidating pair to perform in front of. Olivier was reportedly no fan of Molière, but he showed up anyway. Leigh announced on arrival that, 'We've come to see your Peter Finch'. Olivier leant forward during the performance, a sign of his confidence in Finch's abilities. When they were finally face to face, Olivier told Finch if he was ever in England to 'Look me up'. The casual nature of Olivier's short invitation seemed designed to hide the immense honour it bestowed on the younger actor. It was a knighting all of its own; a veritable kingmaking. They would serve as parting words too; Leigh and Olivier shortly left Australia by boat for New Zealand. They looked back fondly on the country which had hosted them, but saw drifting political and cultural allegiances. Olivier said of Sydney that it 'not only claimed to be as sophisticated a city as could be found in the civilized world, but wished one to be aware that if it was influenced by anyone it was by America rather than Britain, and so indeed it seemed'. This might have been true of other Australian cities too – and Australians themselves might have felt it – after the war, but Britain still held sway and attracted its share of expatriates.

FINCH AND TCHINAROVA PACKED UP THEIR LIFE IN Australia on the strength of Olivier's recommendation, and arrived in England at the end of the year. It was a repatriation for Finch, but only just. While Finch had been born in London, he had spent very little time there before being sent to Paris. The drab grey weather which greeted Finch and Tchinarova had a foreign and alienating feel. To one journalist, writing a profile of Finch at the time, it was 'evil-smelling' and 'undeniably the most cheerless city in the world'.[9]

The journalist behind the piece was Australian critic and novelist George Johnston, who provided the first longform, in-depth profile of Finch, written as a dispatch from London, detailing the young actor's early successes. Later on, Johnston, who would famously base himself and his family on the Greek island of Hydra, hit hard times while there, and Finch loaned him money for 'another year on the island' and to 'have a go at another book'.[10] Finch was also said to be interested in buying the film rights to a book Johnston had co-authored with his wife Charmian Clift. Johnston repaid the favour by transforming Finch into Archie Calverton in his Miles Franklin award–winning novel *Clean Straw for Nothing*, which fictionalised Finch's benefactor act – 'in this way, aggressively, almost as though he hated both of us for the situation forced upon us, it was Calverton once again who came to the rescue' – but also put him in the middle of a complicated yet platonic love triangle with the fictional stand-ins for Johnston and Clift (it is widely believed that Clift's anxiety about her depiction in *Clean Straw for Nothing* aided in the depression that ended her life in 1969, the year of the novel's release). Johnston largely stayed true to the biographical details of Finch's life – although he killed Calverton off in a fictional car accident in the book's final pages – and he provided the reader with a series of perfect, concrete physical descriptions of Finch including his 'young-old face' with the 'sharp deep-set eyes and gaunt cheekbones, the big sensual mouth and the spiky tangle of hair'.[11] In 1985, the *LA Times* reported a film adaptation of the novel was imminent, to be directed by Gillian Armstrong and starring Mel Gibson. It would be filmed in Greece and the material reworked as more of a biography of Finch. Nothing came of it.[12]

Long before life on Hydra, Finch found a flat to live in in London and began to call the Oliviers, in the hope of finding an audience. The Oliviers weren't in the best of shape after their Australian tour. Olivier had done his knee in on the trip, and Leigh's underlying mental health condition – manic depression – had been tested throughout. It was a painful wait for Finch and Tchinarova, as the social call was essential to Finch securing work. They were eventually invited to attend a small cocktail party. Sherry and biscuits were served, but the Oliviers had to rush off to another party shortly after the Australian couple arrived. It was a disappointing reception. Olivier, however, was good on his word. He signed Finch to a five-year contract with the newly established LOP – Laurence Olivier Productions – an attempt to go independent after his own contract with the Old Vic was not renewed. Finch debuted in *Daphne Laureola* for LOP, playing a young Pole who is infatuated with a middle-aged English woman. After a nerve-wracking opening night, it received strong notices. Finch's role was minor in the play, but it was blown up at home as a major heroic act. Morsels of praise the performance received in England made their way back to Australia – seemingly always a country whose media would heed the opinion of the homeland. The *Sun* practically screamed, 'Sydney Actor Hailed in London.'

Olivier didn't have another play lined up for Finch right away. As he had in Australia, Finch took on minor film roles in the background. British cinema had come into its Golden Age in the 1940s. Directors David Lean and Carol Reed, and the pairing of Michael Powell and Emeric Pressburger, were working steadily. Finch wasn't up to working with their likes yet, but he secured work in more modest fare, which gave him the space to stand out. He cut through in *Train of Events* – an uneven anthology of stories in the lead-up to a train crash – as a young man who murders his mistress. *Variety* in the US, in a short capsule review, singled him out:

> Acting plum falls to Peter Finch. His tense overwrought emotions, depicting how war can turn a harmless nonentity into a murderer, are convincingly and forcefully portrayed.[13]

It was clear, however, from *Train of Events* that Finch would never be the traditional leading man. Despite the clean lines of his face and sharp jaw, he was, overall, too intense, inward-looking, searching and profoundly quiet. So he would often show up late in movies, playing an intense quasi-love interest, disrupting the main plot, occasionally underwritten, but never not fully present. His skill, from all that radio training, was to give warmth to his words, sounding full and rounded, but in such a way that made the viewer aware that he was always holding back an acid tongue. That lashing tongue would make its presence known in his personal life.

FINCH WAS WORKING ON A SMALL SCALE UNTIL HE CAME face to face with one of the biggest icons in cinematic and theatrical history. The meeting would happen away from the cameras. In 1951, Laurence Olivier convinced the titan Orson Welles to travel to London and mount a limited run of *Othello*. Welles had only recently wrapped a troubled stop-start film adaptation of the play, which he had self-financed, taking him three years to complete as he propped up the production by taking on different jobs. His *Othello* – eventually released in 1952 – had been shot across Italy and Morocco, using as many real locations as possible, and Welles wanted to bring the spirit of invention with him to Olivier's stage. News spread through theatre circles that Welles didn't wish to cast anyone with experience playing in Shakespeare productions, a directive that ruled out most of the country's top-tier acting talent. Most British actors started actively downgrading their CVs, putting strikes through appearances in Shakespeare plays. Indeed, Maxine Audley, who would play Emilia for Welles, had in fact played that very part before, and did a very good job of hiding it.

Welles' unusual casting call left Finch in a good position to snare a role. Olivier went in to bat for Finch with Welles, convincing his American friend that Finch should be his Iago. Finch wasn't exactly ecstatic about Olivier's campaigning on his behalf. He was feeling burnt out from having taken on too many acting commitments since landing in London. Film offers were coming in too – and with them shorter schedules – but Olivier was convinced that Finch wasn't ready to take them on, and told him so. Still, Finch couldn't turn down the opportunity to stand directly across from, and whisper in the ear of, the giant he had so admired from such a great distance back in Sydney. (It is unclear whether Finch ever mentioned to Welles the influence on his Sydney troupe, and the pinching of the Mercury name.)

Typical of the *Citizen Kane* director, however, Welles didn't quite live up to his outsized reputation. His professionalism was wanting. Rehearsals were chaotic. Welles threatened his players; if they weren't up to his standard, he would swing a 20-foot pole, normally used for adjusting stage lights, and make them jump over it. He was more interested in recounting stories from his own life than having anyone practise Shakespeare's lines. Welles kept repeating a story of John Barrymore picking up an actress and throwing her into the wings. There is a difference between holding an audience captive, and holding your cast mates hostage. At a certain point, Finch had had enough, telling Welles in a rough Australian accent: '*Fuck you*'.

Welles' unprofessionalism did not end there. He refused to rehearse on stage with the cast, sending his understudy to perform beside them. When he did take to the stage, he would skip lines and rush through to the end of his soliloquies. He instructed the cast that under no circumstances must they touch him, creating even more distance between them. A week before opening a touring preview in Newcastle, Welles disappeared. He had gone to Italy for a party.[14]

It was clear, as the production was rolled out for a regional opening tour, that Welles himself had not memorised the play properly and was improvising, casually adding some lines not taken from *Othello* at all. He entered the stage from unexpected directions and moved around in ways that were not rehearsed. This threw his cast off, and might have been deliberate: he refused to be upstaged by any of them. He put on padding and stepped into 4-inch stilted shoes to bring his already tall frame to a towering six foot six inches. In a moment of great deflation, it became obvious that Welles had deliberately filled out the cast with shorter actors than himself.

Finch, however, continued to stand up for his cast mates off the stage. Welles would insist that the cast join him for drinks after each performance, boring the troupe with longwinded, self-promoting stories. Finch tried to shut down Welles' endless self-mythologising by one-upping him, calling on his own set of colourful stories from back in Australia. In doing so, he managed to do what few had ever managed: he shut Orson Welles up. Once they had left Welles' suite, a cast mate, in the grips of getaway laughter, exclaimed to Finch: 'You've done it! You've won by a knock out!'

These verbal contests remained in place for the rest of the Newcastle tour, but at least there was a sense of sport to them now. Welles remained unsporting on stage. Far worse than that, he was physically violent throughout the rest of the run. One night, he was overly enthusiastic in play-strangling Gudrun Ure in the role of Desdemona, and, on another, he threw a bag of coins at Maxine Audley, cutting her face and drawing blood.[15] It was no wonder that his supporting cast didn't give their best performances on *Othello*'s opening night at St James's Theatre – Welles was lucky they gave him anything following his ongoing oppressions – and, consequently, reviews were mixed. Finch was more decisive in his thinking on Welles:

I learned from him not to have so much talent that it explodes in all directions. I was usually the recipient of the explosions ... If he offered me £70,000 – I wouldn't act with him again.[16]

Welles didn't completely scare Finch off Shakespeare. He signed up for Mercutio in *Romeo and Juliet* the year after starring in *Othello*. The rendition – widely praised – would prompt his return to film acting. Vivien Leigh, having taken in Finch's Mercutio, appeared at his door at 2 am, in the grips of a hypomanic episode, brandishing the script for a film titled *Elephant Walk*, a romantic melodrama, whose producers were hoping would recapture some of the magic of *Gone With the Wind*. The film was scheduled to begin shooting in a week in Sri Lanka and, at that point, was without a male lead.

The producers had offered the part to Olivier, which would have allowed him to work alongside his wife, but he had bowed out citing exhaustion and commitments to the stage (Olivier later rebuffed the idea: 'I've never been exhausted by anything in my life. I just thought it was a fucking awful film.'[17]) Paramount Studios, who were producing, had tried to secure the likes of Clark Gable and Marlon Brando without success. The approach to Finch was made as a last-ditch attempt to fill the role and save the production. He didn't have the standing typically required to land the male lead in a Hollywood production of that size. And, with a budget of $3 million, it was Paramount's biggest movie of the year, but Leigh was insistent. She wanted to work with Finch.[18]

Irving Asher – the Warner Bros envoy who had played a central role in discovering Errol Flynn with *Murder at Monte Carlo* – was running *Elephant Walk* for Paramount, and it was he who relented, giving in to Leigh's demands. Finch agreed to the part enthusiastically, enticed by the Sri Lankan shoot and appearing opposite Leigh. Prestige went along with her wherever she went. A year earlier she had won her second Oscar, for her performance as high-strung and strung-out Blanche DuBois in Tennessee Williams' *A Streetcar Named Desire*. In purely clinical career terms, there was no way Finch could turn down such an opportunity. He might well have come to regret it. The fact that Leigh was knocking on his door after midnight should have been ominous enough.

The cast's nerves were on edge from early on. The plane they had boarded to Sri Lanka had, just two flights later, crashed, killing all aboard. That disaster gave flight to a disastrous romance: Finch and Leigh were falling for each other. Parties until 2 am were regular occurrences. They were a heady, potentially toxic mix, dangerously suited to each other. The pair had both spent parts of their childhoods in India, and both liked to drink. After a night out, Finch could keep it together on set the next day, but Leigh was struggling to deliver anything resembling a performance.

Olivier was called to fly in to check on his wife. He was confronted with an anxious Leigh, still in the grips of an extended manic episode, experiencing the increased sex drive that is one symptom of that condition. He left as soon as he had arrived, uncertain how he could be of help in a situation without a clear remedy.

Production wrapped on external shots and the cast and crew were to fly to Hollywood to film the interiors on set. On the first leg of the 72-hour journey to California, Leigh escaped from her seat moments after take-off. She was shaken by news of their previous aircraft having crashed, and her own memories of having survived a plane crash with Olivier in 1946, when an engine of a passenger liner leaving La Guardia airport had caught fire; the pilot miraculously landed in Connecticut. Now years later, she was inconsolable and so uncontrollable. She bashed her fists against a window and began to take her clothes off. Finch and an air steward attempted to hold her down, but she threw them off and repeated the attack against the hull. A sedative was administered, and peace descended on her at last, but it wore off later on, and Finch had to restrain her yet again. Demonstrating how contagious anxiety can be, Finch would develop his own fear of flying following the incident, which would place serious limitations on his career. It is hard to be a true itinerant if you can't fly. He refused unless it was completely necessary, taking time-consuming sea and rail trips instead.

Once the cast arrived at Paramount Studios – they were on the biggest soundstage on the lot – matters would hardly improve. Leigh, still clearly confused, started calling Finch 'Larry' and she started inserting dialogue from *A Streetcar Named Desire* into her *Elephant Walk* lines. It continued until she collapsed on set, unable to stop crying. David Niven – an old friend – swooped in, bundled Leigh up and drove her to his home. A panicked Finch absented himself, unable to cope with the extreme situation. Olivier later damningly noted in his memoirs, 'Where the hell was he by the way?'[19] It wasn't a good look for Finch to run out when the going got tough, but he didn't disappear entirely: the film still needed finishing. The studio replaced Leigh with the much younger Elizabeth Taylor, who had only recently shaken off her status as a child star (the cinemagoer is naturally forgiven if they forget she was in *Lassie* and *Come Home*). Finch was deeply concerned about the nearly 20-year age gap between Leigh and Taylor. To play against Taylor would be to appear in a completely different film from the one he had been shooting in Sri Lanka with Leigh. It would undeniably change the nature of the relationship between the two characters, but he had no choice except to press on.

After all that turmoil, the resulting film is *fine* but forgettable. The seams showing where Leigh was cut out from the Sri Lankan shoot are not visible enough to transform it into the curio it could have been. Instead, it stands as an uncritical piece of colonial art, too bloodless to become objectionable agitprop, not passionate enough to become something worth fighting with. The whole production only comes roaring to life in its last scenes when a herd of its titular elephants storm – running not walking – Finch and Taylor's sprawling estate, knocking down and accidentally setting walls ablaze, bringing down the old colonial mansion.

Finch is serviceable in the film, although Bosley Crowther at the *New York Times* had him down as 'just plain bad'.[20] It was, ultimately, the sort of role he would perfect later, that of an aloof husband figure, prone to drink, but with a romantic residing deep within. The studio heads at Paramount were impressed by the performance, offering Finch a seven-year contract, which the actor took into consideration. But, as it would turn out, Finch hated – *hated, hated, hated* – Hollywood. It failed to live up to his expectations. For Finch, the glamour was gone and the lights dimmed. He was expecting the freewheeling scenes he had heard about happening during the Golden Age, but instead he found closed-shop communities and gated-off stars. If he was being charitable, he would call the atmosphere of Los Angeles as one of 'relaxed hysteria'.

Finch later told a television interviewer, 'I thought it was a hideous existence in Hollywood'. He gamely recounted having visited Marlon Brando's house and finding that it 'was like trying to get into San Quenton prison with sliding doors, and dogs and secret microphones' with Brando's wife throwing bricks through the windows. With such discoveries, combined with his personal experiences with Leigh, it was all too much: there was a psychic disturbance in the air.

Finch would acutely feel Los Angeles' bad influence on his appetites and try to resist them. Warner Bros, however, forced him to give into his impulses in New York when he was promoting the Roger Moore – co-starring *The Sins of Rachel Cade* for them in the early 1960s. The studio people pressured him to run up a big bill at the hotel he was staying at in order to push a story. They suggested he order Moët et Chandon, Chivas Regal, caviar and to complain about the suite. 'They love cunts at the front desk,' the publicity director at Warner Bros suggested. Finch wouldn't oblige; an Australian austerity came over him. According to his second wife, 'by the time we flew into LA we were already known as a couple of weirdsies.'[21]

He had her drive him around in a Cadillac, drinking tequila together. When he refused to show her Hollywood, she threw him out of the car on Sunset Boulevard and he disappeared around a corner. It brought out the worst in him. Perhaps Finch was simply wise to the end of the studio system – of which *Elephant Walk* was certainly a minor portent – and that the New Hollywood was still some time off, and that, whenever it did arrive, he would likely be too old for its youthful inventions. So, ever the vagabond, Finch turned down the offer from Paramount and made his way back to England, returning to the rain, ready to resume his career there.

CAST MATE: DIANE CILENTO

British cinema in the 1950s was floundering in ways familiar to Hollywood. The studios were facing cinema's great technological competitor – television – as the boxes were being installed in homes across the country. Finch, despite having turned down Paramount, still signed a binding, multi-year contract with a British studio. He put ink to a five-year deal with the Rank Organisation. Rank – with its distinct, oddball opening logo of a bare-chested man hitting a large suspended gong – had been the defining British studio of the 1940s. The company was named after its founder, J Arthur Rank, an industrialist with a background in the deeply un-cinematic world of flour milling. Rank had strong ties with the Methodist church and when the church began to decry the negative impacts of American films on families in Britain, religious agitators and wowsers suggested that homemade production companies should start to provide alternatives. Rank, dusting himself off, took up the challenge.

Rank would play a part in the death of the Australian film industry in the 1950s – when his company bought its controlling interest in the Greater Union theatre group, it showed that it was more interested in pushing its own British product than investing in Australian films, protecting their own interests in the same way the Americans had. Finch had first worked for Rank on *Train of Events* and they were proud to have welcomed the actor back into their fold in the wake of a huge Hollywood production such as *Elephant Walk*. Their chief production officer announced excitedly to the press: 'We are going to build Finch into a major British star'.

Finch, however, was hardly happy with the partnership. He saw Rank as a living testament to the troubles of British cinema. Indeed, he might have largely agreed with François Truffaut's offside assessment that there was 'incompatibility between the terms "British" and "cinema".'[22] Finch denounced Rank's output as 'very British stiff upper lip, unimaginative and pandering to popular taste at an unnecessarily low level.'[23] He wasn't off the mark. The eight films he made with Rank are difficult to, well ... rank. Their quality varies but only ever by increments. *Passage Home* (1955) – the first film Finch would make under his new contract – at least showcased his dramatic range, appearing as a tyrannical, often drunk captain of a merchant ship. It would not be the last time he would be cast in a movie set on the seas (he would play Lord Horatio Nelson late in his career). There was understandable concern among actors in Britain that they risked being typecast in nautical fare, which was churned out at high rate. Finch would tell the *Los Angeles Times*, quoting character actor, Sir John Mills, that it was a matter of having 'to fight the naval hat.'[24]

Passage Home saw Finch cast alongside a younger unrequited love interest played by Diane Cilento, another Australian who found herself working in theatre and film in the United Kingdom. Blonde-haired and boundlessly bright, Cilento was born in Mooloolaba, on Queensland's Sunshine Coast, and raised by her notable doctor parents. She was sent to study in New York, where her father was posted at the United Nations, as part of an early delegation of the World Health Organization. Cilento had joined him after being expelled from a local high school, but she continued her rebellion in America, spending afternoons in the museums and cinemas instead. Her truancy was eventually discovered and her parents relented, letting her drop out of formal education to pursue her passion for dramatic arts. Echoing Finch, she ended her time in America with a tour of Molière's *The Imaginary Invalid*.

America wasn't forever. Her father was sent to the Middle East and her mother did not want the family to stay in New York without him, so they made their way to Britain. There Cilento successfully auditioned for the Royal Academy of Dramatic Art. Conventionally attractive, she had no problem finding work, appearing as a back-up dancer for John Huston in his *Moulin Rouge* (1952), before being professionally courted by Merle Oberon's intimidating ex-husband Alexander Korda, signing a contract with his studio British Lion Films. Cilento would appear in a string of films distributed by the company throughout the 1950s. British Lion was frequently bailed out by the British government and so Cilento was amused to find herself in the rare position of being an actor who was, in effect, a 'civil servant'.

Through the shooting of *Passage Home*, Cilento found Finch to be a roguish co-star. He cornered the other male lead actor on the film – Anthony Steel, a graduate of Rank's 'charm school' – into a destructive pissing contest, challenging Steel to try and drink as much as possible before a scene was shot and ruining his performance in the process. Cilento disapproved of the loutish behaviour but felt a familial connection with Finch. He reminded her of her brother – sharing a 'voraciousness for life' matched with a 'covert vulnerability'. Like Finch, Cilento continued to pursue stage work to break the monotony of the poor-quality films she was starring in. It was while working on a taped production of Eugene O'Neill's *Anna Christie* for ITV that she first collaborated with a young actor who would become central to her celebrity and destructive to her career. An ambitious young Scot,

Sean Connery had, until recently, been a body builder and a background extra on films, including the unexpected and not entirely successful Errol Flynn musical *Lilacs in the Spring* (1954).

Cilento and Connery found each other long before the bright heat of his James Bond fame. Their romance was slow going at first. Cilento was already in a loveless marriage with an Italian suitor – she had survived a suicide attempt made after living with his oppressive family – to whom she was newly pregnant, so her relationship with Connery was platonic at the outset. She returned to Australia, without her ex-husband or Connery, to have the baby – a natural birth, guided by her mother, who had 'birthed half of Queensland' (her mother would publish 24 popular books across her lifetime, starting with *Square Meals for the Family* in 1933).

As their relationship progressed, Cilento and Connery's acting careers ascended too. For a brief moment, in both Australia and Britain, she was more famous than he was and she counselled him on taking roles, giving him strong notes for his audition for Bond. Connery snared the role and would be busy in Jamaica filming *Dr No* (1962) while Cilento was filming the adaptation of Henry Fielding's ribald 1749 novel *Tom Jones* (1963), which would see her nominated for a Best Supporting Actress at the Academy Awards (this despite a later confession by the director of photography that her best scenes were edited out). A conservative urge – perhaps brought on by professional jealousy – had begun stirring in Connery. He certainly shared some of the coldness and unfeeling attitudes of the character who made him globally famous, as well as Bond's retrograde gender politics. It was at this point that Connery demanded that Cilento stop working, effectively curtailing her career. He wanted a 'wife' and Cilento felt herself 'dwindling' into that role and that role alone. There were no other parts he would let her play.

Connery was not always successful at suppressing Cilento's ambitions. The demands of being Bond wedded the couple to the British film industry, but both Connery and Cilento carved out time to make professional inroads in America between entries in the spy series. They travelled together to Los Angeles with a newborn son – their first and only child together – so that Connery could work with Alfred Hitchcock on *Marnie* (1964), taking up residence in Sammy Davis Jnr's home – a 'pad' Cilento was sure 'had never housed a nun' – for the duration of the shoot (the lounge furniture 'reeked of orgies' and there was a projector that could play porn at the push of a button). It wasn't necessarily the ideal setting for a young family. They would return to America later that decade to work on projects that would see them in a professional couple swap – Connery working with Joanne Woodward on *A Fine Madness* (1966), Cilento working with Woodward's husband, the all-American Paul Newman, in the sundrenched western *Hombre* (1967).

Returning from Arizona, where *Hombre* was filmed, for pick-up shots in Los Angeles, Cilento was invited to lunch by Warren Cowan, one of Hollywood's most powerful publicists (a 'star at promoting stars' according to his *NYT* obituary). Cowan pushed a package of artificial sweetener across the table to Cilento and said that his skill was that he could make anyone in America taste it just once – 250 million people – and he could do the same for Cilento. The audience would then decide if they wanted more. Cilento was tempted, but turned Cowan down. It was partly her own decision – her 'boredom threshold' had been met with full-time acting – but she became aware of Connery's displeasure at her progress there too. She was on a phone call to her UK agent at this time when he broke the news: the word was being put out that 'if anyone employs you, Sean will never work for them again'.

While Connery was working with Sidney Lumet on the paranoiac military prison drama *The Hill* (1965), shooting in Spain, a far more serious transgression took place, about which Cilento would go into remarkable detail in her late-in-life memoir. Cilento said she had no intention of talking about the incident until she read a *Playboy* interview with Connery, in which he confessed, 'I don't think there is anything particularly wrong about hitting a woman'. Staying in a three-star hotel on the coast, overrun with celebratory members of a wedding party, Cilento had been invited to dance and drink with the revellers. She later looked around the hotel for Connery, but could not find him, and so she stumbled upstairs to their room to go to bed; when she opened the door, he struck her across the face. As she wrote in her memoir, 'the violent, oppressive nature of the film spilled over into ordinary life in the hotel'.[25] Indeed, if Cilento's allegations were true – and Connery's comments to the press over his lifetime would seem to corroborate them – then Connery had missed the anti-violence message so clearly laid out at the end of Lumet's great film, in which he begs his fellow prisoners not to beat their abusing officer when given the chance.

This stark physical assault was only one part of the abuse she experienced at his hands. Connery's demands that Cilento stop work were part of an overall coercive control of her finances – despite his astronomical paycheques for playing Bond, he paid her a strict, measly 'housekeeping' wage, which he often withheld out of spite. His systematic dismantling of her career kept her reliant on him and his money.

It is difficult to envisage what Cilento's career would have looked like if Connery hadn't entered her life. The films she did star in during her short career have struggled to cut through in the years since and it's hard to identify which work she is ultimately best remembered for. The pagan worship horror *The Wicker Man* (1973), true to its plot, has a cultish devotion among movie audiences. *Tom Jones* is frequently recalled, but only to be cited as one of the worst – if not *the* worst – of the Academy's Best Picture winners. The rest remains murky. Cilento reunited with Finch in one of his least well-known films, *I Thank a Fool* (1962), a needlessly complex Hitchcock knockoff, in which she plays the distressed, housebound wife of Finch's cold, controlling lawyer.* It's a sad reality that a great actor might be forgotten altogether – no matter their skill, their natural charm – if they never manage to star in a memorable movie. Cilento might not have cared either way. There was an undeniable restlessness about her artistic pursuits. She completed a pair of novels – *The Manipulator* and *Hybrid*; Connery painted a cover for the former (he didn't seem to have a problem with her working as a writer). She translated plays from Italian. Susceptible to spiritualism, she gave away great deals of labour for free at a cult-like working farm, being ordered to watch over food at night to make sure no one ate, and eventually made documentaries inspired by the movement. After the troubled couple divorced in 1974, Cilento would return to Australia to live the rest of her life in

---

* In turn, Finch would work with Connery on his own forgotten film, *The Red Tent* (1969), a Russian–Italian co-production about the rescue mission following the crash of the Italia aircraft during a polar expedition. Connery plays the ghost of the doomed Norwegian explorer Roald Amundsen – under dusty white make-up – who haunts Finch's Italian aviator. The Russian cut of the film ran nearly three hours. The international release would lose an hour and much more in translation.

Far North Queensland, building a community theatre on her rainforest property. She died in 2011, and many of the news reports led with her marriage to the more famous man, cruelly reducing her to 'Mrs James Bond'. Connery got his way, even in her death.

THE PASSAGE HOME (1956–1962)

In the same year that Cilento and Finch appeared on screen together in *Passage Home*, Finch co-starred in another film, alongside another Australian actor. Re-enter Errol Flynn. *The Dark Avenger* (1955) – worked over as *The Warriors* for the US – was a pasty retread of Flynn's earlier action pictures that, by most accounts, he did for the cash and the cash alone. Finch apparently signed up for the film for the opportunity to appear opposite his fellow countryman. Flynn would prove a bad influence, approaching an impressionable Finch with spectacularly wrongheaded advice: 'You're *acting*. Don't act. I don't act, that's why I'm a star'.

How could an actor who had studied the art so seriously – read its history, taught it to others, had harboured ambitions for a national theatre in Australia – have listened seriously to such counsel? Finch was straying from his former ideals, perhaps slouching towards middle age. If he entertained Flynn's defeatist approach, it also spoke of Finch's desire to always have an out. This they shared and there was a poetic, uniquely Australian resonance between them. To wit: an eager fan had once gatecrashed Finch's dressing room, wishing to praise his performance. Finch snapped back at her: 'I'm not an actor. I'm an Australian bum. And a poet'. Flynn noted in his memoir: 'I was a Tasmanian-Irish bum, and I didn't mind

THE FORGOTTEN ELITE: PETER FINCH

going back to being that'.[26] (A crude reduction: where Flynn ran over his own dog, Finch saved a friend's from drowning.)

Bums both, there were subtle differences in these bolshie attitudes. Flynn saw the bargaining power such a dismissive attitude had. To threaten the studios with walking away – and to do so convincingly – was leverage, and it made him richer than many of his contemporaries. Finch seemed to eye the exit less as a business strategy than as a potential personal salve. Still, it was clear that Finch cared about the art. By the time they worked together, Flynn couldn't give a fuck, whereas Finch was deeply ashamed of his performance in *The Dark Avenger*.* Between the strong wills of Laurence Olivier, Vivien Leigh and Orson Welles – and the contagion of antipathy from Flynn – Peter Finch was an actor pushed and pulled by the actors nearest to him. This might have been understandable for a younger actor, but Finch was never that young around these key players in his career; he was in his late thirties by the time he starred in *Elephant Walk*. It might have had to do with his being Australian; looking, like that nervy nation often did, towards America and Britain to guide and grant self-

---

* Finch and Flynn would intersect again after Flynn's death. In 1969, Finch volunteered for a 20-minute screen test film directed by Robert Aldrich, who Finch had worked with twice before. Aldrich intended the test footage to demonstrate the value in ABC Pictures investing in *The Greatest Mother of 'Em All* and the capacities of a relatively unknown younger actress. Finch forwent any fee in order to play a character called Sean Howard. He was, in fact, playing a fictionalised version of Errol Flynn, and the story was based on Flynn's relationship with Beverly Aadland and her mother. There were some differences: Howard was a film director, rather than an actor, but the core story was the same. Aldrich's film was never approved for completion and Australians were robbed of a strange superimposing of two of their leading actors atop one another. They would intersect once more after death: Peter Finch Avenue heads towards Errol Flynn Boulevard at the Disney Studios Australia complex.

115

worth. However, as he hit 40, Finch did something very few Australian actors had done to that point: he went home.

This move would establish a tradition of internationally successful Australian actors returning home to appear in local films, whether seizing an opening in their schedules, hoping to visit family and old friends, or to pursue work with a particular sought-after filmmaker. But it was remarkable that Finch made it back to set such a precedent. Australian cinema, in the mid-1950s, was heading towards its lowest ebb. By one count, just 25 films were made in the 1950s in all of Australia. In the middle of the decade, in 1955, only one film was made all year. If you watched a film a day, you could watch every Australian film released in the 1960s over 17 nights. It's a quick study to become an expert in mid-century Australian cinema.

Without Cinesound playing a role in the market, the entire industry had practically come to a halt. Any postwar prosperity didn't reach the nation's screens, and local producers had all but given up fighting against American cultural domination. In the words of Andrew Pike and Ross Cooper, two leading Australian film historians, the long reign of prime minister Robert Menzies resulted in a 'public and governmental preoccupation with material well-being and political security [that] made the absence of an Australian film culture a matter of little general concern.'[27]

Hollywood and the British studios were happy to take advantage of Menzies' disinterest and step into the cultural vacuum he had created. The majority of their efforts fell within the Western genre, telling frontier stories. Ealing Studios – now best remembered for its series of 'Ealing Comedies' with Alec Guinness – produced *The Overlanders* in 1946, about a cattle drive across Western Australia and the Northern Territory. Ealing were also behind *Eureka Stockade* (1949), which told the story of the uprising on the goldfields and Peter Lalor's political agitation.* They were clear efforts towards national myth making for Australia, but they were done with British talent behind the camera. *Eureka Stockade* was delayed so its script could be reworked, and its cast revised, so that it fit within the guidelines of the British quota system.

The British were interested in setting up a permanent film unit in Australia and creating a steady stream of productions. Whereas the Americans often only came for a single film – directors flying in and out – and were interested in Australia as a foreign location, which had the potential to attract audience members who couldn't afford to travel, who could see it instead for the price of a cinema ticket. Foreign production, in this case, was simply another built-in selling point, another way to cut through the market.

The Kangaroo Kid (1950) and *Kangaroo* (1952), for instance, were both clearly trading on the international name recognition of Australia's most prominent marsupial. *The Kangaroo Kid* is forgettable, but *Kangaroo* – not to be confused with DH Lawrence's novel of the same name – is notable for starring Rat Pack member and JFK's pretty brother-in-law, Peter Lawford. *Kangaroo* was a 20th Century-Fox production, where they finally came good on their decades-old promise to make a film in Australia – the country's first Technicolour production – but, like *Smithy* before it, it was a cynical commercial exercise, a deliberate attempt to unfreeze capital

---

* Finch had a small but effective role in *Eureka Stockade*, working with its director Harry Watt, who had also ushered in *The Overlanders*. Curiously, Watt later admitted that both Charles Chauvel and Ken G Hall had advised him against employing Finch for *The Overlanders*, although it wasn't clear exactly why they went against their former player.

through local investment and the creation of saleable product.

Lewis Milestone – who had directed Errol Flynn and Judith Anderson in *Edge of Darkness* – was hired by Fox to take charge of *Kangaroo*, which had a long and troubled production. Filming was moved from New South Wales to South Australia, because location experts thought the NSW locations looked too much like 'Southern Arizona or California',[28] leading the filmmakers to question why they were shooting in Australia at all. They may have wished that they had stayed home, as the Americans weren't entirely welcome either. Actors' Equity protested the use of American stars in the film, and, in particular, publicised the fact that the American producers were paying First Nations extras lower wages.

Finch eventually came home as part of this influx of international activity, but he first returned to Australian cinema without having to actually leave England. In 1956, he reluctantly signed up to star in a film based on Nevil Shute's wartime novel *A Town Like Alice*. Both book and film had key scenes set in the Northern Territory, but the adaptation was, in fact, primarily filmed in London, at Pinewood Studios. The ending featured exteriors were shot in Alice Springs, but none of the film's stars travelled to shoot there (a local chemist, with only his back showing, stood in for Finch in these scenes).

Finch initially resisted taking the role, telling his agent that it was a 'woman's picture', and having his character only appear halfway through the film was beneath him. His long-suffering agent, knowing that he would cut through in a smaller role, insisted he take it. She was proven right. The pushback showed that Finch didn't always have the strongest head when it came to strategising career steps. *A Town Like Alice* is a brisk black and white melodrama, largely set in a prisoner of war (POW) camp in Malaysia. Working with the British director

Jack Lee, Finch plays an Australian for the first time in years, and he would be able to draw on his experiences during the war in doing so. Lee had used Finch in a single scene role in *The Wooden Horse* (1950) – another POW drama – and would become enamoured with Australia and live out the rest of his life.*

FINCH MADE IT BACK TO THE REAL AUSTRALIA IN 1956. He arrived in Sydney, and headed straight to the Journalists' Club, an old drinking hole, with a mate. He was snubbed when he arrived, with the patrons believing he thought he was too good for them. They cut him down to size. His friend reminded him of the tall poppy syndrome, and then suggested maybe he shouldn't have walked into the Journos; 'maybe you should have *crawled* in.'

Finch travelled to Alice Springs to attend the premiere of *A Town Like Alice*, where locals, donning rugs and chugging ciggies, reclined in deck chairs to take in the film during an outdoor screening on a late winter night. The star of the film could be there in person because he had boarded a cargo boat back to Australia to take up the lead in an adaptation of D'Arcy Niland's short, hard-nailed novel *The Shiralee* (1957). Ealing Studios would return to Australia for the production after a seven-year absence. An associate at Ealing had read Niland's novel in proofs and immediately wanted to buy it to turn it into a film. The head of Ealing was shocked at Niland's rough language and needed convincing. The script

---

* Lee couldn't get many films up off the ground after this, but took up a bureaucratic role as the Chairman of the South Australian Film Corporation which would become central to the revival of Australian cinema.

was cleaned up and the green light given. Filming was to take place in regional New South Wales, in the towns of Scone, Coonabarabran and Binnaway.*

Finch was enlisted to play the novel's main character Macauley, an itinerant swagman who hits the road with his young daughter. It was, in many ways, a precursor to Peter Bogdanovich's *Paper Moon* (1973), which would be built on a similar father-daughter plot, shot in black and white. It was clear that *The Shiralee* meant something to Finch and it is certainly his best performance from this era, underpinned by a winning conviction. Was he more at ease 'at home'? Finch certainly found eerily autobiographical aspects to the plot of *The Shiralee* – he played a father taking his child away from his mother, having accused her of adultery. Like George Finch, Macauley didn't really want anything to do with his child once in his possession, but made the point to remove her from the custody of her mother partly out of spite, after she had cuckolded him. Peter Finch had, at this point, his own child with Tamara, a daughter, and he too was no model parent – often absent in the same way his father had been. The autobiographical drive of the story provides us with more of a rough-hewn Finch on screen – he's simply a bit of a shithead, and is, perhaps, at his best playing a shithead.

---

* Diane Cilento entered discussions with Ruth Park and her husband D'Arcy Niland to buy the rights to Niland's novel *Call Me When the Cross Turns Over*, intending to develop it as a project for Sean Connery, so that the couple could spend some extended time in Australia. Connery was 'cagily interested' but 'leery of finding his way into the notoriously difficult Australian accent'.

THE FORGOTTEN ELITE: PETER FINCH

FINCH WOULD RETURN TO ENGLAND, BUT HE WAS BACK again in Australia the very next year for another film. *Robbery Under Arms*, a popular bushranger novel first published in 1888, had already been adapted for the screen four times before Jack Lee arrived to mount another version (when the cinemagoer today complains about the glut of unnecessary remakes and reboots they are often forgetting how baked into the business model this approach was from the very start, even in places like Australia). In fact, it was adapted twice in 1907 alone – by one company in Sydney, and the other in Melbourne; a perfect cinematic showing of the cultural rivalry between the two cities.

In the early 1900s, it was not so surprising that the novel proved to be such a hot commodity. Australia's earliest filmmakers and their audiences were besotted with bushranger stories, and the strong anti-hero narratives that drove them. This was so much the case that the NSW government banned bushranger films in 1911, warning against their 'injurious influence' on young audiences. The ruling stalled the production of what was otherwise an incredibly popular genre, and moralistic interventions such as these would prove fatal to the industry.

Finch was invested in the film, though he was displeased with the state of the script when he read it and worked on parts of it himself. He performed heavy lifting elsewhere. Indeed, his roguish charm carries most of *Robbery Under Arms* (1957). Clad in head-to-toe black – a highly impractical shade in the Australian desert heat – he plays the bushranger, Captain Starlight, in the manner of the ambiguous anti-heroes who had populated so many American Westerns. In fact, Finch was anticipating the Spaghetti Westerns that were to boom across Europe, and Italy in particular (thus *spaghetti*), in the

1960s. He wrote a note back to England that his interpretation of Starlight had 'come out like some terrible Sicilian bandit ... as cheeky as hell and a killer at the same time'.

The film would also anticipate the actor's love affair with Rome. Shooting on *Robbery Under Arms* would prove to be the last time Finch would step foot in Australia. Instead, he became a cosmopolitan identity, looking for a home elsewhere. In Rome, he became extremely close with the Australian poet BR Whiting, who lived in the city with his wife, the painter and sculptor Lorraine Fraser (sister of the future Australian prime minister, Malcolm Fraser). Finch loved Rome, where no one seemed to care about his station. Back in England, he hosted expatriates, including Patrick White, who arrived on Finch's doorstep, invited by his second wife, the actor Yolande Turner, who Finch had met on a beach in South Africa. Finch had no idea who Patrick White was; Turner had to remind him.

Finch's films started to rove the globe too. He frequently appeared as a mid-level professional moored in a colonial outpost.* The typecasting might have related to the fact that it felt authentic for an Australian to be stationed in such settlements. As a result, watching the films feel a lot like doing work too. *Windom's Way* (1957) – set during the Malayan Emergency but shot on Corsica – is a particular challenge to get through. Fred Zinneman's monastic melodrama *The Nun's Story* (1959) at least brought some glamour via Finch's co-star

---

* In the case of 1966's *Judith* – a bombastic Sophia Loren vehicle, which never quite lives up to the promise of its Nazi revenge plot – Finch takes a more active role in the history of colonisation, playing a commander of the Haganah – the Zionist paramilitary group – in the last days of the Mandate for Palestine, as Britain planned to cease their administration of the region.

Audrey Hepburn – although she was deglamourised in the role itself, playing a nun torn between her desire to do scientific work and the demands of the church. The film was set and shot in the then Belgian Congo. *The Nun's Story* was a huge hit and was followed for Finch by *The Sins of Rachel Cade* (1961), largely damned for being a close retread of its predecessor; an unsurprising criticism given it was also set in the Belgian Congo (though filmed in Los Angeles). Again, here was Finch playing an atheist in Africa with his female co-lead (played by Angie Dickinson) playing a missionary. Hollywood's propensity to hit the same notes again for profit could not be denied.

Finch was back in Britain and given ample room – and added girth – to roam in the title role in *The Trials of Oscar Wilde* (1960). He gained a significant amount of weight through a diet of champagne and potatoes. Actively pursuing weight gain for an acting role has become a stereotypical approach of Method acting that is trotted out again and again by Oscar-baiting hopefuls. He stayed in character for much of the production, and would spend nights reading Wilde's poetry while crying in bed. Wilde was a complex historical character to resurrect, both in his comic form – one-liners galore – and in his tragic element, a downfall ignited by homophobia and flamed by his own hubris. Finch was awarded Best Actor at the British Academy of Film and Television Arts (BAFTA) for his performance. Finch, in fact, to this day holds the acting record for winning the most BAFTAs, a total of five across three decades – for *A Town Like Alice, The Trials of Oscar Wilde, No Love for Johnnie, Sunday Bloody Sunday* and *Network* – a sign of his towering status among his contemporaries in Britain.

Despite the relative assuredness of his professional standing, his personal life was far from straightforward. Finch was brought face to face with his real father after a simple ring

CAST MATES

at the doorbell. Jock Campbell, a broad-faced Scottish army officer who had had an affair with Finch's mother during the war, announced himself to the stunned actor. It was obvious enough based on their looks that the familial connection was genuine. In that moment, Finch's distant Australian relatives were suddenly foreign to him. His eccentric grandmother, who had influenced the wayward direction of so much of his life, was no longer his blood relation. At least some of his life story started making more sense: his Australian father hadn't wanted him because the boy wasn't his in the first place.

His professional career had chaotic scenes too. Finch would be reunited with Elizabeth Taylor for one of the most notoriously difficult productions of all time, *Cleopatra* (1963), which nearly bankrupted its studio, 20th Century-Fox, as they sank incredible amounts of money into the flailing film. Finch was cast as Julius Caesar, given the eponymous Caesar cut, and befitted in robes. As shooting began, however, Taylor fell critically ill and was flown back to America. Production rolled on, if only so that the producers could continue collecting the insurance covering the film. For this to happen, Finch, in Taylor's absence, was taken to the set each day and ordered to perform the same shot over and over again. Echoing Vivien Leigh's dramatic dropping out of *Elephant Walk* because of a breakdown, Finch was in a position where he could not mentally go on with filming – or, rather, he could not go on *not* filming. He broke too, and was put in the care of a 'nursing home' for two weeks, trying to recover. The studio had put in $7 million dollars and only had 12 minutes of footage to show for the investment. Finch left the film and was swiftly replaced. He lost a credit on the film and the conflict in scheduling also meant that he had to withdraw from playing Captain Bligh to Marlon Brando's Fletcher Christian in *Mutiny on the Bounty*

(1962), although the pain inflicted by *Cleopatra*, at least, saved him from being terrorised by Brando's notorious behaviour on the set of that film.

Cleopatra is often cited as the endpoint of the old Hollywood. Finch seemed to agree telling the *Los Angeles Times* in 1962 that the star system was dead, 'healthily so', and that 'Hollywood is through as the centre of the film industry'.[29] In 1968, Finch starred in Robert Aldrich's *The Legend of Lylah Clare*, which partly parodied the death rattles of the old ways of working. It was 'high kitsch' according to Renata Adler in the *New York Times* and 'a takeoff on some of the highly serious tragic movies Hollywood has made about itself' but one 'so faithful in spirit that it is almost indistinguishable from its model'.[30] Finch had recently worked with Aldrich on the aircraft disaster film *The Flight of the Phoenix* (1965) and appeared in *Lylah Clare* as an ageing film director working with Kim Novak's titular star, with Novak deliberately evoking her dual roles in *Vertigo* (1958). It turned out audiences weren't interested in seeing a movie about a moribund industry. In a later interview, Aldrich thought there were about 25 reasons the film failed so spectacularly, and one of them was 'Who cared about Peter Finch?'.[31]

POINTS OF DEPARTURE (1963–1977)

Across the 1960s, British cinema was undergoing similar changes to those in America. Outdated systems were being overturned. The old ways of working were fading fast. Ealing Studios had released its last film in 1959. *The Siege of Pinchgut* was, somewhat surprisingly, another production in Australia. *Pinchgut*, a thriller set entirely in Sydney, largely on the city's pristine harbour, follows a group of petty criminals as they overtake Fort Denison (it is worth tracking down for the incredible black and white photography of mid-century Sydney). The producers flew Hollywood star Aldo Ray in to play the broad meathead ex-crim, who took the island hostage, and aimed a disused Second World War cannon at a munitions ship across the harbour, intending to blow up most of North Sydney.

A sense of destruction and renewal pervaded global cinema too. In the mid-1950s, a group of young Britons got together to establish the Free Cinema. Sometimes labelled a movement, the push was originally only intended as a program of curated short documentaries to counter more conservative mainstream efforts. It was simply a practical effort by a collective of aspiring filmmakers to have their work shown. But they wrote down a manifesto in their third program:

> British cinema [is] still obstinately class-bound; still
> rejecting the stimulus of contemporary life, as well as the
> responsibility to criticise; still reflecting a metropolitan,
> Southern English culture which excludes the rich
> diversity of tradition and personality which is the whole
> of Britain.

Free Cinema would be an essential part of the British New Wave and their guiding statement had resonances with Finch's own ambitions for the Mercury Theatre back in Australia. Finch's cinematic career would be revitalised by the movement. Throughout the 1960s, he would be flitting between American and British productions – often co-productions between the two countries, as was the case with the Greece-set *In the Cool of the Day* (1963), co-starring a young Jane Fonda – and these

THE FORGOTTEN ELITE: PETER FINCH

were often among his most conservative films. In the films made by younger British filmmakers, it felt like the times had caught up with Finch's sense of spirit and style, but he was not quite of their generation. Their films would skew towards stories about troubled teens and twenty-ish tyros struggling in poverty. The angry young men were not exactly in short supply. Luckily for Finch, someone had to play the square the youth rail against.

In both *No Love for Johnnie* (1961) – his last film for Rank – and *Girl with Green Eyes* (1964) Finch would play the older man to a much younger love interest – an outdated, overused and leering plotline in cinema, but one that is at least tested within the stories themselves, particularly in the latter film, where Finch came up against Rita Tushingham, the energetic face of many early British New Wave efforts, in the green-eyed title role. Finch was similarly recruited to play the older, clingy suitor Farmer Boldwood to Julie Christie's Bathsheba Everdene in the 1967 adaptation of Thomas Hardy's 1874 novel *Far from the Madding Crowd*.

He would ultimately make two films with *Madding Crowd*'s director John Schlesinger – a heady filmmaker who set the nerves of some critics on edge with his high-energy efforts. Schlesinger was often dressed down for his shakily composed and choppily edited films, but they had wide appeal, and he would certainly coax two of Finch's best performances out of the actor. Schlesinger, born in London to an upper-middle-class Jewish family, had a background in acting himself. He had, in fact, appeared with Finch back in Powell and Pressburger's *The Battle of the River Plate* (1956). Finch could see the advantage in Schlesinger's acting background when it came to directing: 'Having been an actor himself he understands all our idiot problems.'[32]

Finch remembered Schlesinger well from *River Plate* and told the *Los Angeles Times*, 'John says he was terrible. I thought he was rather good. He got stuck in the German helmet – it's very unfair for a good Jewish boy, he never played anything but beastly Germans'. Schlesinger shied away from acting after that, pivoting to directing documentaries for the BBC. He was a contemporary of the Free Cinema crowd, but never signed up to their manifesto, and occasionally tried to distance himself from them, perhaps from a sense of competitiveness. There was significant shared ground though: Schlesinger, like his Free Cinema contemporaries, used the skills he had learnt from directing nonfiction films to drive and energise his features. It worked for him. His third feature film, the swinging 60s raver *Darling*, broke big in America and landed him a Best Director nomination at the 1966 Oscars and clinched its young star Julie Christie, at 26, the Best Actress award. Schlesinger, at the zenith of his professional career and with America calling, decided to go out to the Dorset and Wiltshire countrysides instead, to make his ten-minutes-shy-of-three-hours adaptation of Hardy's novel. To go after Hardy with such sincerity was an unexpected move – as it is for any director of the contemporary moment moving backwards into stately historical fiction – and admirable in its ambition, but Schlesinger would come to regret the decision. He was exhausted by a long and hard shoot and was despondent at the cold critical and commercial response to the film.

In Schlesinger's opinion Finch was too suffering during filming – juggling two separate intimate relationships, one being his future wife Eletha – and there is a sense that this personal defeat comes across on the screen.[33] Schlesinger thought only Finch truly captured the 'classic doom' of the novel.[34] Boldwood was wounded throughout by Bathsheba

THE FORGOTTEN ELITE: PETER FINCH

Everdene's persistent rejections of his advances, hurtling him towards Hardy's bleak and violent ending. The film was likely too long and too much of a downer to capture the imagination of audiences, particularly those who were waiting on something as zippy as *Darling*. Schlesinger, however, bounced back by finally making a film in America, as the Americans had long wanted him to, with the New York–set *Midnight Cowboy* (1969). The film, which centres on a hustler and was an adaptation of a queer novel, won Best Picture and secured Schlesinger Best Director.

Schlesinger used *Midnight Cowboy*'s capital to make a personal statement in his next film with Finch, *Sunday Bloody Sunday* (1971). If Schlesinger had hinted towards homosexual themes in his earlier film, here he was crafting a more open story about his own sexuality, effectively coming out on celluloid. Not everyone was willing to go all the way with him. Ian Bannen – Finch's co-star on *The Flight of the Phoenix* – was initially cast as one of the leads but couldn't play the queer scenes without plying himself with gin. Schlesinger was left desperate. Finch's agent called him in Rome and asked that he get on the next available flight back to London. Finch proved again to be a quick study. *Sunday Bloody Sunday* was a daring story for its time, focusing on the open relationship between a young bisexual man (Murray Head), a divorced job consultant (Glenda Jackson) and a Jewish doctor (Finch). After the 'tic-ridden'[35] performance by Dustin Hoffman as Rizzo, hobbling and spitting through all of *Midnight Cowboy*, it is incredible to watch Schlesinger elicit such a serene, still performance from Finch. He was willing to fully commit to the role on screen, gamely getting in bed with Head and playing the queer aspects of the story – for want of a better word – straight.

Finch's performance would be acknowledged with his

first Oscar nomination, an unexpected recognition, though he eventually lost out to Gene Hackman's turn as the rough-headed cop Popeye in *The French Connection* (1971). The nomination brought Finch the American attention that had long eluded him, although he struggled to land another film that would extend the capabilities he had developed working with Schlesinger. Most actors can capitalise on an Oscar nomination to reel in better roles. Not Finch. What, for instance, brought him to consider taking the lead in a production like *Lost Horizon* (1973)? It was technically his third disaster film in the space of a decade, but unlike *The Flight of the Phoenix* and *The Red Tent*, 40 minutes in, after a plane is hijacked and crashed into high mountaintops, *Lost Horizon* takes a breakneck detour, becoming a full-blown Burt Bacharach musical. The film was a disastrous flop and it would take Finch a number of years before he found another project worthy of his talents. In fact, he decided he would prefer farming instead, moving to Jamaica to grow bananas.

FINCH'S RETURN TO CINEMA WOULD BE PRECEDED BY a real-life violent act on screen. In 1974, the 29-year-old Christine Chubbuck, a Florida-based newsreader, shot herself live on air. Before pulling the trigger, she informed her audience:

> In keeping with the WXLT practice of presenting the most immediate and complete reports of local blood and guts news, TV 40 presents what is believed to be a television first. In living color, an exclusive coverage of an attempted suicide.

THE FORGOTTEN ELITE: PETER FINCH

It was an outrageous moment that seemed destined to attract the attention of New Hollywood. Explicit scenes of violence were one of the key markers of difference from what had come before. Indeed, the start of New Wave in America is often credited to the moment when Warren Beatty and Faye Dunaway, as doomed criminal lovers, are violently shot down at the end of *Bonnie and Clyde* (1967). The Old Hollywood was dead at last.

Bonnie and Clyde's bold director, Arthur Penn, had worked with Finch on the London stage a decade prior, but it seemed unlikely that Finch, even with his prior connection to the director, would have any association with New Hollywood. An opportunity, however, presented itself in the middle of the 1970s. Paddy Chayefsky, one of the few 'name' screenwriters in Hollywood, had developed an ambitious new screenplay, based on immersive research into the inner workings of the NBC television newsroom and ideas about what exactly was wrong with America (Chayefsky had previously explored the ins and outs of an institution in 1971's *The Hospital*, for which he had won his second Oscar for Best Screenplay). The current national malady, for Chayefsky, was an excess of media and everything else besides. *Network* was to be the diagnosis, telling the story of a news anchor – Howard Beale – having a live breakdown on air, and how those around him try to capitalise on his madness to run up the ratings at their flailing station. It was unclear if Chayefsky had seen the footage of Christine Chubbuck, but he made note of the incident in one draft of his script. Like Chubbuck, Howard Beale declared to his audience, matter-of-factly, that he intended to shoot himself on air.

The demanding role would prove extremely difficult to cast. High-profile actors were courted. An early wish list included the all-American names of Henry Fonda, Paul Newman and Jimmy Stewart. The consensus among most was that Beale was too vulgar a role to take on. The technical difficulty of the character's rolling monologues may have dissuaded some of them too. Finch, living in semi-exile in Jamaica, was as unlikely a prospect as anyone to land the part, but after reading the script, he desperately wanted it. He told his American agent so, who responded that he would need to fly to meet with the creative team behind the film. Finch roared back: 'You mean they want me to *audition*? Tell them to go fuck themselves', and hung up on his agent. Finch called back straight away and apologised: 'Sorry, darling, I forgot I was an actor.'[36]

Those behind the camera would need serious convincing when it came to Finch. Howard Beale, like most of the characters in the script, needed to be as American as a box of Graham crackers to make the satire inherent to the script work. *Network* was, according to its director, 'the quintessential American story, and the actors had to be American.' Subsequently, its producers had been extremely reluctant to audition anyone with a non-American accent. Newsreading in America presented a very specific form of vernacular. On the big nationwide networks, the newsreader had to front up and speak to the entire country in a voice everyone would understand and, more importantly, trust. This needed to be the baseline of the Beale character before his spectacular live-to-air breakdown.

It wasn't impossible, though, and Finch simply did what any good actor would: he did his homework. He went directly to the source, watching tapes of the leading newsreaders, including Chayefsky's friend, news anchor Walter Cronkite. Based on these studies, he wisely decided the accent could not be 'perfect regional American nor non-American'. Finch decided it would have to be 'Eastern Standard'.[37] He played the middle and it was his genius move.

To meet with the production team, Finch flew to New York, paying for his own flights. His hunger for the part was obvious and he was as nervous as a beginning actor auditioning for their first role. Chayefsky and Lumet met him at his hotel, accompanied by a producer from MGM, and together they planned to walk to another hotel for an informal script reading, which would stand in as his audition. What little Finch said on the walk between hotels secured him the part. There was no concern about his accent; his close studying had paid off. During rehearsals, Finch and Chayefsky visited the Rockefeller Center to watch an airing of the nightly NBC news broadcast. Finch was spontaneously invited to sit in the chair and read from the teleprompter, which he hastily accepted. He said thank you 'in his "Aussie accent"', sat down, and in flawless "American" began to read the newscast'. He impressed the newsreader, who thought he could do the job for real.

NETWORK WOULD STAY IN NEW YORK FOR MOST OF ITS production. It would not be shot in Hollywood. Finch would find himself on the east coast rather than the west, reporting to a quintessentially New York director in Lumet. The prolific, workaholic Lumet was part of a new generation of directors who preferred filming at home in New York rather than trying to lead a false life in Los Angeles. Lumet simply couldn't do it: 'When I leave New York for any other place in the United States, my nose starts to bleed'.[38]

Other than being a proto New Yorker, Lumet was often

cited as being the 'actor's director', in that he was both beloved by them but also expert in their handling. He was keener on rehearsals than most directors, insistent in some instances. This came from personal experience. Lumet, like Schlesinger, had himself started out as an actor (indeed, this meant that Finch's two Oscar nominations were secured working with directors who had themselves worked as actors). In turn, it could be convincingly argued that Finch was an 'actor's actor' – deeply respected for his work by his peers, but never quite capturing the popular imagination until *Network* became a hit.

It is extremely telling then that both of the major biographies of Finch's life were written by actors he had known both personally and professionally. *Peter Finch: A Biography* was written by Trader Faulkner, a former student of Finch's at the Mercury Theatre in Sydney. Meanwhile, the buzzy *Finch, Bloody Finch* was authored by Elaine Dundy, an American actress best known now for her memoir-like novel *The Dud Avocado*, who travelled to Australia to interview countless subjects connected to Finch (Dundy even had a small cameo during a party scene in *In the Cool of the Day* appearing as a young woman who briefly approaches Finch's character). Faulkner travelled to America, but was blocked by many who had already spoken with Dundy and who counted her as a friend, including Sidney Lumet.[39]

Going into *Network*, Lumet was coming off the back of one of his most actor-focused films, in which he had encouraged improvisation and cross-talk. *Dog Day Afternoon* (1975) – the sweltering hostage movie, starring a pacing, sweaty Al Pacino – had been shot in Brooklyn and New Jersey. For *Network*, it was important that Lumet translate the streets of New York to film. The story is one that takes place in high-rise offices, tight apartments, and television studios. The most critical of Finch's scenes, however, were helmed in Toronto, partly to cut costs and partly because the television studios in Los Angeles were off limits. The former boy star of ABC radio in Sydney was playing a New York newsreader in Canada; Finch would have brought some of his knowledge of working in a broadcasting studio to the role. Lumet too was returning to his roots of working in live television where he had gained his start in the early 1950s.

It would prove a demanding schedule shooting in the news studio. Finch had to make his way through Chayefsky's incredibly wordy, precise monologues. His eternally famous 'Mad as Hell' speech, however, was done in two takes. Lumet was a quick director, falling back on a televisual approach and relying far more on the preparations via rehearsals than multiple takes. Finch was also aware that the demanding speech would take too much out of him if there were too many repeat takes. In the film, Faye Dunaway, playing a sharp-eyed producer, watches on, her eyes fixed and widening, knowing the quality of what she has on her hands. Speaking to no one in particular, she beams that the station has hit the 'motherlode' with Beale. Anyone watching Finch must have been thinking the same.

Network predicted the power of the viral moment – a pre-internet meme, Beale's ravings were the stuff of wildfire. In the film, the audience watching at home got out of their seats, and instead of hitting 'share' on some device, repeated the catchphrase aloud, screaming out windows as Beale had told them to. In real life, Howard Beale's cry has been shorthand for decades now for a political exasperation. It continues to play today; the long-running ABC political commentary show *Mad as Hell*, first aired in 2012 and retired in 2022, takes its name from Finch's monologue.

CAST MATES

It seemed that Finch was a lock for the Academy Award as the season progressed, even after his untimely death. He was running against his co-star William Holden in the same category. Holden was old-world Hollywood royalty, best known for being found floating dead in Norma Desmond's pool in Billy Wilder's *Sunset Boulevard* (1950). Now, however, his face was weathered and voice cracked by alcohol abuse, but he still exuded a transfixing confidence, baked into the leathery lines of his skin. Part of Finch's power in the role, and why he won over an old hand such as Holden, is that many of the audience had probably not seen a Peter Finch movie before, or if they had they didn't remember the Australian actor. It wouldn't have been possible if his career had been more of a success.

Finch had long avoided accepting offers to work in television, and despite *Network's* anti-television leanings, his last film was a made-for-TV movie, *Raid on Entebbe* (1977), in which he played the Israeli prime minister. It will always be unclear where his career might have gone from there if he had lived – what roles he might have traded his Oscar win in for. He was reportedly signed on for Warren Beatty and Buck Henry's screwball revival *Heaven Can Wait* (1978), which would have reunited him with Julie Christie. When he died, he had a meeting due with an executive about taking on the role of America's Founding Father, George Washington. It would, no doubt, have lodged in further in the minds of Americans.

THE MORNING AFTER THE ACADEMY AWARDS WERE handed out and Finch was announced as the first posthumous winner for an acting award, Faye Dunaway rose for a 6.30 am photo shoot. The night before, her assigned photographer

THE FORGOTTEN ELITE: PETER FINCH

Terry O'Neill – later to become her second husband – had been scouting for somewhere for the actress to pose. O'Neill knew that the more interesting story he could tell with her would be found in the light of the morning after, so he instructed Dunaway to meet him poolside at the Beverly Hills Hotel at first light. She came out wearing a dressing gown and stilettos. On a small round table next to her, her Oscar stood tall, aside a tray with tea and a Coke. Dunaway posed looking wistful, remorseful, contemplative, bored. Newspapers reporting the events of the ceremony from the night before were strewn around her feet.

The most prominent masthead positioned – the *Los Angeles Times* – carried a bold headline, which read 'Posthumous Oscar for Finch'. In more than one image from the shoot, Dunaway can be seen stepping on the front page and on that headline; treading the sole of her heels into news of Finch's postmortem victory. The carelessness of the act wasn't lost on some; nor was the sour fact that the shoot was being done in the exact same hotel where Finch had died just two months earlier. In the photograph, Finch was quite literally yesterday's news. In death, he was transformed into a prop in a staged exercise in LA glamour. It was a premonition that Finch's legacy would be one of gradual dilution. For many, he has been reduced to a single scene in *Network*, and for some, boiled right down to the three words 'Mad as Hell'. The truth is that actors don't get to choose what we remember them for.

Following his fatal heart attack, Finch was interred in the Hollywood Forever Cemetery, buried in a city he had long hated, but which had, in the end, ensured his fixed place in our collective cultural memory.

PART 3
THE RIGHT STUFF:
DAVID GULPILIL AM

In 1947 Peter Finch took on an unexpected job as assistant director on a documentary about the First Nations people of the Northern Territory, commissioned by Gaumont-British Instructional Films, with the Rank Organisation signed on to distribute the film globally. The actor flew, with director George Heath (who had worked with Finch as a cinematographer on a number of his early Australian films), to Arnhem Land to begin work on the production, which was going under the unfortunate, backwards title *Primitive Peoples*. It is unlikely that Finch, camping out under the stars, would have had any clue whatsoever that Australia's most significant – and historically consequential – actor would come from the very region he was seeking to document.

And so it was to be: David Gulpilil, the Yolŋu actor and dancer, came racing into cinema's consciousness in 1971 after being cast in Nicolas Roeg's *Walkabout* as a teenager. When he was offered the role, Gulpilil assumed he was being asked to play a cowboy. During a lively conversation with critic

Margaret Pomeranz, Gulpilil told a Melbourne International Film Festival audience in 2015: 'I thought I was going to be John Wayne'.

Gulpilil was a sight better than the burly, broad-chested actor donned The Duke. He was faster, funnier, freer in his body. Gulpilil was also – unlike Wayne, who reportedly hated horses – something of an actual cowboy, having worked as a stockman at Bulman Station in Arnhem Land. The pair did, however, share the fact that they were both commanding and distinctive in their movements, identifiable by gait alone. Gulpilil later observed, 'so, instead of struttin' around like John Wayne ... I got to strut around like David Gulpilil'.[1]

His very first scene in cinema proved that no one else moved quite like him. In a wide shot in *Walkabout*, Gulpilil was introduced moving over a hazy desert horizon. Dashing and darting, in what could have been mistaken for dance, save for the fact that he was, in fact, in a fleet-footed goanna hunt. On camera, the lizard turned and locked its head to take in the young man coming fast towards him, like a reptilian stand-in for the film's awed audience.

Few people would have seen anything like Gulpilil's movements on screen at that stage. With a little context, the young actor's extreme grace and fluidity wouldn't have come as a shock. Gulpilil was first and foremost a dancer. He had won eisteddfods in Darwin in his youth. The activist, historian and actor Gary Foley called him the 'Aboriginal Nureyev'.[2] In the history of cinema, it is not unusual for a dancer to transition to acting, but no actor had ever come from the world of dancing Gulpilil belonged to. One can watch Cyd Charisse or Gene Kelly or Fred Astaire or Ginger Rogers or Channing Tatum move across the screen powerfully and call it a transcendent experience – and it is often exactly that – but you would not say any of it was connected to multi-millennia-old acts of deep cultural practice and storytelling.

IN SONG AND DANCE (1971–1984)

The filmmakers working behind the scenes on *Walkabout* had been specifically looking for a dancer. A young Australian production manager working on the then untitled film, Grahame Jennings, wrote to HC Giese, the Director of Welfare for the Northern Territory Administration, to request help in casting the part of a 14–16-year-old, stipulating:

> He should be good-looking, have a good sense of
> rhythm and dance, and some knowledge of English.

Giese wrote back, requesting more details on the story – 'if only in outline ... so that we could get some idea of the sort of contribution which the lad will be required to make' – and the length of time the filming would take. The bureaucrat did, however, already have someone in mind in that very first reply, writing that while there were several young men who had given outstanding performances at the Darwin Eisteddfod who might fit the bill:

> One of these – a lad of 15 years of age from Maningrida
> in Central Arnhem Land – won the open dance item in
> the Eisteddfod against some very strong competition by
> experienced and older dancers.

The young man had, in the words of Marcia Langton, been raised 'in the Djinba world ... speaking his mother's language

Ganhalpuyngu and his father's, Manydjalpuyngu.[3] He was born on Gupulul Marayuwu land in Ramingining. Gulpilil was moved to Maningrida, a three and a half hour drive away, to attend a missionary school and it was here that Nicolas Roeg would travel to meet him and, ultimately, offer him the role in his movie. Gulpilil might have been better prepared for the audition than most, because he was an avid film fan. Films were shown on the 'end wall of a school' on Friday evenings, with people watching on 'chairs or rugs', and Gulpilil would attend regularly and enthusiastically. One of Gulpilil's former art teachers recalled that 'the next day he would often come to me and retell the whole movie, complete with actions.'[4]

Roeg was unusually well positioned to capture Gulpilil's dramatic leap from dancer to actor. When the director was preparing *Walkabout,* he was fresh off his solo debut – the aptly titled *Performance* (1970) – in which he had tailored a lead part for Mick Jagger, and he would go on to make David Bowie's alien-ness literal in *The Man Who Fell to Earth* (1976). Roeg clearly knew he had found that elusive rock star charisma that existed in a Jagger or a Bowie in the young dancer, one which was potently translatable to the big screen. Roeg, however, faced challenges with Gulpilil that he didn't with Bowie or Jagger. Working with his production man, Roeg had to enter into lengthy correspondence with Giese and the 'Aboriginal Welfare authorities' in Darwin, negotiating with the government body about Gulpilil's participation in *Walkabout.* What other actor needed governmental permission and administrative oversight to work on a film?

That first film made more effort at least than later ones to accommodate Gulpilil's needs. In part to counter cultural isolation, it was agreed that Gulpilil would be accompanied by his close friend Dick Bandilil. The production had recruited a science teacher to join the shoot to provide schooling for all children on set. Giese wrote that:

> It is felt that they would obtain a great benefit from learning the technical and production requirements in the making of a feature film and I would, therefore, be pleased if a qualified teacher on your staff could direct his instruction to these aspects during the period that David and Dick are in your company.

It is highly unlikely that Giese was thinking strategically about the potential impact such exposure to film production might have on First Nations filmmaking. Gulpilil and Bandilil's regular teacher had gone on unexpected leave and wasn't able to provide handover notes to the film production's recruit. Still, it was the first sign that the means of production might be handed to Gulpilil one day – an important step towards self-expression and creative independence.

On its release, reviews for *Walkabout* were mixed – Roeg's jumpy acid trip direction wasn't for everyone – but a *Sydney Morning Herald* correspondent who saw the film in New York sent back one of the first positive notes, writing that: 'If Aboriginal actor David Gumpilil [sic] doesn't win an Oscar next year I can't imagine who will'. (Gulpilil wasn't nominated, but if he had been he would have been running against Peter Finch for *Sunday Bloody Sunday*.)

Gulpilil was miscredited as 'Gumpilil' in the credits, and most of his early press clippings can only be found under that name. He deadpanned that the producers might have mistakenly thought that he 'came from a gum tree' (Gumpilil), but he also saw the disrespect shown by the oversight, thinking that it made him 'sound like a bloody childhood toy', and he later pointedly noted that no one ever apologised for the mistake either.

The headline accompanying the article, which miscredited Gulpilil, excitedly announced: *'"Walkabout" Good for Tourism'*.[5] This reading would be one embraced by Australians again and again about their films; that local films needed to be something more than an artistic effort, they also needed to have some sense of being a nation-boosting commodity to achieve any real worth.

20th Century-Fox bought the theatrical rights to *Walkabout*. As part of their promotional efforts, they designed a plan to send Gulpilil on a global tour. It was an ambitious itinerary. They agreed that Bandilil would accompany Gulpilil once more (Gulpilil and Bandilil had also travelled to Japan together the year before as part of a dance troupe for Expo '70). The pair would spend four days in Cannes at the famous film festival, two days in London, 12 days in New York, and two in San Francisco, and finish the official trip in Los Angeles, before returning home (with a two-day stopover in Fiji for a break). Bandilil would play the Didgeridoo as part of the tour, leaving hoteliers confused about the bass-heavy sounds coming from their rooms above.

In New York, Gulpilil and Bandilil played at being tourists, taking in the Empire State and United Nations buildings, and tracing the island of Manhattan by boat. They weren't overly impressed, with their official companion from 20th Century-Fox writing, 'They did not go for New York much (neither did I!)'. Gulpilil was interviewed on *The David Frost Show*, sang the Beatles on radio, and lunched with the *Sydney Morning Herald*'s US correspondent. He wrote to the Welfare Branch of the Northern Territory from the historic Warwick Hotel – built by William Randolph Hearst and the one-time residence of Cary Grant – to report back on his travels, saying that he had seen *Walkabout* in New York for the third time and that audiences were asking him all about Australia. He signed off the letter, David Gulpilil Film Star of the NTA (Northern Territory, Australia). In another letter from the same period, he underlined 'filmSTAR'. Gulpilil knew – and stated – his worth from the very beginning.

From New York, Gulpilil and Bandilil flew to San Francisco, before heading down to Los Angeles, where they would end the trip at Disneyland. A staff writer for the *LA Times* – Mary Murphy – was present when Gulpilil was invited to dance at the 20th Century-Fox publicity offices. Murphy wrote up the scene she witnessed in slightly purple prose, straining to make meaning out of what went on:

> As if the haunting sound of the digeridoo [sic], a primitive musical instrument played by his traveling companion, touched the very base of his nervous system, Gumpilil [sic] moved his face and body in a fluid poem to death. He twisted and writhed and almost pushed himself into the floor taking over the publicity office at 20th Century-Fox for a few moments. Everyone watching was oblivious to the obvious trappings of modern Hollywood.[6]

Murphy suggested that once the music stopped it was Gulpilil who was out of step: 'transported into the technological era with little preparation'. This might have felt true for Murphy, but Gulpilil more than fitted in with any historic scene around him. He would command attention and often boasted of hangouts with Bob Marley, Marlon Brando, Bob Dylan, John Lennon, Muhammad Ali and Bruce Lee, where he was very much their equal on the icon status level. He took particular pride in repeating the story of having shared an intimate audience with Queen Elizabeth. Stepping into Gulpilil's unbeatable filmography, one question keeps looping back around: what stopped him from becoming just as famous around the world as the outsized icons he danced circles around? At the end of his grand tour of Europe and America, he went back to working as a stockman at Bulman Station, and it would be years before he made another film.

In 1971 – the year of *Walkabout*'s release – the so-called New Wave of Australian cinema was yet to fully crest. After years of next to no production, there were promising signs of rejuvenation about the industry. Still, the two most significant films released that year – *Walkabout* and *Wake in Fright* – continued the tradition of international directors arriving in the country to make films of uncertain national origins. Ted Kotcheff, who directed the eerie outback thriller *Wake in Fright*, was Canadian. His film was an international co-production between two independent Australian and American companies. When Roeg arrived to make *Walkabout*, he was not new to the role of interloper in Australia. He had been in the country before, working as a camera operator on *The Sundowners* (1960), the sheep-shearing Western, in which Fred Zinnemann tasked Robert Mitchum to attempt an Australian accent, setting him up for certain failure. That production had Warner Bros behind it, and so there was no doubting that it was anything other than American-owned property. Zinnemann's film had flopped in the US, but performed relatively well in Australia. The effort rankled for the young film critic Sylvia Lawson, who, writing for *Nation* in December 1961, detailed her shock in finding local audiences gasping and laughing appreciatively at any familiar representation of themselves on screen. Lawson countered:

It is horrifying – that we should have to be so touchingly grateful to Warner Brothers for giving this continent a pat on the head, for throwing a few pink galahs on the screen ... Those gasps of joy were the clearest possible demonstration that we need our own film industry ...[7]

The Sundowners would, however, prove central to the revival of the Australian film industry, because it was while he was in Australia working on the film that Nicolas Roeg read *The Children*, the short novel on which *Walkabout* is based. His imagining based on what he read would crystallise into an alluring work. Studio heads at 20th Century-Fox's New York office had been so excited by what they had seen of Roeg's finished adaptation that they pushed to enter the film into the Cannes Film Festival as Australia's first serious contender. One telegram in the tranche of early correspondence with the Northern Territory Administration suggests that the effort was troubled:

Australia has not supported entry of *Walkabout* in Cannes Festival in spite of many attempts by producers.

According to film historians, both *Walkabout* and *Wake in Fright* were denied entry into the festival as Australian submissions when the Film Board determined that they 'were not genuinely "national" productions'.[8] In the press, the uncertainty instigated a heated debate as to whether *Walkabout* was an Australian or British production (to confuse matters more, the $1 million budget came entirely from American sources). *Walkabout* would finally be submitted as a British production, but the fact that there was a debate at all signalled a powerful shift in the Australian industry. The eventual renaissance of Australian cinema can largely be credited to government interventions from consecutive conservative and progressive parties – led by their prime ministers John Gorton and Gough Whitlam respectively – making strategic attempts to revive a long-dormant industry.

The very start of this revival, however, could be attributed to both their predecessor Harold Holt announcing the formation of a new body to oversee the government's investment in the arts, before his extremely cinematic – but ultimately off-screen – disappearance in the waters off Cheviot Beach in 1967. Gorton – Errol Flynn's old schoolmate – would replace Holt, as a compromise candidate, and would be the one to implement the lost man's vision, establishing the Australia Council for the Arts in 1968. In a surprise development, a Film and Television Committee would muscle its way into the line-up of 'high culture' art forms (opera, ballet and so on). The committee put forward three key recommendations: the establishment of a film and television school, a development corporation, and a rolling fund for experimental films. Movement on all three was underway when Gorton was deposed by his political challenger Billy McMahon, who initiated a controversial period of 'de-Gortonisation', with the film school as one of the potential cuts. In doing so, McMahon nearly single-handedly killed the industry that would later make his son, Julian, a Hollywood player. Julian, square-jawed with a wide white-toothed grin, would have made a successful retail politician, a potential successor to his father, but went on instead to a promising career in prime-time American television, leading him to the coveted role of Dr Doom in the cartoonish *Fantastic Four* (2005) and its sequel *Fantastic Four: Rise of the Silver Surfer* (2007).

The federal election of 1972 brought Gough Whitlam into power after his Labor Party had spent 18 years in the wilderness. Whitlam would revive Gorton's policies relating to the film industry and see through the launch of the Australian Film and Television School in 1973. It was one of the strongest signals of an active desire to nurture future generations of filmmakers (Gulpilil would eventually join its student body, not without controversy). At the opening event, Whitlam spoke about the international ambitions of the work to be produced, warning in his typically exacting style: 'There is no room for mediocrity'.

Mediocrity, however – indeed, the opportunity to fail – was a necessity as the nascent industry rediscovered itself. This period in Australian film history is heavily romanticised and lauded, even if, in reality, its results were not always of the highest quality. While the New Wave is often associated with a handful of historical prestige pictures – adaptations of the literary novels *Picnic at Hanging Rock*, *The Getting of Wisdom* and *My Brilliant Career* – most of the films were B-movies. Whitlam saw Bruce Beresford's bawdy *The Adventures of Barry McKenzie* – the only film ever to be entirely funded by the Australian Film Development Corporation – in a cinema in Potts Point on Christmas Day in 1972, 20 days after becoming prime minister. It was a wonderfully crude, crass pick for Christmas viewing, and it would have been highly unlikely that Whitlam watched Beresford's B-movie that day dreaming that he would appear in a sequel.[9] In 1974, Whitlam became the movie star prime minister, appearing, alongside his wife, Margaret, in a cameo at the end of *Barry McKenzie Holds His Own*, appointing Edna Everage a Dame – not a ceremonial function a prime minister is permitted to perform – while flashing his own high-wattage smile.

THE RIGHT STUFF: DAVID GULPILIL AM

Whitlam's moves to boost the Australian industry were being noted in America. Jack Valenti, a one-time LBJ aide turned powerful president of the Motion Picture Association of America, was considering a total boycott of Australia after rumours flew that the Australian government was planning to cap prices on the sales of American content and act as direct buyers. Valenti flew to Australia in 1972 to lobby Whitlam and his new minister for media, Senator Douglas McClelland. At a hotel reception for Valenti, a crowd of 200 protested out the front, including a pair in koala and emu costumes, wearing placards reading 'Help save Australian film' and 'It's time to end 50 years of US Domination of Australian content'. One placard went so far as to read 'Stop Cultural Genocide'. The young director Peter Weir was said to have taken to a loudspeaker on his way into the venue, attempting to play broker, perhaps self-interestedly: 'Sincerely, kids, we want to see complete cooperation between us'.[10]

Whitlam and Valenti would meet again on the sidelines of a trip to Hawai'i after further proposals recommended a forced divestment of Australia's cinema chains. Whitlam was clearly willing to entertain the lobbying. It was Doug McClelland, however, who proved the soft touch – almost a living embodiment of Australia's servitude to the American film industry. He would capitulate to Valenti – an embarrassing leaked letter showed that he had asked the American for advice on names to appoint to the country's Film Commission, and personally lobbied for a job for his daughter. It was a time of tension between Australia and America, as the latter figured out exactly how big a threat the former's new industry would pose to it.

There were at least some signs of productive, if fraught, collaboration. The hectic bushranger biopic *Mad Dog Morgan*

(1976) would star a genuinely deranged and dangerous Dennis Hopper. Philippe Mora's grimy, grim feature was Gulpilil's first film in five years and his first since *Walkabout*, and Mora wrote the part of Billy with Gulpilil in mind. In the film, Billy befriends Hopper's livewire outlaw, as the infamous criminal escapes law enforcement across the east coast countryside, and teaches the bushranger much of his craft. Gulpilil received a credit on the film for 'Aboriginal songs and Didgeridoo'. Billy is barely fleshed out as a sidekick, and yet, nonetheless, Gulpilil gives him energetic life. Gulpilil, not for the last time, becomes the best part of a film that is often falling down around him.

Dennis Hopper hailed from Dodge City, Kansas – Errol Flynn called through to promote his film that was set there in the late 1930s[11] – and, like Gulpilil, spent his boyhood acting out scenes from films he'd seen. Hopper, who had started his career as a teen actor beside James Dean in *Rebel Without a Cause* (1955) and *Giant* (1956), had arrived in Australia in the midst of a career lull after he had followed his wildly successful solo directorial debut *Easy Rider* (1969) with a flop of equal proportions, *The Last Movie* (1971). He was in a deep struggle with substance abuse and was airdropped into the country to give the Australian production name recognition in the American market. Mick Jagger had similarly starred as a noted bushranger in *Ned Kelly* in 1970 to boost sales.

Gulpilil and Hopper didn't get along immediately. The two weren't exactly equal when it came to know-how on set. Hopper was used to riding 'Hollywood horses' – which a 90-year-old could mount safely – while the horses used on the film were barely broken in. Footage of Gulpilil tearing through the bush on horseback is some of the most magisterial that exists of the actor and show his complete mastery of riding. Things would come to a head in a story fondly (and often) repeated by Mora, when Gulpilil walked off the set of the film to go and consult with the Kookaburras and the trees about his co-star. The Kookaburras reported that Hopper was, indeed, fucking crazy. Once that assessment was settled, the pair shared a room for much of the rest of the shoot. Gulpilil would later visit Hopper as a friend in America.

Hopper brought with him to Australia his immersive Strasberg approach to acting. For Hopper, there was method in the madness, but the madness was also The Method. His character Daniel 'Mad Dog' Morgan, known for his violent mood swings, would be seen swigging rum throughout the film, so Hopper naturally felt he needed to consume similar amounts of hard liquor for the sake of verisimilitude. The high-energy actor would eventually be deported from Australia after being arrested driving a car while he was over the legal blood alcohol level. According to the judge reviewing Hopper's tests, the amount of alcohol consumed should have left him 'clinically dead'. He was banned from driving and ordered to leave the country. This story is often told in a kind of mythologising, serving to romanticise a cult figure's alcohol consumption. It's a form of forgiveness for 'cheeky' behaviour, one which would never stretch to include First Nations people such as Gulpilil. Indeed, when Gulpilil and Hopper frequented country pubs during the shoot, Gulpilil would be refused service.

To Gulpilil, he and Hopper became one and the same: 'Him and me was a *bastard*'.[12]

GULPILIL COMPLETED JUST TWO MORE FILMS IN THE 1970s. In the same year as *Mad Dog Morgan*, he starred in the adaptation of beloved children's novel *Storm Boy* (1976), which would have school-age adolescents around the country enraptured by his winning presence. This breakthrough role would lead to important work in schools across the country. Gulpilil's household name recognition was radical. First Nations actors who had come before him, much to the Australia's shame, had not received the same level of public acknowledgement. In their remarkable essay, 'The Challenges of Benevolence: The role of Indigenous Actors', the performance scholars Maryrose Casey and Liza-Mare Syron suggest that 'the dominant belief' in Australia was 'there were no Indigenous actors' and 'that Aboriginal people could not act'.[13]

Yet they existed, and worked hard. Like Gulpilil after them, Henry Murdoch and Steve Dodd – who both appeared in *The Overlanders* and *Bitter Springs* – worked as stockmen and both would be typecast as sidekicks to white characters. Dodd had a career that spanned seven decades but was never offered anything approaching a lead role in his lifetime. Most First Nations actors made a transition into important advocacy work. The groundbreaking co-stars of *Jedda*, proud Arrernte Anmatjere woman Rosalie Kunoth-Monks and Tiwi man Robert Tudawali, both moved into significant roles in political activism in the Northern Territory, Tudawali campaigning against stockmen's poor wages, which led to the Wave Hill walk-off of 1966.

Gulpilil was back in a supporting role in Peter Weir's anticipated follow-up to *Picnic at Hanging Rock* (1975). Weir's *The Last Wave* (1977) remains truly difficult to make sense of. An environmental disaster film with a strong current of quasi-mysticism running through it, Weir's sophomore effort has the usual problem of an artwork stretching for profundity – you're more likely to see the reach than what it is aiming for. The fact that three white screenwriters were projecting magical properties on to their First Nations characters for the sake of plot renders it a discomforting watch today. Indeed, the Biripi actor Brian Syron, who worked as a cultural consultant on the film, serving as the key liaison for the First Nations actors, suggested that the film was 'far more Mexican than culturally relative to Indigenous Australians'. Some American reviews were attuned to this artificiality; others seemed to like it (it was popular with stoners in LA), but Gulpilil was consistently singled out among the cast. Critic Peter Travers' overall drubbing offered that 'In Gulpilil's eyes are a world and a history that haunt you in a way the phony horror film setups of *The Last Wave* never do. He's the genuine article'.[14]

At home, while Gulpilil's standing in the industry then was much surer, in part thanks to the mainstream embrace of *Storm Boy*, the following decade failed to offer him much more than what had come before. This was at a time when many of the Australian New Wave directors, along with their lead actors, were marshalling an exodus to Hollywood. Gulpilil would pick up a small part in *The Right Stuff* (1983) – Philip Kaufman's masterful three-hour adaptation of Tom Wolfe's space race nonfiction novel, a pissing contest replayed as epic poetry – but he was mostly found starring in the hokey, market-hopeful films Australia was becoming known for pumping out at the time. Two of them centred around Australia's most famous reptile: 1987's clunky crocodile horror movie *Dark Age* (a genuine croc-of-shit*) and Paul Hogan's

---

*   *Dark Age* at least brought together the charismatic Gulpilil and the great Woiworrung and Yorta Yorta man Burnum Burnum. On set, Gulpilil would teach him how to throw a spear and speak some language for the film, lessons sadly necessitated by the fact that Burnum Burnum was of the Stolen Generation, taken from his family when he was just three months old.

international blockbuster *Crocodile Dundee* (1986). Gulpilil's two brief scenes in the latter film would introduce him to his biggest audience yet – the biggest audience for any Australian film ever – but unlike its main star, there would be little profit from the film's immense success.

CAST MATE: PAUL HOGAN

It is, unfortunately, impossible to write about Gulpilil's relationship to Hollywood without making an extended detour into the career of non-Indigenous actor-writer Paul Hogan. They prove an interesting comparative pair, and their commonalities can be as telling as their differences. Hogan – like Gulpilil – had also entertained thoughts as a child that he would grow up to be John Wayne. He mused in his late-in-life memoir that 'every boy wanted to be The Duke' and that when he was young, Wayne's films – many directed by John Ford – had captivated him: *Fort Apache, Rio Grande, Red River, The Sands of Iwo Jima*. Decades later, the then Sydney-based comedian was in Los Angeles to film a prime-time television special when he had the chance to meet Wayne – as the iconic actor lifted himself out of a pool at the Beverly Hills Hotel, surrounded by palm trees and pastel pink furnishings, Hogan watched on, before blurting out, 'G'day Duke' and getting a one-line reply: 'And a good day to you too, young fella'.[15]

It was a boyhood dream come true, and many of Hogan's boyhood dreams did come true, which leads to questions about who in Australia is afforded such good fortune. Hogan, after all, had much of Hollywood accessible to him following his meteoric rise. His very first feature film rapidly became the highest grossing Australian film of all time – both at home and internationally – and it has remained in that exact position, unbeaten, since its release more than 35 years ago. Its commercial performance meant that its cultural reach was all encompassing. The phenomenon hit my life extremely early: in a home movie, taken at my christening party, my dad, carrying a heavy portable video camera on his shoulder – while recording straight on to big clunky VHS tapes – did a mock interview with one of my first cousins, Beau, about him having just caught a crocodile, a fantasy brought on by the croc-mania in the air around us. 'Say something to Sam about the crocodiles you saw today ... how big were they? Were they 20 foot? You better say something! This is all going on the news tonight ... How big was the crocodile you caught this morning?'

'Five ... ten foot!' he says.

'Ten foot? That's only a little one,' my dad prods.

'Nah ... 30 foot!'

'Thirty foot? That's more like it. That's a big one, isn't it.'

A little later dad starts speculating what might be next for the child prodigy crocodile hunter in front of him. 'Are you off to New York next week? What are you going to do over there? Are you going to see all the film stars? Go to all the parties?'

'Catch more crocodiles.'

'Catch crocodiles in New York? That would be excellent. I don't think anyone has ever done that before ... not for a longtime anyway.'

This escalating exchange of exaggerations was driven entirely by the recent release of Hogan's *Crocodile Dundee* (1986). In the same home movie, my grandfather comments that my father looks like Paul Hogan / Crocodile Dundee – a comparison many Australian men must have heard in the aftermath of the movie. It was proof of how adored Hogan was at home that year, but he had an unusual, winding pathway to the kind of global fame that would result in misquotations at family BBQs. Indeed, the laconic Hogan became a leading man about as late as you can get in Hollywood; he was 46 when his film hit with American audiences. To Americans, the *Crocodile Dundee* character might have come out of nowhere; to Australians it was a clear linear career progression, a logical projection of Hogan's onscreen persona, only now outfitted for a much larger screen. Pre-fame, he worked as a rigger on the Sydney Harbour Bridge, but while still perched high above the waters, he wrote a letter requesting to audition for a televised variety talent competition. He went on the show primarily to take the piss out of it, but he was such a hit he was invited back again and again. Hogan leveraged his appearances into a popular television career, resulting in his own long-running sketch comedy program, *The Paul Hogan Show* (1973–1984).

It was not, however, Hogan's sketch comedy background that best set him up for international success. It was his work in advertising. Hogan had built connections with firms throughout his television years, becoming the spokesman for various brands, which would get his face in front of overseas audiences and train him to sell an idea of Australia to the world. He first fronted a series of popular TV ads played at home, launching the Winfield brand of cigarettes, by adlibbing lines and using his rough accent to appeal to working-class audiences (often stressing that at 40 cents a pack they were the best value cigarette brand – the cigarettes were said to be the most smoked brand in Ramingining). Later, Hogan would be similarly employed to sell the largely unloved Foster's brand of beer in both the UK and America.

The most memorable of these advertisements would see Hogan become the face of Australia itself via the landmark, folksy tourism campaign 'Come and Say G'day'. A series of television advertisements featured Hogan, at his absolute breeziest, talking directly to the camera, backdropped by a series of inviting, handsomely filmed locations, casually pitching a trip to Australia to Americans. The campaign's breakthrough success was in selling 'personality' and a mutual friendliness to Americans (and that this would be best expressed by Hogan). The ad even came with its own cut-through catchphrase, which is still quoted to this day: 'slip an extra shrimp on the barbie' (translated for the Americans from an original line, 'pop another prawn on the barbie'). And it worked: as a result American tourism to Australia increased by a remarkable 22.8 per cent in 1985. The Australian consulate in Los Angeles had to stay open during their lunch hours to process the unprecedented number of visa applications streaming in. The *LA Times* reported that Hogan had boosted tourism to Australia 40 per cent overall.[16]

Hogan was, however, selling a very particular vision of Australia. That image was blond-haired, blue-eyed and noticeably untroubled. Hogan was the essence of 'no fuss', not even asking to be paid for appearing in the ads – perhaps anticipating that they would pay off in other ways down the track. Indeed, the idea behind his eventual record-breaking pay-off, *Crocodile Dundee*, came to the comedian when he was in New York, on a trip for the advertising campaign. Hogan was struck, walking the heaving, densely populated streets of Manhattan, that an outback frontiersman might be the most out-of-place person you could drop on to such iconic avenues.

On his return to Australia, he fleshed the idea out into a

feature-length script and recruited Peter Faiman to direct. Faiman came to the feature from working on *The Paul Hogan Show* and was primarily versed in television production, which showed in parts of the movie. The Australian-set section of the film, however, felt sweepingly cinematic – it owed much to the camera work of acclaimed cinematographer Russell Boyd, who was a frequent collaborator with Peter Weir. In this sense, *Crocodile Dundee* benefited – and directly profited – from the early aesthetic successes of the New Wave. That is to be expected as an industry builds on its own skills, but it was evident that *Crocodile Dundee* could not have been made a decade earlier, and not without the artistic innovations of better films. But *Crocodile Dundee* owed an even greater debt to the landscapes Russell Boyd's camera shot. The long establishing shot landscape scenes were cut in to give a proper sense of place, documenting and using the traditional lands in Kakadu. The scenes set at the Walkabout Hotel were filmed around the McKinlay Shire in Queensland, that the Shire had acknowledged were traditionally owned by the Kalkadoon, Yulluna, Mitakoodi and Mayi peoples. It was a debt that would have ramifications when Hogan came to mount a sequel.

Revisiting the comedy more than 35 years later, it is genuinely surprising to find that the story of *Crocodile Dundee* is stripped of the usual beats that make up a feature film. The character of Dundee is introduced to a Sydney-based American journalist, Sue, who, from her harbour-view home office, has convinced her New York superiors – including her newspaper mogul father – to send her to interview the weathered bushman following his survival of a recent crocodile attack. She's overwhelmed in the outback and falls for Dundee on his home ground. The script is flipped when Dundee follows Sue to New York. The production of the film more or less mimicked the movie's narrative: a ragtag Australian film crew found themselves out of their element shooting on the streets of New York. Like any local production, they had to win over the Teamsters – the strong-arm labour union who ran most on-location film sets in Manhattan – and Hogan has proudly suggested that the larrikin Australians got on with them better than anyone since.

The working relationship with the unions might have been an early sign of how the film would win over American audiences. Indeed, Paramount Pictures, who bought the rights to release the film in America, were closely watching the film's performance in Australia, and soon began to excitedly expand their own plans, shifting to a wide release across the US. The film became the second highest box office success in the US in 1986 (second only to another Paramount venture, the decade-defining military excesses of *Top Gun*).

AT THE HEIGHT OF HIS FAME, IT WOULD HAVE BEEN hard to name a better-known Australian internationally, and Hogan remains, for many, shorthand for Australian success, cinematic or otherwise, in America. By the 1990s, however, Hogan's legacy was ripe for ridicule. In a fondly remembered episode of *The Simpsons* titled 'Bart vs. Australia', the bratty eldest son of the Simpson family is extradited to the antipodes after he makes a prank call to an Australian family and, using reverse charges, runs up an expensive phone bill on their behalf. Evan Conover, a member of the US State Department – with the official title of 'Undersecretary for International Protocol: Brat and Punk Division' – is sent to the home of the Simpson family to explain their part in the ensuing geopolitical conflict. The envoy sets up a slideshow, over which he soberly observes that:

> Unfortunately, Bart, your little escapade could not have come at a worse time. Americo-Australianian [sic] relations are at an all-time low. As I'm sure you remember, in the late 1980s, the US experienced a short-lived infatuation with Australian culture.

Conover then clicks through a series of slides featuring Crocodile Dundee, a Koala Blue shopfront,* ex-footballer Mark 'Jacko' Jackson promoting the Energizer Battery, and a fictional footlong Subway sandwich spread with Vegemite. It's a brutal reduction.

There could have, however, been an alternative ending. In her book *The Birth of Korean Cool*, the American–Korean journalist Euny Hong outlines the South Korean government's decades-long policy of building soft diplomacy through cultural production.[17] *Hallyu* – meaning the Korean Wave, or K-Wave – takes the same approach Australia showed to its film production in the 1970s, but applies it to all cultural production. The Ministry of Culture in Korea has been far more strategic than their rough counterparts in other countries, but Australia might have come close in the 1980s with the back-to-back successes of its American-targeted tourism ads and *Crocodile Dundee*. Certainly Gorton's and

---

* Koala Blue was a kitsch fashion venture launched by *Grease* star Olivia Newton-John and her business partner, opening its first shopfront on Melrose Avenue in West Hollywood, in 1983. The concept included a milk bar, where customers could buy meat pies. The brand went bust after a rapid expansion to 60 stores internationally proved unsustainable.

Whitlam's level of strategic investment in the arts – where bold policies prospered – laid the groundwork for *Crocodile Dundee*'s unprecedented success. But that reading belies the fact that the film itself was much more the deliberate product of a free market mentality. The billionaire Kerry Packer, who owned Channel 9, had, after all, mentored Paul Hogan throughout his television career. Packer had worked closely with *Crocodile Dundee II* director John Cornell on launching World Series Cricket (Cornell was best known for playing the dropkick of a sidekick Strop on *The Paul Hogan Show* and had produced the first film).

Independent investment in *Crocodile Dundee* was widely promoted as a tax write-off for those who agreed to come on board. In the 1980s, private financing in film had been encouraged by a division of Australian taxation law, the infamous incentive 10BA, which gave financiers a 150 per cent concession, meaning they only paid tax on half of any profits from their investment. It is of little surprise then that *Crocodile Dundee*'s success was mounted in the same decade that saw the ascension of Robert James Lee Hawke as prime minister. Despite being a Labor figure and a long-time union leader, Hawke's best-remembered economic achievements are floating the Australian dollar on the world market, and removing controls on foreign exchange.* Hawke was a globalist and he was conveniently PM when Hogan's 'Come and Say G'day' tourism campaign came across his desk. There was considerable pushback within Cabinet about how Hogan's broad accent would play in America. According to

---

* A recent study by the Australian historian CJ Coventry revealed that Hawke was an active informant for the US government during his time as the head of the ACTU, from 1973 to 1979, spanning the Nixon, Ford and Carter presidencies.

Hogan, Hawke simply stared down his ministers and asked, 'What's wrong with his bloody accent?', knowing full well how close his own speaking voice was to the ocker comedian's. Hawke instinctively knew that he and Hogan were cut from similar cloth; Hawke was most famously the president of the Australian Council of Trade Unions (ACTU) before wrestling the leadership of the Australian Labor Party, and Hogan himself had done a short stint as a union official early in his career while working on the Harbour Bridge, although he eventually walked away from his union position, feeling he wasn't up to the task.

Hogan, however, believed Hawke had lied when he told a reporter he had seen *Crocodile Dundee*. And yet it is easier to imagine Hawke watching the film and wishing it was he who was up on screen, than to imagine Whitlam watching *Barry McKenzie* and thinking the same. Neither Hawke nor Whitlam would have had anything on Ronald Reagan though, who not only kept abreast of the big American releases, but also could – and would – play his own films back during his presidency. Reagan screened *Crocodile Dundee* at Camp David in 1986. The movie-mad president would watch a surprising number of Australian films during his years in office, including *Breaker Morant* (1980), *Gallipoli* (1981), *The Year of Living Dangerously* (1982), *The Man from Snowy River* (1982) and *Phar Lap* (1983). He watched the early efforts of the Australian New Wave directors in America too: Bruce Beresford's *Tender Mercies* (1983), Fred Schepisi's *Roxanne* (1987) and Peter Weir's *Witness* (1985) over two consecutive nights. Australia's New Wave cinema had, however, first entered the presidential viewing logs when Jimmy Carter watched Gillian Armstrong's *My Brilliant Career* on 1 March 1980, but no president watched anywhere near as much Australian fodder as Reagan.

THE RIGHT STUFF: DAVID GULPILIL AM

It is unclear what Reagan thought of any of these films, but it was obvious that he considered film as partly educational. Reagan watched *E.T. the Extra-Terrestrial* (1982) at the White House with several astronauts and director Steven Spielberg and told the room, 'everything on that screen is absolutely true'. The next morning Reagan received a briefing on the US Space Program.[18] Movie culture could provide a common language. Reagan would screen *Crocodile Dundee II* at Camp David on 6 June 1988. Seventeen days later the ageing president would meet with Bob Hawke for the last time. Two days beforehand, Hawke had delivered a speech to an economic forum in Chicago, in which he employed Hogan's film as an accessible touchstone for the foreign audience. In trying to impart a message against national protectionism, and to encourage support for opening free markets on a global scale, Hawke introduced himself as 'the Prime Minister of Crocodile Dundee country' and reached for the famous scene where Dundee sizes up a mugger's blade and flashes back his own hunting knife. He told the audience he had no knife but:

> I do however come with a weapon. It is the
> weapon of logic, honed by the concern of my fellow
> Australians at the damage being done to them and
> to the prospects for global economic security by the
> irrationality of the policies of the world's major player.
> Like Mick Dundee I produce the weapon, not to hurt,
> but to provide understanding of what is enlightened
> self-interest.[19]

It was nowhere near as succinct as Hogan's iconic 'That's a knife' line reading, but it does show just how far and wide

Hawke was pushing his agenda for global reform, and how willing he was to try to translate political policy into a popular language. Australian cinema was finally in reach as a translation device. Every boom, however, eventually goes bust. Australia went into a recession in 1990, and Hawke was ousted as prime minister two years later, at the exact same time that Hogan was struggling to figure out his ongoing place in Hollywood.

Hawke's successor, Paul Keating, would try to rinse Hogan's influence clean from the nation's image of itself, to start the new decade afresh. Keating, having seized control, now wanted the country to look a lot more like him. In an interview, he said that he would prefer that Australia represented itself by its more 'clever and cultivated achievements' than Hogan's simplified 'shrimp on the barbie' slang. Hogan in turn, took great offence, and the prime minister eventually issued a series of back-downs. In rejecting Hogan, it was clear Keating was pushing back on Hawke's image too, but he was also running from his own origins. Keating, like Hogan, had grown up in Sydney's western suburbs – he was raised in Bankstown, not that far from Hogan's Granville. Keating should have foreseen that Australians would come to identify themselves with so-called 'westies' and that his hometown would become a contested battleground for future control of the country. To this day, hopeful prime ministers still chase the larrikin confidence of Hawke, and the iconography that goes with it, just as every modern national tourism campaign chases Hogan's.

Back in *The Simpsons* lounge room, the US state official finishes his slideshow documenting Australia's cultural stranglehold over the United States with the observation:

'For some bizarre reason, the Aussies thought this would be a permanent thing. Of course, it wasn't.'*

Still, you could imagine Hogan thinking the ride would last longer than that. The sequelising of Dundee signalled as much. *Crocodile Dundee II* was a success, if not quite as much as the first film. Hogan wasn't the only one interested in capitalising on the character: Paramount Pictures reportedly wanted to parachute the Dundee character into *Beverly Hills Cop III*, but Eddie Murphy wisely vetoed the idea.[20] Still, that didn't stop Hogan from making a third Dundee film in 2001, *Crocodile Dundee in Los Angeles* (which, given its title, should be central to the thesis of this book but has nothing interesting to say at all).

Dundee remained out there, roaming the wider cultural imagination, as an undead intellectual property. A new sequel was teased for months in 2018, featuring a plot focused on the American-born son of Mick Dundee, in what was eventually revealed as a fake-out: the ads pointed to nothing more than a new Australian tourism campaign designed to debut during the Super Bowl and hoping to reclaim some of Hogan's original 'Come and Say G'day' magic. There were cameos from latter-day Australian stars: Russell Crowe, Hugh Jackman and Margot Robbie – teasing the non-existent film. It was a logical conclusion for this particular film series to eventually mutate into pure advertorial content.

---

* The final slide in the series shows a cinema with the marquee letters reading 'Yahoo Serious Festival' but the cinema is boarded shut. Middle child Lisa utters, 'I know those words, but that sign makes no sense'. Yahoo Serious – a true outlier in Australian culture – was the better comic performer than Hogan, so much closer to the physical comedy giants of Buster Keaton and Chaplin. That he was reduced to a punch line isn't as painful as the fact he only ever made three films.

The actor, after all, had long seemed uninterested in trading in on his newfound success in Hollywood in any traditional manner. He showed little to no interest in transitioning to dramatic roles (despite flirting with such a prospect by starring in the 1985 miniseries *Anzacs*).*

Hogan turned down actor-for-hire gigs with big commercial plays like *Three Men and a Baby* (1987) and *Ghost* (1990) and instead went ahead with his own productions. Hogan's first non-Dundee film, the mawkish melodrama *Almost an Angel* (1990), which saw Hogan play an ex-crim who, after a near-death experience, comes to mistakenly believe he is dead and an angel, feels like it might have come straight from Hogan reading the script for *Ghost* and mistranslating its appeal.

Hogan seemed indifferent to film culture beyond the success of *Crocodile Dundee*. It's impossible not to come to the conclusion that Hogan never really wanted to be John Wayne – an actor who starred in over 150 films. The idea of the old Hollywood workhorse clearly didn't really appeal. He didn't want to be Clint Eastwood either, an actor who used his early successes to transition to directing, working well into his eighties and now into his nineties (both Hogan and Gulpilil would meet Eastwood in America; Gulpilil met with Eastwood on the actor's ranch on a trip to America for a prospective meeting about collaborating, but nothing came from their discussions).

---

*   Decades later, the more traditionally handsome Eric Bana – born Eric Banadinović to first-generation migrants – would rise from very similar sketch comedy origins to Hogan and happily move to leading-man status in Hollywood, going from Poida, a tinnie-swilling, blond-mulleted bogan, an extremely Hogan-inspired creation indeed, to accepting the lead role as a traumatised Mossad agent in one of Steven Spielberg's darkest dramas, 2005's *Munich*, via an acclaimed performance in the crime indie *Chopper* (2000).

Is it any wonder then that Hogan never reached out to Gulpilil to offer something more to his co-star? There is surely a scenario in which Gulpilil's role is expanded in the *Crocodile Dundee* sequel – or, indeed, an alternate universe where Gulpilil is Crocodile Dundee, in which the fish out of water elements play more convincingly than a white colonial settler walking around another white colonial settlement. Gulpilil's early experiences promoting *Walkabout* in Los Angeles and New York would have provided autobiographical material for such a take on the role. It might have been a deeper, more emotional film. When he was in New York in 1971, he told a reporter, 'I just want to get back to the land. I miss my father very much.'

Unlike the other subjects in this book, however, Gulpilil was likely never given a break in Hollywood because the idea of casting a Yolŋu actor in anything other than an Australian-set film probably never occurred to anyone there. The *New York Times* made this explicit in 1979, when its critic Richard Eder, writing a short notice on *The Last Wave* on its American release, suggested that: 'because Gulpilil is a full-blooded Australian aborigine [sic], there probably will never be many movie roles for him.'[21] Eder's frank observation underlined the reality for First Nations stars on the rise such as Gulpilil: that their aspirations and potential work opportunities were always curtailed. There was little imagination for casting Indigenous actors in anything other than tribal roles, or as subjects in issues-based films directed by non-Indigenous filmmakers.

The term 'Aussie invasion' – often wheeled out to describe Australian actors dominating the competition in Hollywood – is misguided at best, given Australia's violent colonial history, but there might be in such terms a form of confession. Who is allowed to play the invader? White actors could travel freely in the 20th century, but this was not always the case for Indigenous actors. The state had to approve Gulpilil's travel on his first trips. State intervention was brutal in the case of actor and activist Bill Onus. The proud Wiradjuri and Yorta Yorta man had appeared in early Australian films *Uncivilised* (Charles Chauvel), *Lovers and Luggers* (Ken G Hall) and *The Overlanders* (Harry Watt). In the wider entertainment industry, he became known for a series of performances in Melbourne, culminating in the presentation of his show *An Aboriginal Moomba: Out of the Dark* in 1951, intending to put a bright spotlight on Indigenous performers. The next year, Walt Disney – likely having heard of *Out of the Dark's* monumental success with audiences – invited Onus to meet in America, but the Australian Security Intelligence Organisation (ASIO) successfully advocated for the US Embassy to block his entry into their country, denying Onus a visa. There is no record of what Disney's intentions were for the meeting, but it would be safe to assume that the Australian government killed any chance of collaboration between the pair and potential investment in an Australian film project.[22]

Gulpilil's career – like that of many film stars – included many missed connections. In an interview in America, Gulpilil expressed his desire to return home to the Northern Territory to make a film about his fellow Yolŋu people. 'We want to live independently and make a true film to show Australians who Aborigines really are. When white people in Australia talk about us, they say, "Culture, culture, dance, dance." They don't understand us, speak our language. I want to film the story of my people how we live and how we used to live in the olden days. Then, maybe, white people will understand more about us.'[23]

THE RIGHT STUFF: DAVID GULPILIL AM

A DARK AGE (1987–2001)

At the time that Paul Hogan was in the lucky position of being able to turn down lucrative roles and to take his time in considering his future prospects, the line had gone decidedly quiet for Gulpilil. In his own words, 'And then there was … nothing'. The 1990s became a stinging dry spell for anyone who had, up until that point, been following the actor's career. The German auteur Wim Wenders opened the new decade with his unwieldy, globe-trotting sci-fi epic *Until the End of the World* (1991), co-scripted by Australian novelist Peter Carey, and featuring Gulpilil in a borderline cameo role saved for the third act. There would be some menial work in television, and a minor appearance in *Dead Heart* (1996), but the actor would not appear in another feature film until the new millennium ticked over. Writing and reference to Gulpilil in America runs dry as a result during the same period. The length of Gulpilil's absence from the big screen feels like an indictment on the Australian film industry given that the cut-through of his role as Neville Bell in *Crocodile Dundee* would likely have catapulted a white actor into steadier, higher strata work opportunities. For his part, Gulpilil would later disparagingly call *Crocodile Dundee* 'bullshit'. He detested how the role had twisted his public image. In his one-man play, he told his audience that the film changed the perception of him, a traditional man, into a 'funny bugger from the city'. His true origins had been washed out. Gulpilil was equally disturbed by his poor profit share from the first film. When Hogan decided to make the sequel to his monster hit, Gulpilil told a Darwin-based journalist: 'They ripped me off. They made so much money. I'm not even getting royalties. I walked out with about $7000 or $8000 and out of that I had to pay tax'.[24]

The article ran with a sensationalist headline: 'Gulpilil Asks $1m for Sequel to *Dundee*'. Gulpilil did, indeed, put this amount to the producers as the condition for his return. Given its astronomical profits, anyone associated with the first film would have been preparing to request some sort of increase in wages for participating in a sequel, but Gulpilil must have known he wasn't on equal footing to ask for any kind of pay rise. Why not swing big and ask for a million dollars? After all, what would a million dollars really mean to Hogan's net worth in 1987 when the film went into production? Rather than pay him what he was due, Gulpilil's character was simply switched out in the sequel. The Yamatji actor Ernie Dingo was cast in a role that seemed created to replace Gulpilil (the fact that Gulpilil and Dingo shared the screen, however briefly, in Wim Wenders' *Until the End of the World* felt like a happenstance rebuke of Hogan – a radical thought that a movie could star more than one First Nations actor).

It robbed Gulpilil of the opportunity to star in a sequel, and with it the potential to extend the life and story of his character. When film critic Jake Wilson was writing a monograph on *Mad Dog Morgan*, he sat down with Gulpilil to rewatch the film on DVD in the mid-2010s, going into the actor's hotel room with the knowledge that Gulpilil often proposed sequels to films he'd already starred in. To Wilson, this began to make sense as Gulpilil 'feels an ongoing responsibility for the characters he's brought to life, developing his own "back stories" in addition to whatever information is given in the script'.[25] Wilson thought this true of most actors, but it might have had a particularly significant meaning to a First Nations actor. As Maryrose Casey and Liza-Mare Syron explain, 'At the end of the day non-Indigenous actors may feel free to walk away from their roles, whereas Indigenous actors cannot or do not. Indigenous actors cannot, or do not, seek to escape their personal, historical, and recent connection to story and character'.

This was almost certainly true for Gulpilil. He longed to make 'The Tracker 2', a follow-up to his beloved 2002 film that audiences would have likely welcomed too. Any attempt could have been of cultural significance. A sequel to *Mad Dog Morgan*, say, might have given Gulpilil the chance to explore the historical background of his character, for which the original was found wanting. Gulpilil asked Wilson: 'What happened to Billy?' It was a question of importance because, in Gulpilil's mind, the director Philippe Mora had left out important cultural details, including which nation Billy belonged to: 'See, he should've went back, the director should have went back, and said Billy, this is where you come from. And then you see the village. See, Mora just got it to halfway, the history halfway'.

While Gulpilil remembered Mora, and most of his collaborators over the years, quite fondly, when it came to Paul Hogan, he didn't hold anything back. In one powerful personal assessment of his former co-star:

> He is big-time Hollywood. I don't like him. I've been watching him on TV and reading about him in America. Congratulations, Paul Hogan. He never, never mentions my name.

It is an extraordinary quote and not only because of its extreme frankness. It also reveals in that devastating final observation – *he never, never mentions my name* – that Gulpilil not only believed he hadn't been remunerated properly for *Crocodile Dundee*, but that it's makers hadn't shared in its non-financial windfall either, failing to give him a greater platform. Gulpilil's career would be a long struggle to receive proper credit for his work. This struggle extended well beyond his experience with Hogan, and spoke to his place in the industry as a whole:

> I was the black face of Australia at that stage and they been using my image in advertising and promotion and portraying me as a stupid blackfella as well as paying me bugger all and nothing was coming back to my people except for the lousy pay I was getting, so I thought I'd try them out.

There seemed to be little thought in the film industry about the cultural ramifications of pay levels for First Nations actors. Whenever he finished a film, Gulpilil would take the money he made back home to Ramingining, and it could all be gone in a matter of hours, redistributed among the community. There were traditional obligations for him to do so. *Crocodile Dundee* caused the 'most lasting damage', according to Gulpilil's future collaborator Rolf de Heer, because it was the one film everyone in the community knew. They were also informed of how exceptionally well it had performed at the box office. According to de Heer, the community knew that the film 'had made an unimaginably large amount of money, that it had made Paul Hogan rich' and that by logical extension, it should have made Gulpilil rich. There were suspicions that Gulpilil was lying when he reported that he had only made $10 000 on the film, and that he might have been hiding his money.[26]

There was also the matter of personal costs accrued in keeping his professional career alive. Gulpilil's agent John Cann relayed a situation where the actor was involved in a television commercial that required international travel to

Spain. The professional engagement might have seemed straightforward but, as Cann explained, even a locally held casting session requires at least two days' transport. In this instance, Gulpilil had forgotten his passport and Cann calmly detailed the lengths the actor had to go to retrieve it. He had to fly from Alice Springs to Darwin, staying overnight there before boarding a light plane to Ramingining, where he had to find a vehicle to drive across Arafura swampland before swimming across a 'crocodile-infested' river, walking 'several kilometres' to his house, grabbing his passport, before walking back, swimming back, driving back, flying back. In Cann's telling, he 'swam back across the river with his passport in his mouth, got in the car, drove back to Ramingining, light plane to Darwin, flight from Darwin to Sydney, where he met me, all smiles.'

Gulpilil repeated a similar story in his one-man play, recounting a time when he had to take a plane to make it in time to film a part in a television adaptation of *The Man from Snowy River* (1995) – suggesting this wasn't a one-time occurrence. The financial burden of exercises like this – particularly hiring a plane between Darwin and Ramingining – likely meant that profits from going through with the gig were all but cancelled out. The material impacts on an actor living remotely as Gulpilil did were evident and it just isn't something ever asked of white Australian actors and, if it were, the complexity would make most quit the industry entirely. Gulpilil's persistence was unquestionable and his determination remarkable.

Gulpilil wasn't alone in facing such challenges and demanding change. In the wake of *Crocodile Dundee*'s success, an independent statutory authority representing First Nations people in the Top End of the Northern Territory – the

Northern Land Council – commissioned a policy document, which proposed a set of protocols for filming on Country. In *Guess Who's Coming to Dinner in Arnhem Land?* – cleverly named after the 1967 Oscar-nominated interracial marriage drama, starring Sidney Poitier – the authors of the report found that every year, 'the Northern, Central, Tiwi, and Pitjantjatjara Land Councils receive something in the order of 400 approaches from filmmakers to film on Aboriginal land and/or with Aboriginal people'. The goal of *Guess Who's Coming to Dinner in Arnhem Land?* was to establish a permit system, designed to stop filmmakers walking onto traditional lands to 'shoot at will'.[27]

Traditional owners had negotiated with Hogan for his use of their land for the first film, but, like Gulpilil, were now seeking fairer remuneration for its sequel. Collectively, the groups proposed rents, which were estimated to cost just 0.04 per cent of the first film's profits. Hogan paid the traditional owners of Kakadu National Park, just $200 000. They warned the producers that if they were refused that amount, the cost would jump another $100 000 and access would be denied entirely from there. The Deputy Chief Minister of the Northern Territory came out in the press and deemed it a 'money-grabbing exercise' and one 'which would drive other film-makers away from the Territory'. The authors of *Guess Who's Coming to Dinner in Arnhem Land?* characterised these press comments as 'attacks on traditional owners' and wryly noted the discrepancy between the producers paying for locations in Australia and America. Hogan, for instance, had no problems paying up to $2000 an hour to use a New York pub in the first movie.[28]

The authors of *Guess Who's Coming to Dinner in Arnhem*

Land? wryly noted the discrepancy between the producers paying for locations in Australia and America. Hogan, for instance, had no problems paying up to $2000 an hour to use a New York pub in the first movie.

The conflict over *Crocodile Dundee II* might have been something of a premonition. It must have been unsurprising for Gulpilil and members of the Northern Land Council to discover, in 2010, that Hogan had been barred from leaving Australia, unable to return to Los Angeles, after being assessed as a flight risk over allegations of historic tax avoidances, including funnelling profits into offshore accounts. It was the 'most expensive tax investigation in Australia's history'[29] and Hogan kept the case in the news by openly antagonising prosecutors, calling them 'clowns' and comparing them to the Taliban.[30] The dispute, which took eight years to resolve, only ended when Hogan reached a settlement with the Australian Tax Office for an undisclosed sum. It was as if Mick Dundee had revealed himself to be a cousin of that other late 1980s icon: Gordon Gekko.

While Hogan was using his profits to buy up an impressive, if odd, real estate portfolio – including a 132-acre property in Byron Bay, an office block in Parramatta, and properties in Santa Barbara and Malibu – Gulpilil was practically homeless for long stretches during his career. In the late 1980s, at a time when the groundswell of land rights challenges were surging, ahead of the landmark Mabo decision, the Hawke government returned traditional lands to Gulpilil. On this site he built two small, inexpensive houses.[31] Their limited fit-outs meant, however, that he could not watch his own movies, an act of remembrance he longed to perform.

CAST MATES

ONE OF THE EARLIEST DOCUMENTARIES FOCUSING ON Gulpilil's life, *Walkabout to Hollywood*, centres on his early ventures in America (rarely seen after it first screened on the BBC in the early 1980s). As its title suggests, the documentary shadowed Gulpilil as he travelled to Los Angeles. He was there, in part, to attend a set of retrospective screenings of his earlier films (*Walkabout*, plus Weir's *The Last Wave*). A loose 50 or so minutes is pulled together from observational footage, some featuring the actor at home in Ramingining. Other sections feature him in Redfern, where he teaches a traditional dance class. Once in Los Angeles, Gulpilil is photographed awkwardly roller-skating around Venice Beach and attending Disneyland with his young family, spinning wildly around on the Mad Tea Party carousel. In a brief scene, Gulpilil is seen excitedly trying on and buying a pair of leather cowboy boots (John Travolta's *Urban Cowboy* was all the rage at the time).

Walkabout to Hollywood was directed by Bill Leimbach, an American who grew up in San Diego and migrated to Australia in the 1970s, after finishing film school in London. He first met Gulpilil as he courted the actor to play Bennelong, in a film exploring the relationship between Bennelong and Arthur Phillip, the screenplay for which Leimbach had written while still at film school. The historical epic ultimately proved too expensive to get off the ground, requiring recreations of tall ships and Sydney's first settlements (this was well before CGI, Leimbach reminded me). The pair went on to make *Walkabout to Hollywood* instead.

Leimbach's documentary elides the fact that Gulpilil was in the US to film a small scene in Philip Kaufman's space race biopic *The Right Stuff* (using the Mojave Desert to sub in for the Australian outback and three African-American extras standing in for Gulpilil's kin). It does make mention, however, of another project Gulpilil was hoping to get off the ground. The actor was envisioning this film as his directorial debut and, for contemporary audiences watching *Walkabout to Hollywood*, unaware of this historical detail, the fact lands as a significant revelation. Gulpilil had told a reporter for the *Honolulu Advertiser*, when he was in that city on a dance tour in 1979, that 'like dancing, I found that film-work came natural to me'. He was thinking ahead about how he could make his own projects: 'For the future, I will try to write some original scripts that will help towards preserving the traditional Aboriginal culture. It is something I want to do for my people'.[32]

As early as 1971, fresh off *Walkabout*, Gulpilil was talking about his desire to make a Western: 'I would like to make a cowboy film – either in America or Australia. I'd like to play a cowboy, you know, a station hand'.[33] The screenplay that Gulpilil dreamed up for such a film was called *Billy West and Lightning Thunderboy*. According to its earliest loglines, *Billy West* was to tell the story of 'an American cattle rancher sent to Australia in the early 1900s to run a cattle station in the Northern Territory'. West, travelling with his Indigenous American wife, was tasked with producing beef supplies to export to American soldiers in the Philippines. Clearly *Billy West and Lightning Thunderboy* would have explored Australian–American relations a good five years before *Crocodile Dundee* exploded onto the scene.

It is not explicitly stated in his documentary but Leimbach was lined up to serve as Gulpilil's co-director on *Billy West*. Gulpilil had been responsible for the story and would direct the scenes with First Nations actors, while simultaneously starring as Lightning Thunderboy. Finances were in place and actors were flown to Australia, meeting in the film's production offices in Kings Cross ahead of the start date for shooting in May 1981. Max Gail – an American actor best known for his role on the popular US police sitcom *Barney Miller* – was invited to take the role of Billy West. Gail had personal connections with Indigenous American activists and introduced Gulpilil and Leimbach to the Canadian-American Buffy Sainte-Marie. The Piapot Cree First Nation singer-songwriter, who is seen jamming with Gulpilil in *Walkabout to Hollywood*, would be cast as the female lead. Despite all this significant groundwork, *Billy West and Lightning Thunderboy* would never eventuate. That fact now feels like a stinging loss, particularly because the prospect of Gulpilil co-directing a fictional feature film would have cemented a genuine milestone in Australian cinema (a number of groundbreaking Indigenous-led documentaries were being made at the same time as *Billy West's* development, largely directed by women, including Essie Coffey, Coral Edwards and Madeline McGrady).

This was not, however, the first time Gulpilil had come close to sitting in the director's chair and had it taken from underneath him. In Derek Reilly's short biography *Gulpilil* – more extended magazine profile than book – the author notes that, in the early 1970s, the actor had been invited to join the newly founded Australian Film and Television School. Gulpilil rocked up to take his place alongside the iconic inaugural intake of students, including the directors Phillip Noyce, Gillian Armstrong and Chris Noonan. Gulpilil's admission into the school could have been read as a strategic step to give autonomy to First Nations filmmakers to tell their own stories. Noyce – who would later direct Gulpilil in *Rabbit-Proof Fence* – told Reilly that the opposite was true, recalling that a short documentary credited to Gulpilil – *Showing Melbourne to Maningrida* – was not, in fact made by him at all. It was instead a case of 'very well-intentioned staff at the film school using him as a subject for a film'. The director sombrely noted that 'Everyone tried to tell him [Gulpilil] what he wanted to do'.[34]

Billy West and Lightning Thunderboy was a chance to right this particular wrong – handing material agency over to Gulpilil – but financing for the film fell apart before cameras started rolling. It wasn't a big, flashy falling-out. The Australian government had, simply, failed to legislate 10BA – the exact tax incentive that would go on to make *Crocodile Dundee* into a reality – in time for its production to start. As a result, the film's existing investors pulled out. Leimbach says the filmmakers lost $250 000 and sets that had been built in Arnhem Land went to waste. The principal players were keen to return to the film in a year's time once 10BA was in law – the tax write-off did end up propelling most film productions in Australia throughout the 1980s – but in the interim the existing sets were burnt down by bushfires in the area. With them went the hope for the first film born from Gulpilil's own imagination. Leimbach was saddened that Gulpilil didn't get the opportunity to direct and that the largely First Nations cast lost out on their roles.

Leimbach said that, over the years, whenever Gulpilil would run into him, the actor would cry out, 'When are we going to do *Billy West*? When are we going to do *Billy West*?' The script for the historical fiction must still be floating out there somewhere, longing to one day be made in Gulpilil's honour. In the meantime, we have *Walkabout to Hollywood*, a remarkable record, capturing Australia's most arresting actor, pregnant with the promise of being able to tell a story of his own invention, on his own terms.

Bill Leimbach speculated that, ultimately, it wasn't possible for Gulpilil to work in America for any extended period of time. 'He was always homesick, and I remember one occasion driving back from the Indian reservation and there was a country and western song on the radio, and he was just streaming down tears, and he couldn't wait to get back to the hotel to make a phone call to Ramingining.'

Unlike David Gulpilil, Paul Hogan got to make his own Western. So where we don't have *Billy West and Lightning Thunderboy*, we do have *Lightning Jack* (1994). Co-starring a young Cuba Gooding Jnr, Hogan's last sole screenwriting credit was his final attempt to lift his Dundee persona and remodel it as a different character for the American market. In doing so, he dropped a minor variation on Dundee in a different era, playing an Australian outlaw obsessed with his own publicity. Hogan was left awed when filming scenes in Monument Valley – known for its starkly red mesas and buttes – and the landscapes are the usual breathtaking vistas, but the film itself had nothing to add to the genre, and barely constitutes a riff. There's a feeling then that towards the end Hogan is just a boy playing with his toys, and, critically, he doesn't let the audience in on the fun. You could never imagine Gulpilil doing the same.

CAST MATE: BRIAN SYRON

While Paul Hogan seemed to be able to get any pet project he liked greenlit, happily turning down others, First Nations writers, actors and directors in Australia struggled to get even the smallest scale productions off the ground. In researching the life of Gulpilil, I somewhat naturally came across *Kicking*

Down the Doors: A History of First Nations Films 1968–1993,[35] a 600-page tome with a simple black cover, housing a monumental intellectual exercise in cataloguing all Indigenous and non-Indigenous films that had represented – or purported to represent – Indigenous life in Australia. It is a wildfire of condemnation and no reader can walk away from reading it without thinking critically about the Australian film industry. The paucity of Australian films through the 20th century can make Australia look like a victim – hurt by the impositions of Hollywood – but it was a perpetrator too.

The book was spearheaded and co-authored by proud Biripi man Brian Syron, who is also widely credited with being the first First Nations person to direct a feature-length film, taking the title that Gulpilil might well have held if *Billy West and Lightning Thunderboy* had been realised. It wasn't until the book kicked down my own door – a giant print-on-demand copy that dropped at my doorstep with a thud – that I realised its author, was a distant in-law relative. Syron was the great uncle of my first cousin – the boy in the home video imitating *Crocodile Dundee*. In the back of my head, I could recall some vague mention of him during childhood at my aunty and uncle's house but it was no strong memory – I could remember the name in passing but not why he was mentioned. That story was the same collectively: Syron's history as both an actor and filmmaker has largely been hidden from mainstream view, as he died shortly after making his debut film. Nor did he live to see the publication of *Kicking Down the Doors*, which was originally printed in a run of just 20 copies. And yet it is hard to deny that he is a historically significant figure, with deep ties to Gulpilil.

Unlike Gulpilil, Syron had an urban upbringing. He was born and raised in an inner-city slum in Sydney's Balmain, and began his creative career as a theatre actor, but potential work as a male model, trading on his striking good looks, would give him the opportunity to move overseas. Syron kept his heritage hidden partly so he could leave the country with ease. He first left Australia for Europe, before moving across to America and finding himself in New York. There Syron used what little money he had saved to sign up to study acting under Stella Adler, the renowned and influential teacher of Stanislavski's Method. Adler, the scion of a Yiddish acting dynasty, had taught with the Group Theatre – co-founded by Lee Strasberg – before training directly under Stanislavski in Paris in the 1930s. Syron would flunk his audition for Adler, but the teacher saw his commitment in the distance he had travelled. He would go on to study under her for three and a half years starting in 1961, supporting himself through modelling work and waiting tables, and by working in the mailroom of the Australian Consulate. His classroom contemporaries included Warren Beatty (a couple of years above), Peter Bogdanovich (a few years above) and, more immediately, Robert De Niro. Gary Foley reported that he was sceptical when Syron, on his return to Sydney, told him who his fellow students had been:

> Brian used to talk about his mate 'Bobby', and I one day said, 'Bobby who?' and Brian replied, 'Bobby de Niro, Baby!'[36]

After graduating with Adler, Syron toured theatrical productions throughout America. In touring the southern states in 1967 – including Georgia, Virginia, Tennessee and North Carolina – Syron wrote that these visits were 'the finalization of my black politicization.' He explained that 'No black person travelling through these States during this period of peace marches, race riots and assassinations could have remained untouched and I had to come home.' In the very same year Australians were being asked to vote in a referendum as to whether the First Nations people of the country should be counted as part of the population.

In a self-taped interview, recorded in his Bondi flat overlooking the beach, Syron explained the exact moment he realised he had to come home. His sister had travelled to America to tour with him and Syron explained that through her, he'd 'had a breath of home'. Later, he realised he didn't want what New York was offering him. Dancing in his apartment by himself, 'pretty high', he caught himself in the mirror: 'I looked to the side, and suddenly I started to change, I became very much like my father, who was Black, and then I changed again, and not only did I change, there were the stars and there were the night sounds of Australia and there was the land, and it called me home.'

On his return to Australia, Syron worked for a theatre company in Perth, but finding the city overly conservative, he made his way back to the Sydney scene once more. He had an eye towards political activism, racial justice, and the burgeoning Black Theatre. He also kept an open line to America. Inspired by his studies in New York, he set up acting classes in his home city. In 1969, he began teaching 'the first group of urban Aboriginal students to ever study Stanislavski from an Aboriginal perspective'. The political leader Charles Perkins, the famed Arrernte Kalkadoon man, offered Syron an office near Central Station to host the classes (Perkins' daughter Rachel would become one of the most significant players in the Australian film industry from the 1990s through to today). Taxis had to be organised to drive students back to

Redfern, to avoid the risk, on the short walk back home, of being arrested by police for being on the streets after 9 pm.

Syron would continue to migrate professionally between Australia and America. He flew to California to work as an attachment on Bogdanovich's slapstick revival *What's Up, Doc?* (1972), with leads Barbra Streisand and Ryan O'Neal, which was filming in both Los Angeles and San Francisco. Syron would spend most of the shoot fronting up to Warner Bros studios in Burbank every day to learn something about filmmaking practice. This back and forth would prove Syron to be one of the most important brokers of meaningful cultural exchanges between Australia and America. He often put his own money down too; remortgaging his home to tour Wiradjuri playwright Robert J Merritt's groundbreaking work *The Cake Man* in the United States.

In 1974, Syron would invite Gulpilil to travel with him to America, for a cultural exchange program with the National Theatre of the Deaf, in Waterford, Connecticut. Gulpilil – alongside old friend Dick Bandilil again – would teach traditional dance and stories from the Dreaming. Syron had sought permission from Worora Elder, Albert Barunga, to share these stories and myths. After Barunga had personally seen the National Theatre of the Deaf perform in Australia, he gave permission because of the 'nature of the company'. Syron said that 'Albert Barunga felt that unlike most white people these Deaf actors showed the same capacity to relate their feelings that our people have known for centuries'.[37]

In the same year, Syron was made the inaugural Honorary Artistic Director of the new theatre at Bondi Pavilion. He launched the venue with a staging of *The Fantasticks*, an off-Broadway musical, from 1960. On opening night, Whitlam arrived wearing a Javanese batik top, in striking red and white. Gulpilil opened for Syron, dancing for the excited audience. It was while working within this role at the Bondi Pavilion that Syron brought Stella Adler out to Sydney. Adler was professionally engaged to teach workshops at the Bondi Pavilion for a month. The *Sydney Morning Herald* excitedly reported 'First Lady of US Theatre Arrives Soon' with a photograph of Adler with Syron's arm around her.[38] On this same trip, Adler tried to convince Syron to take over running her acting studio in Los Angeles. He said he would think about it and accepted her invitation after being unable to secure work as a film director in Australia. In 1975, he was at work, instead, on Hollywood Boulevard, teaching John Barrymore Jnr, the scion of Errol Flynn's former drinking buddy, sitting among former cowboys and teen idols – 'film stars and potential film stars' – looking to further their dramatic skills.

During this time, the Whitlam government started to cement its film industry policies as physical institutions. Much of Syron's scholarship, in surveying Australian films in *Kicking Down the Doors*, documents how these well-meaning institutions failed First Nations filmmakers over and over again. The doors were double-bolted. This was true of the Australian Film and Television School and it was certainly true of funding through bodies such as the Australian Film Commission (AFC). As Syron made clear, much funding for Indigenous filmmaking came, not through official film channels, but via educational and health departments and, subsequently, these opportunities were limited to documentary-making. This produced important work, but writers and directors who wanted to make dramatic, fictional works were overlooked. Syron repeatedly made the point that First Nations filmmakers were constantly expected to make films about 'causes and issues' whereas non-Indigenous filmmakers could make film 'for the track record and the fun of making it'.

In place of being given the resources and autonomy to make his own films, Syron was hired to work as a 'consultant' on films led by white directors that featured Indigenous actors and storylines. He worked on two Gulpilil-starring productions in this role: *The Last Wave* and the made-for-television literary miniseries *Naked Under Capricorn* (1989). It was a role that Syron would come to resent. In many cases, Indigenous actors were being asked to rewrite dialogue and rework scenes, with a view to verisimilitude, but they were given no real credit for this work. It was Syron's firm belief, for instance, that Gulpilil should have been given a scriptwriting credit on *Walkabout* given the extent of his contributions to telling its story.

In some cases the filmmakers needed direct intervention to save them from themselves. During the pre-production of *The Last Wave*, Gulpilil and his Indigenous cast mates protested that the dialogue was inauthentic and, with the backing of the Aboriginal Cultural Foundation in Darwin, sat down with Weir and his co-writers to rework parts of the script to better reflect their culture. Again, no screenwriting credit was handed over. Syron explained that:

> As with everyone, I often gave contact names of my people throughout Australia and many times when I was asked to consult on scripts I made suggestions to overcome problems that I saw in terms of the writers' lack of knowledge on this Koorie.

THE RIGHT STUFF: DAVID GULPILIL AM

In some cases, he discovered that Indigenous contributors had their creative credits removed altogether at the last minute, scrubbing them from the record, and robbing them of potential future work. Syron noted too that when Jack Davis – the groundbreaking Noongar poet and playwright – was cast in the CBS-produced TV movie *The Blue Lightning* (1986), Davis was delivered a script in which his dialogue was invented gibberish. Davis was expected to adapt this scripted placeholder nonsense into his own language without any acknowledgement of his creative labour. Syron thought this was particularly noxious on this project, given Davis's recruitment confirmed to him that 'the presence of Aborigines is a big draw for American audiences'. Syron watched this happen first hand. His work on Bill Bennett's feature-length thriller *Backlash* (1986) was based on a treatment of just 27 pages long and without any written dialogue. The actors were asked to improvise the dialogue. So who was really writing the script?

Syron wrote *Kicking Down the Doors*, in part, to know the history behind him while forging ahead to make his debut film. *Jindalee Lady* (1992) is a romantic comedy about a First Nations fashion designer, her cheating white boyfriend, and the Black filmmaker attempting to win her over. He cast Kuku Yalanji woman Lydia Miller, who had been his cast mate in *Backlash*, in the lead role. The film was made under trying circumstances. Syron signed on to direct the film aware he was likely dying. Knowing this, he wanted to leave the finished film behind as part of his legacy. He explained: 'It's my bark painting'. In making a culturally significant work, he had to face opposition to the film and a lack of support from mainstream funders. Unable to secure support from the AFC and knowing that time was not on his side, Syron went ahead and directed the film anyway on a budget of just $30 000, shooting over 21 days and calling in various favours. Syron's real fight, however, would come in trying to secure funding for the post-production of the film, which would prove much more costly. Having a finished film – and one of such landmark significance – Syron thought the AFC would want to sign up to support it on its way to the big screen.

As part of the Hawke government, Paul Keating had opened the new Film Finance Corporation (FFC) in early 1989 as an alternative funding body to the AFC. Syron was suspicious that the FFC would not provide to First Nations filmmakers, given that the AFC hadn't funded a First Nations director to make a feature film in its 20 years of operating (the AFC would finally offer funding to Tracey Moffatt in 1991 to make her debut feature, *Bedevil*). A British bureaucrat import, Peter Sainsbury, would be appointed the general manager of the film development division. David Stratton reported that many referred to Sainsbury as 'the Mikhail Gorbachev of the Australian film industry', perhaps pointing to him being a unifier, but Sainsbury would soon become Syron's chief antagonist.[39] Sainsbury pointedly refused to support *Jindalee Lady*, and would often overstep his mark in commentary on the quality of the film, in meetings and behind closed doors:

> One is left simply embarrassed rather than inspired.
> The fact that some of the characters concerned are
> Aboriginals is, I think, tragic rather than laudable.

Syron had been extremely careful to consult with his community on the handling of subject matter in the film. He sent the script to ten organisations, including the Aboriginal Medical Service, legal and education services, and land councils. Syron changed details of the plot based on advice received, redrafting the script so that the male lead didn't drink. In subsequent meetings, Sainsbury would reportedly comment to Syron about the 'low artistic standard' of his film. Sainsbury was reported to have said that 'the AFC would be the laughing stock of the film industry if they supported *Jindalee Lady*'. Syron fought back.

The AFC knew they were in trouble with Syron and attempted to make amends by reviewing their position on the film, but in doing so only exposed their shortcomings. The actor Justine Saunders, a proud Woppaburra woman from the Kanomie clan of Keppel Island, had been engaged by the AFC to reassess the film on their behalf and told a journalist, 'They were afraid of the film. I believe the commission feared the film because it contained images of Aboriginal people which have never been seen before in films in this country'.[40]

Having been repeatedly rejected by Sainsbury and the AFC, Syron made a last-minute attempt to secure funding for post-production from the Aboriginal and Torres Strait Islander Commission (ATSIC), which had been established in 1990. ATSIC awarded Syron $30 000. He still thought it important that the AFC eventually come on board, even if only on symbolic grounds. In the meantime, Syron began to investigate the extraordinary step of having his case heard by the Human Rights and Equal Opportunities Commission of Australia. Aboriginal Legal Services agreed to take on his case, but much of the research needed in bringing forward a complaint would have to be done by Syron himself. The AFC eventually backed down, agreeing to fund the film for its post-production and committing to employ an Aboriginal consultant for future work.

While awaiting the final decision and, later, the transfer

CAST MATES

of funds, Syron still needed to get the film completed, and without support at home, he had to look towards America for much-needed assistance. He lamented that he didn't 'want to take this offshore because all of the work needed can be done by the local industry. The local industry can ill afford at this time to lose work when it is in such a depressed state. But I have no choice if Australia is not interested'.

An American film editor, having viewed some of the dailies, agreed to work on a cut of the picture, and 12 rolls of film were sent to Los Angeles, where Syron would travel to work as co-editor. The pair set to work in an editing suite of a studio on South Victory Boulevard in Glendale. Syron took the street name, 'South Victory', as something of a good omen, a portent of potential success. Chemical odours in the cutting room, however, were overpowering. Syron fell ill and had to absent himself from the studio, spending the rest of his time in LA recovering his health. America, however, while not attempting to kill him, continued to show more material support for the film than it was getting at home. When it came to finding stock footage of an aeroplane, Syron was turned down in Australia. Qantas rejected his application to use footage of one of their fleet. A corporate spokesperson issued a statement: 'The film is not the sort of image that Qantas wishes to be aligned with. There is nothing in it for Qantas and Qantas is very fussy about where it puts its image'. An American company, North West Airlines, stepped in instead, providing Syron with the imagery he needed to complete the film.

Jindalee Lady never received a wide release in Australia. The Sydney Film Festival invited Syron to show it on a television set. Five local distributors were invited to an investors' screening; none showed up. Syron reflected: 'This says so much about Australia.' There are, as a result, few contemporaneous reviews and the film itself remains difficult to find. In stark contrast to the Australian response, the film was embraced on the festival circuit in America, finding particular support in Hawai'i, where it played a film festival and was nominated for an award. It played in Canada too. A critic for a newspaper in Alberta wrote that:

> *Jindalee Lady* gives North American audiences a different, and often compelling, view of urban Australian Aboriginal life. It's a view, however, that Australians themselves may never get to see. For reasons that make little sense, this film ... was rejected by film distributors in that country. It is their loss.[41]

Loss is the right word. *Jindalee Lady* has not completely evaporated, as *Billy West* has. It exists, after all – it is out there to find if you make the effort, but few have. Watching it now, it is clear Syron had revisionism on his mind. His wasn't as explicit as Tracey Moffatt's deliberate reworking and partial rebuke of *Jedda* in her 1989 short film *Night Cries*, but *Jindalee Lady* was a chance for Syron to rewrite Charles Chauvel's famous film too: this was no doomed romance. The upbeat ending of *Jindalee Lady* left some people thinking they had watched a soapy melodrama, and, in the few critical notices, this was used against the film. Syron, however, never overhyped his finished product. If there are amateur elements to the production, how can this be a criticism of its makers when they were locked out of professional funding, and so the opportunity for professional development too, for decades? Ahead of his time, Syron reframed the project from the start, noting it as making a great pilot for a television show (decades later Ivan Sen's lyrical crime movie *Mystery Road* would continue as a popular ABC television series under the same name). It was also only a debut; if Syron had lived to film another work, or to continue to advocate for a viewership for his film, who is to say where he would have gone?

Some of the most arresting images in the film are ones that address this, documenting First Nations cultural activity in the early 1990s that would grow to have even greater influence as the years went by. For her fashion show, Lauren enlists a dance troupe to craft a narrative around her clothes. Syron himself hired the fledgling Bangarra Dance Theatre – to whose early artistic director, Stephen Page, Gulpilil had taught dance – for this scene, and *Jindalee Lady* contains some of the first footage of the historic company.

Syron died in 1993, at the age of 58. He didn't live to build on his work in *Jindalee Lady* or *Kicking Down the Doors*, nor see where his activism would eventually lead. He had sensed this would be the case for a long time. During his lifetime, Syron experienced more success in America than most non-Indigenous filmmakers and actors. At the same time, he could see that the way other Australians looked towards Hollywood was heavy with colonial reverb. He delivered a powerful blow in one of the many cutting lines in his written history: 'Non Indigenous Australians are always seeking foreign confirmation, maybe it's because they are still calling out for more reinforcements to shore up their position in Australia.'

UNTIL THE END OF THE WORLD (2002–2021)

After its unbecoming war with Syron in front of the Human Rights Commission, the AFC established an 'Indigenous

THE RIGHT STUFF: DAVID GULPILIL AM

Branch' in the year of his death. Three years later, it would present its first initiative to the public, releasing a collection of short films titled *From Sand to Celluloid* (1996). Two of the directors from this inaugural group – Dunghutti woman Darlene Johnson and Kaytetye man Warwick Thornton – would make short films starring Gulpilil during his remarkable career revival. Gulpilil would make a brief appearance in Thornton's art market satire *Mimi* (2002). He would also appear in the feature films of First Nations filmmakers, appearing in a small but significant role, in Ivan Sen's mournful crime film *Goldstone* (2015), a sequel to the earlier Blak-noir *Mystery Road* (2013). In *Satellite Boy* (2012), by Gunai/Kurnai woman Catriona McKenzie, Gulpilil features as a grandfather of the title character, living in a disused drive-in cinema, which is facing the threat of complete destruction by a mining company – a record of film infrastructure under threat. The lasting impact of Gulpilil's screen presence was on the mind of many filmmakers during this second act of his career.

Darlene Johnson, out of all his collaborators, seemed most invested in Gulpilil's legacy. Her 2002 documentary *Gulpilil: One Red Blood* – titled after a uniting catchcry of Gulpilil's – would begin a period of reflection on his career and place in history. Gulpilil approached Johnson with the idea for the documentary, having seen and been impressed by her earlier *Stolen Generations* (2001). It was a powerful pairing. Johnson provided audiences with an alternative to *Crocodile Dundee* when she worked with Gulpilil again, collaborating on a short fictional film called *Crocodile Dreaming* (2007). Johnson and Gulpilil developed the story, working carefully in consultation with the Yolŋu community. Gulpilil explained that '*Crocodile Dreaming* is my mother's dreaming ... It's not *Crocodile Dundee* ... It's my true story'.[42] The film united Gulpilil with Murrungun man Tom E Lewis – who had starred in *The Chant of Jimmie Blacksmith* (1978) – making the short something of a First Nations equivalent to Robert De Niro and Al Pacino playing against each other for the first time in Michael Mann's *Heat* (1995).

Johnson was clued into film history, parodying Gulpilil's Hollywood standing. He is introduced to the audience wearing a Rat Pack–style tuxedo, filming an advertisement directed by Johnson, making a Hitchcock-like cameo in her own film. *Crocodile Dreaming* had ambitions that were much larger than its relatively short runtime. Through working with Gulpilil and his family, Johnson had worked towards establishing proper cultural protocols, as well as developing non-Western ways of telling stories on film. Johnson would produce another documentary, *River of No Return* (2008), focusing on Gulpilil's niece Frances Djulibing, exploring Djulibing's love of Marilyn Monroe – the documentary was named after the 1954 Monroe-starring Western. Djulibing would wisely advocate with Gulpilil for a not-for-profit casting agency for Indigenous actors.[43] Johnson explained to a film academic:

> You can't be a dictator and a control freak. You can't want to do things this way or that because, well, you know, that's the Western model for making films – the idea that the director has got to be the leader and you're supposedly controlling everything on set; the idea that the film is about what you ultimately want.[44]

This sense of decolonising filmmaking as a practical effort would be important in the relationship between Gulpilil and his most enduring collaborator, the non-Indigenous, Netherlands-born, Adelaide-based filmmaker Rolf de Heer.

In making *One Red Blood*, Johnson was in part documenting Gulpilil's return to feature filmmaking for de Heer's *The Tracker* (2002). That film was the roundabout way the actor finally did get to make his own Western. Rolf de Heer took up the challenge of reintroducing Gulpilil to mainstream audiences in a work designed to rectify some of the past wrongs in the way he was presented on screen. Tellingly, it was Gulpilil's first lead role.

Rolf de Heer is an outlier of the Australian independent film industry, keeping Adelaide as his base. He had managed to bring Miles Davis to Australia to star in *Dingo* (1991), in his only acting role. Acknowledging Gulpilil's vast talents, de Heer crafted *The Tracker*, an Australian version of the revisionist Western, which had been popularised by Clint Eastwood's sparse and violent *Unforgiven* (1992). It was a simultaneously regenerative and self-critical genre piece. Gulpilil would reappear in a role as a tracker in the very same year, in Phillip Noyce's reckoning with the Stolen Generations, *Rabbit-Proof Fence* (2002), and was arguably typecast in the role by the time he rode into the Nick Cave–scripted *The Proposition* (2005). Regardless, the sustained work clearly meant as much to Gulpilil as it did to local audiences. When he won Best Actor at the Australian Film Institute Awards, he looked out at the audience and correctly declared: 'I deserve this'.

Rolf de Heer's films with Gulpilil both amused and bemused critics in the States, but they at least returned Gulpilil to the pages of their periodicals, if not to their shores. Writing in the *New Republic*, famed critic Stanley Kauffmann noted that: 'Film in Australia has not made an icon of the outback as thoroughly as we have done with the West, but Australian "Westerns" occur. An exceptional one is *The Tracker*, which has the shape of an offbeat American Western ... the feeling that this might have been Arizona, with a sheriff's posse guided by an Apache scout, does not last long'.[45]

Why did the Western – that most American of genres – mean so much to Gulpilil? It might have been a case of foundational 'first love', watching John Wayne in the first film he ever saw up on the big screen. There might have, however, been a deeper cultural connection to the genre. The hero in most classic Westerns exists in a frontier not yet settled by laws and exists on the land with a sense of freedom. In his classic essay, 'The Westerner', originally published in the *Partisan Review*, Robert Warshow asked why the Western had a particular hold over American audiences. His answer: 'it offers a serious orientation to the problem of violence such as can be found almost nowhere else in our culture'. The Western might be a space to directly confront colonial violence (although the American hero, almost exclusively non-Indigenous, is more often than not a perpetrator of such violence even if he resists the law of the land). Warshow's sharp description of the Western hero, however, could stand as one of Gulpilil on screen too: he 'fights not for advantage and not for the right, but to state what he is, and he must live in a world which permits that statement'.[46]

Gulpilil's fight in a world which wouldn't permit such statements would continue to be one of seeking due credit. Through the success of *The Tracker*, Gulpilil would receive writing credits on two documentaries about his life, both of which tell much larger stories than the fictional films he has starred in. The director credit, however, remained elusive. There is no doubt Gulpilil wanted to make his own films. Before working together on *The Tracker*, Gulpilil invited de Heer to Ramingining, a 14-hour drive from Darwin. Gulpilil wanted de Heer to make a film on his Country after *The*

Tracker. According to de Heer, 'David had ideas for a lot of films, and he wanted them all shot up there.'[47] He wanted to transform Ramingining into Arnhem Land's Hollywood and was harbouring an ambitious slate: a cowboy movie, a massacre film, and a story based on a cattle drive (Howard Hawks' *Red River* might have been circling in his mind). It was possible that among these was a hope to resurrect the long-dormant *Billy West*. Rolf de Heer thought about it, and finally decided that the only way to make a production shot on location in Ramingining would be to make Gulpilil co-director. Once more, however, this title would slip away from Gulpilil. Before shooting began on what was to become *Ten Canoes* (2006) – a film that included a great deal of Gulpilil's family lore and starred many of his kin – tensions arose between Gulpilil and his community, and he fled for Darwin. He would provide the narration for the film, but wasn't anywhere near as involved as originally planned.

Peter Djigirr, Gulpilil's younger brother and a widely respected Gurruwiling Ranger for the South East Arafura Catchment, would step in for his kin. Djigirr would return to produce and co-star with Gulpilil in the actor's final fictional collaboration with de Heer, *Charlie's Country* (2013), which was also shot largely in and around Ramingining. Widely regarded as a semi-autobiographical work, the actor, finally, had a co-writing credit on a feature project. The film came together after Gulpilil was released from a stint in prison and de Heer simply wanted to find a way to help his friend out. In de Heer's mind, getting back to work and making a film together was the best option. The confiscation of Charlie's spear by local police kicks off the plot of the film. When Gulpilil presented in court in 2006, on charges relating to carrying a machete, the magistrate joked, 'What happened to that film you were going to make about police in the Northern Territory?'

CAST MATES

If the magistrate was belittling Gulpilil's standing in Australia's movie culture, the actor would get one up on him: his performance in the film 'about police in the Northern Territory' won him the Best Actor award in the Un Certain Regard competition at Cannes in 2014.

Gulpilil's last film was the elegiac documentary, which rebuked the fact that a certain collaborator 'never, never mentions my name' with its declarative title *My Name Is Gulpilil* (2021). It would see him receive a producer credit too. Gulpilil had announced in 2019 that he had been diagnosed with lung cancer two years earlier. He outlived doctors' expectations, and co-existed with the disease until his death in 2021. On his passing, his image – in the form of scenes from his films – were projected onto the hard-tiled sails of the Sydney Opera House, sitting as it does on Bennelong Point, named after a famous First Nations figure Gulpilil had once signed on to play. He was layered into the cultural history of the city and his country. It shouldn't have taken a de Heer to get Gulpilil's career on track, nor to hand over storytelling autonomy, but these were the circumstances of Australian cinema in the second half of the 20th century that audiences will have to face as they look upon their history. Gulpilil broke so much ground on his own during his lifetime that you can only hope that the singular significance of that work will not be ignored or forgotten, but continuously, and purposefully, built upon.

At the end of *The Tracker* Gulpilil is given the literal last laugh – a dry, persistent chuckle his character sounds out in response to his surrounding circumstances and what he has survived through the film – and one can hear it still, reaching out from the memory of the movie, and echoing far into the deep time of cinema's long future.

PART 4
THE INTERPRETER:
NICOLE KIDMAN

The 1990s saw a boom in multi-screen suburban cinemas – in 1985 there were just 167 screens in Australia's suburbs; by 1995 there were 500 – and this was where my chronic movie-going was enabled. A Westfield shopping complex opened ten days shy of my tenth birthday, in nearby Tuggerah, and it changed the cultural landscape of the suburbs around my hometown. Housed within the complex was an eight-screen Greater Union multiplex. Movie attendance became a free babysitting opportunity while parents shopped. At the same time Australians were also the biggest owners, per capita, of videocassette recorders in the world – another free babysitting service. I would spend my weekends cycling down to Top Video in Budgewoi to return home with a plastic bag of seven weekly rentals, the plastic bag tied precariously to the handles, the block-like cassette covers often knocking against the frame.

There might have been another reason that Hollywood had lodged in my head as a kid. When I was growing up my hometown harboured a longstanding rumour that the Texas-born actor Matthew McConaughey had gone to my high school. The likelihood of this being true felt slim at best. Gorokan High School, after all, is settled in a low-socioeconomic lakeside suburb of the central coast, a one and a half-hour drive north of Sydney. It would have been an unlikely spot for an Australian celebrity to call their alma mater, let alone an America movie star of McConaughey's stature.

The story, as I had heard it, was that McConaughey had been on a Rotary student exchange program – Rotary being one of the world's largest community service organisations, having started in Chicago in 1905 – and was living with a host family out in the bush, and that he still sent letters and presents for birthdays to everyone in the family. There were, however, few ways to confirm all this detail back then. Even at the height of his mid-90s fame – when you could see his lithe, tanned face and slicked-back hair floating around video stores on VHS covers – it didn't seem to hold much weight. After McConaughey's fame took a dip when he failed to capitalise on the success of his breakout role in Joel Schumacher's adaptation of a John Grisham courtroom potboiler, *A Time to Kill* (1996), the chance to confirm the story seemed long gone.

Then came what *New Yorker* critic Rachel Syme handily summarised as the McConaissance – a career renaissance for the actor. The McConaissance arguably took hold in 2011 with another legal thriller – *The Lincoln Lawyer* – and reached its peak in 2014, when McConaughey came out with the buzzy HBO limited series *True Detective* and won his Best Actor Oscar for the faux-prestige of the *Dallas Buyers Club* (2013). Rachel Syme figured that the McConaissance had an

THE INTERPRETER: NICOLE KIDMAN

'unusually organic quality' to it, and perhaps that quality was what drove journalists to try and decode its origins.[1]

It certainly meant that there was enough intense and sustained interest for Australian journalists to go digging into his rumoured local connections and so there, at last, was that longed-for corroboration: McConaughey had indeed attended my shithole of a public high school (I use 'shithole' with the utmost affection – it's a shithole, but it's *my* shithole and it's a proudly public shithole too). McConaughey had attended Gorokan High for about five months in Australia's bicentennial year – 1988 – while living in glorious Warnervale (Warnies to the locals). I knew Warnies intimately, largely for its train station – it was my gateway to Sydney throughout young adulthood – and for the fact it was basically one large failed real estate tract. McConaughey looked the part, too, in photographic evidence of his stay uncovered by news sites. The proof shows an impossibly tanned McConaughey smiling into the camera, holding a can of Foster's (the famous Australian beer that no Australian drinks), while a friend clutching a can of Tooheys Draught grins fawningly at the future movie star in drunken stupor.

In 2020, McConaughey released his memoir *Greenlights*, which went into surprising detail about his time in Australia. (McConaughey visited the Gorokan school library – a place where I bunkered for many afternoons discovering the usual under-undergraduate Americana – to borrow a copy of the poems of Lord Byron, which he took home and masturbated to.) His stay in Warnervale reads like a high-school remake of *Wake in Fright*, with McConaughey relentlessly antagonised by his 'host father', to the point he put his fist through his bedroom door and retracted it 'bloody and pierced from shards of plywood'.[2] The most hyper-localised stretch of the book details the beginning of this fraught relationship, in which McConaughey describes the drive from Sydney airport, where the father of his host family progressively lied to him about where they were going. As the outskirts of the city faded behind them, he insisted that they lived in Sydney, then just outside of Sydney, then Gosford, then Toukley, before finally coming clean and admitting they lived in Warnervale as they turned up a dirt road and to their driveway.

As McConaughey was driven across the Harbour Bridge, one of the Sydney turn-offs he was forced to skip would have taken him to Longueville, the languid, leafy north shore Sydney harbourside suburb, only two suburbs back from Greenwich, where Peter Finch had spent his childhood. Longueville was a conservative stronghold and home to one of Australia's acting giants. The the young Kidman family felt like outsiders. Antony was active in supporting the Labor Party. Janelle was involved in the Women's Electoral Lobby and there was a political dynamic to dinner table conversation. Their daughter Nicole Kidman would be roped into handing out how-to-vote cards on polling day – a 'doomed duty' as the novelist Thomas Keneally put it in an early profile of the actor published by the *New York Times*. To avoid detection from her peers, Kidman would don a baseball cap, and pull it down to cover her face.[3]

Born in Hawai'i in 1967 – just two years older than McConaughey – Nicole Kidman naturally rewires the internal logic of a history of Australian actors, for the simple fact that she had shared American citizenship by birth. It was as if the movements of her future career, gliding back and forth between the two countries, were predestined. Her parents – Antony and Janelle – had been living in Honolulu, where Antony was a graduate student at the University of

Hawai'i at Mānoa. The young, mobile family were bound for Washington DC – for further study, and often found attending anti-war demonstrations – before returning home to settle in Sydney where they would raise their two children in upper-middle-class surrounds. They were an ambitious Sydney family. Kidman's father, like Peter Finch's, was an author with a scientific background – Antony was a psychologist and biochemist, and his books included the self-help titles *How to Change Your Life: Tactics for Moving from Thought to Action* and *Staying Sane in the Fast Lane: A Guide*. The Kidmans' first daughter was something of a child prodigy, keenly pursuing her unusual childhood hobby, acting. Her sense of separation from mainstream Australian activities was evident from the start of her life. Due to her fair skin, she wasn't allowed to sit on the beach during the midday sun, and was instead permitted to make a sandwich and retire to bed with a book of her choosing, a kind of Proust of the north shore.

Kidman credited her parents' personal library for her interest in acting. In that childhood home, Kidman would become the characters within the pages she read. She moved on to plays next, and inhabited every role in Chekhov. She took her private enthusiasms public when she was drawn to weekend study in the city, signing up to acting classes at the Phillip Street Theatre, and later moving across to the Australian Theatre for Young People (ATYP). In this version of Sydney, Peter Finch's aspirations for a children's theatre and an acting school had been realised. At ATYP Kidman performed in a revival of Frank Wedekind's *Spring Awakening* – a popular play for youth theatre groups given its ample cast of teenage characters to fill. Wedekind's erotically charged morality tale works as the Kidman urtext – stepping into Wedekind's world at 14 was a powerful premonition of her later transition to starring in two adaptations of works by Arthur Schnitzler, a close contemporary of Wedekind, 15 years later: *The Blue Room* on the stage and *Eyes Wide Shut* in cinemas. Kidman has long thrived on outré European sensibilities – working from under the Brechtian layers piled upon her by the likes of Lars von Trier and Yorgos Lanthimos – and queer American camp. She would play a crazed woman who would urinate on Zac Efron's character to take the bite out of a jellyfish sting for Lee Daniels' pulpy, homoerotic *The Paperboy* (2012) and she recalled working on the Wedekind play with Daniels for Andy Warhol's *Interview* magazine:

> ... in that, I had to ask the boy to beat me, in the amazing scene where she finds a switch and tells him to hit her with it. Because she is sort of confused as to why she was feeling pleasure. And at 14 to be dealing with that subject matter was really extraordinary for me.

Sitting in the theatre, watching the 14-year-old onstage, was the New Zealand–born director Jane Campion, who hoped to cast Kidman in her final student film – *A Girl's Own Story* – at the Australian Film Television School. It was not meant to be. There have been conflicting stories as to exactly why not – some suggest the headmistress at North Sydney High intervened, refusing to let Kidman take the time off to participate in case it distracted her from schoolwork. If the story is true, she needn't have been concerned about Kidman's schooling; she would drop out before her final year. Kidman herself later told the *Hollywood Reporter* that she was the one to pull out of Campion's project, not wanting to wear a 'shower cap on my hair and kiss a girl'. Upon learning of Kidman's refusal of the offer, Campion sat down and wrote to the young actor on the back of a postcard, kindly suggesting, 'I think you made the right decision and I hope one day we will work together. Be careful with what you do, because you have real potential.' Campion went a step further: 'Protect your talent.' It was a potent message to pass on to a 14-year-old.

Campion was not alone in wanting to give Kidman advice. It seemed many had invested concerns for her career direction. Another director warned her off attending the National Institute of Dramatic Art (NIDA). He told her: 'Don't go; they'll destroy you.'[4]

NIDA was established in 1958 as a theatre school, but the Australian New Wave soon fished some of its leading stars from the alumni pool, including Mel Gibson and Judy Davis. It must have been difficult for Kidman to resist signing up. One of the central keys to understanding Kidman is acknowledging her persistent enthusiasm for study. At the height of her early global stardom, she would be found in the Lake District taking a Wordsworth-inspired poetry course. Even when she had made it to America, with a decade's worth of film credits behind her in Australia, she was *still* signing up for acting classes. The fact that she fronted up to the Actors Studio in New York could be read as her attempt to legitimise – or, indeed, *Americanise* – her style, but it also serves to confirm her status as the forever student.

BOP GIRL (1983–1994)

It is easy to forget that Kidman was ever a child actor. Her height, there from the very start, could obscure such a memory. At just 13, she loomed at 175 cm tall. Revisiting her earliest films, you are quickly reminded of just how young she was. Films for children in Australia in the 1980s were not as forward-thinking as they might have been, often harking back to a bygone era. Indeed, Kidman was 'introduced' to Australian cinema audiences in the 1983 remake of the Rank Organisation's 1947 *Bush Christmas*, a toothless children-in-peril tale that had more in common with hoary British pantomimes than anything truly cinematic. The 1983 redo was directed by Henri Safran, who was trying to recapture some of the magic of his Gulpilil-starring film *Storm Boy*. He unquestionably failed: *Bush Christmas* was born anew, but was dead on arrival.

The urge to remake a so-called Australian classic was in keeping with the lack of original thought during the notorious 10BA era. In a desperate search for adaptable material, producers began to revive older properties at a remarkable clip, many made for television. There were, for instance, three new versions of former Peter Finch vehicles alone: *A Town Like Alice* (1981), *Robbery Under Arms* (1985) and *The Shiralee* (1987), were all reworked. It was a strange pursuit of nostalgia for a cinema that was never particularly beloved in the first place.

Which audiences were producers chasing with such efforts? They certainly weren't going after the youth market. The totemic early entry in Kidman's early Australian filmography, *BMX Bandits* (1983), however, at least tried to reach kids wheeling around in the suburbs. Its affable director Brian Trenchard-Smith was one of the chief drivers of Australia's B-movie engine room and had just dropped the cheap and nasty dystopian exploitation picture *Turkey Shoot* (1982) on unsuspecting audiences. Although its target audience was younger, *BMX Bandits* shared with *Turkey Shoot* a distinct lack of constraint – Kidman's frizzy hair, seemingly at the height of its powers, could barely be tamped down by the dome of her bright yellow bike helmet, and the plot of the film was similarly freewheeling, descending into a prolonged chase scene around the halfway mark that never breaks. Shot in Manly – a film made on Kidman's side of the Harbour Bridge – *BMX Bandits* focused on its three teen leads finding themselves in a tight love triangle, as together they try to hock some stolen police radios they have discovered in a bag submerged under water. The mercantile plotline serves to underscore that *BMX Bandits* was among the first onscreen appearances of Australia's Gen X. Bored, disaffected but with a secret entrepreneurial streak, they were ready to take control. Some of Kidman's own moxie was present in the movie. Indeed, Kidman had picked up the phone as a young teenager and cold-called an agent, June Cann, securing a place in Cann's busy books.

The Gen X march towards yuppiedom continued apace in the Boomtown-set *Windrider* (1986) – a rare Australian film produced in Western Australia – starring Kidman and her soon-to-be real-life boyfriend Tom Burlinson, a Canadian–Australian crooner who had broken out big in *The Man from Snowy River* (1983). Burlinson plays a windsurfer out to impress his businessman father and when the film's director signed on, it was decided that *Windrider* would be an opportunity to follow in the profitable footsteps of American 80s teen comedies echoing erotic dreams of self-realisation and emancipation from parental control. It was a boys' world, however, and Kidman was cast adrift, watching Burlinson make waves on the beach while she was stuck in the 'girlfriend' role. A more interesting film might have been constructed out of her fleeting subplot as the lead singer of a New Wave band. Kidman certainly had the CV to carry it.

In 1983, she appeared in Gillian Armstrong's music video to Pat Wilson's bouncy debut 'Bop Girl'. There, somewhere out in Sydney's eastern suburbs, Kidman was filmed floating in an above-ground pool, casually smoking a cigarette, furnished with a paperback titled *Virgin Kisses*. Armstrong was well versed in the aesthetics of early 1980s music, having directed the pop punk musical *Starstruck* (1982). Kidman was too: she had formed her own covers band, Divine Madness, which mostly traded in Blondie hits – 'Call Me' and 'Heart of Glass' – dreaming of Debbie Harry's peroxide glam.

Windrider and *BMX Bandits* with their active, sports focus – there were also Kidman films about running, horse racing and mixed martial arts – did well as exports, all regularly run on American cable television throughout the 1980s. They were part of a rolling supply of excess filler. The quality issue in Australian film during the 10BA era wasn't just the rampantly quick production turnaround – the exhausting edict was for films to be produced within a single financial year – it was also that many of the best directors who had built their careers on the back of the assertive reforms in the 1970s had already made for the exits and were working in Hollywood. Bruce Beresford would guide Robert Duvall towards securing his Best Actor Oscar in *Tender Mercies* (1983). Fred Schepisi made a handful of journeyman efforts. Gillian Armstrong would return to the classicism of her debut *My Brilliant Career* in America with the Pittsburgh-set *Mrs Soffel* (1984), a quietly deranged prison romance, hidden away within the respectability of its period piece outfitting, featuring Diane Keaton and Mel Gibson as a pair of doomed lovers on the run. Peter Weir fled to work with Harrison Ford on a back-to-back pair of eccentric, effective dramas – *Witness* (1985) and *The Mosquito Coast* (1986).

THE INTERPRETER: NICOLE KIDMAN

The mass exodus must have had a disorienting effect on the industry, leaving it feeling directionless – or, at least, director-less – for a time. Acting newcomers in the 1980s, in particular, must have felt the sting of not being able to work with the best filmmakers of the 1970s, watching that opportunity go to young Americans. Kidman, however, would be one of the lucky few to benefit from working directly with two major New Wave directors who remained in Australia – George Miller and Phillip Noyce – both knowing the independence working at home granted them.

They stayed behind, in part, to work towards a new Australian studio model, taking the profits of the 1970s and investing them in the 1980s. Kennedy Miller was the production company forged by George Miller and his producing partner Byron Kennedy in 1978 ahead of their first film together, *Mad Max*. Funded and propelled by that film's unexpected success, the pair moved to Sydney from their Melbourne base in the early 1980s and began expanding the scope and ambition of their projects. That included travelling to Los Angeles to try to figure out just what kind of cinema studio Australia could sustain. The pair spent time on the ground essentially conducting research, in what amounted to a reconnaissance mission. Splitting the workload, Kennedy looked into distribution practices, while Miller enrolled in acting classes. Hollywood, chasing *Mad Max* money, offered Miller directing work, which he turned down, including refusing the debut of the tortured tale of Vietnam vet Rambo in *First Blood* (1982). Ted Kotcheff, director of *Wake in Fright*, took up the challenge instead.

After these mild flirtations with Hollywood, Kennedy and Miller ultimately decided to return to Australia to invest in *Mad Max 2* (aka *The Road Warrior*) with its promises of a

CAST MATES

new boost in capital. Hollywood wouldn't hold all the answers. In fact, they might have been looking towards higher climes in the state of California for inspiration, to San Francisco where key New Hollywood talent had attempted to work out of the typical zoning for American movie production after the fall of the old studios. Indeed, Phillip Noyce suggested they were attempting to establish a directors' collective based on Zoetrope Studios – later American Zoetrope – the independent production company founded by the directors Francis Ford Coppola and George Lucas in 1969.[5] Zoetrope first moved into a warehouse – replete with a lobby fitted out with pool table and espresso machine – but soon took hold of the Sentinel Building, a copper green–tinged flatiron-style building in San Francisco's North Beach district, which had housed a theatre used by stand-up comics in the 1950s. Kennedy and Miller would similarly move into the art deco Metro Theatre in Kings Cross in Sydney, also projecting their ambitions partly through design architecture to evoke past tenants. (They might not have had a pool table or coffee machine, but Noyce was known to play video games in the Kennedy Miller offices.)

It wasn't a complete rejection of Old Hollywood ways. Noyce explained that Kennedy Miller dreamed that a 'number of directors would be on permanent payroll' in the style of the old studio systems, where 'directors received their next assignment with the Sunday *Los Angeles Times*'. They would pick and choose from both Old Hollywood and New. Indeed, what was once a deficit in Australia – the lack of cultural infrastructure for film – was now seen as an enviable opportunity to start again and do things right. Miller wasn't afraid to rub this fact in Hollywood's face, telling a *Los Angeles Times* reporter, 'We're in a situation in Australia where we can do films without a lot of the impediments that come with the job here. The machine here is so big that there's a real inefficiency. So many things get in the way of making a film – the deal, the package, the career – that it's a wonder fine films are made at all'.[6]

Kidman came into contact with this new system following grave tragedy. Byron Kennedy died at just 33 in a helicopter crash in 1983. Miller marched on, regularly attempting to honour his former partner, launching in the same year the first of a series of ambitious six-hour miniseries. The television networks had been chasing prime-time dramas that could pull in big audiences. Kennedy Miller signed with Channel 10, then in Rupert Murdoch's possession, to produce one-off series with production values closer to those of films. The deal between Miller and Murdoch was closed via a simple handshake and an edict to make 'bold television'.[7] Kidman would benefit from that declaration, breaking out in *Vietnam* (1987) – an ambitious docudrama designed to reckon with Australia's support of the American war in Vietnam and the lasting effects of a grim, lottery-like conscription policy at home – which would be followed, in Old Hollywood studio player style, with a work written specifically for her (*Bangkok Hilton*, made in 1989, would air in America on TBS, the pay television network owned by media giant Ted Turner). Kidman was incredibly across the film historical approach Kennedy Miller was attempting: 'If it had been the 1930s I would have signed to them'.[8]

While they were dancing around American ways of working, the directors at Kennedy Miller were thinking about Australian identity. Tall, droll Phillip Noyce seemed particularly preoccupied with such thoughts. His historical drama *Newsfront* (1978) had eulogised Ken G Hall's era of newsreels, showing deference to the history of Cinesound. As if reanimating the credo of Charles Chauvel, Noyce was not shy in voicing his patriotic belief that the boom in filmmaking in Australia was down to a 'new nationalism'. Unlike Chauvel, however, this nationalism longed to divorce itself from the Commonwealth, emerging in the late 1960s and 1970s, peaking with the election of Gough Whitlam's social democratic government at the end of 1972. For Noyce 'making and screening Australian film was a declaration of our cultural independence from the US and the UK', the country's 'old cultural, economic and political masters'.[9]

The Australian filmmaker could not be wholly isolationist. Kidman's cut-through feature film – with Noyce as director and Miller as producer – *Dead Calm* (1989) was an Australian adaptation of an American novel of the same name by Charles Williams. Orson Welles had attempted to shoot the thriller in the late 1960s as *The Deep*. Welles saw the story's commercial prospect, but struggled, as ever, to work to a typical shooting schedule. He began shooting in 1966 and worked through until 1969. The film was never completed, and a final nail was hammered in its water-logged coffin when its star Laurence Harvey died. There was no way to salvage what remained. Welles' loss, however, was Phillip Noyce's gain. The novel had been sitting on a shelf without an adaptation.

The rights for the material had been hotly contested in Hollywood ever since, but they had landed in the hands of the Croatian actress Oja Kodar, Welles' long-term de facto partner, who had played the lead role of Rae Ingram (the part Kidman would eventually inherit). Kodar didn't want anyone in Hollywood to have the rights to make the movie, because she begrudged how poorly many in the industry had treated Welles throughout his career. One streetwise actor-turned-producer, who had long hoped to adapt the novel himself, knew of Kodar's strict edict and knew that it ruled him out, but he also thought Phillip Noyce might have a better shot. He handed a photocopy of Williams' novel over to Noyce and told him, 'You've got water in Australia – see if you could make this down there'.[10]

Enter the special envoy. George Miller was sent to America to plead a case to Kodar. Noyce knew that Miller's professional background as a doctor meant he had a 'great bedside manner'. Whatever diplomatic magic he cast, it worked: a ragtag Australian team took hold of a prized American novel. With rights secured, the story was Noyce's to tell. It wasn't all smooth sailing. Kodar briefly changed her mind, but Miller and company threatened to sue, and she backed down. Kennedy Miller forged ahead with casting. Noyce considered a number of American actresses for the part, but after he watched *Vietnam*, he wanted Kidman for the role. However, her youth, and how it would change the role, was unavoidable. Noyce developed a five-month training program for Kidman, intending, in part, to make her seem much older than she was. She worked with a vocal coach trying to deepen the sound of her voice and was paired with a movement coach to mature her body language and posture. The intention was to age her up from 19 almost ten years to a semi-convincing 28 years old. She was playing against Sam Neill, the notable New Zealand expat, who was freshly 40. Not only this, she was also expected to play a grieving mother, as Noyce and company had added a prologue to the film showing that the protagonists had lost their young child in a car accident.

Kidman's and Noyce's careful work showed dividends. Warner Bros had bought international rights and were so confident in the film that they released it in American cinemas before it had been tested in the Australian market (a reversal of Paramount Pictures' approach with *Crocodile Dundee*). Kennedy Miller, in turn, sent Kidman to Los Angeles. She met with agents and producers trying to find an American debut and eventually signed with Sam Cohn, the 'first superagent of the modern age', with clients including actors in the ranks of Meryl Streep and Sigourney Weaver, and directors including Robert Altman, Bob Fosse and Sidney Lumet.[11]

Despite the powerful representation behind her, she missed out on roles in *The Silence of the Lambs, Sleepless in Seattle* and *Ghost*.* The eventual cataclysmic shift in her career was initially downplayed in a brief notice in the *Sydney Morning Herald*, informing readers that Kidman was on her way 'to Hollywood for possible chats about a possible movie with none other than teenie heart-throb Tom Cruise'.[12] It was the first mention of the pair together in print, the first rolling snowball in what would become an avalanche of press for the next decade. Kidman flew into Los Angeles – with a head cold – from Japan where she had been promoting *Dead Calm*. Eventually, she signed on for the rumoured movie, then going under the working title *Daytona*, pulling out of a production at the Sydney Theatre Company to clear her schedule. *Daytona's* young producer and star, Cruise, had been shown a print of *Dead Calm* at a private screening, and had been enraptured by it, asking to meet with Kidman. According to Phillip Noyce,

---

* Given she unsuccessfully auditioned for it, and he claims to have turned it down, there is, in a parallel universe, an alternative reality out there where Nicole Kidman and Paul Hogan co-starred in *Ghost* together and that is a reality that must be stopped at all costs, lest the vision of them at the pottery wheel together enters our world.

the young actor had already fallen in love with her, just through seeing her on screen.

Unimpeachable as a screen presence, Cruise had spent the first half of the 80s starring in synthetic, stylised sex drama-comedies – the Reaganite *Risky Business* (1983), exploding teenage fantasies of adult independence on screens across the world – before pivoting to prestige roles that cast him as the fiery upstart against older stars – critically *The Color of Money* (1986) with Paul Newman – who lent him credibility as a serious actor. The brothers Ridley and Tony Scott provided consecutive mid-decade turning points – casting him in the overblown fantasy *Legend* (1985), which flopped at the box office, and the militaristic peacetime propaganda of *Top Gun* (1986), which did anything but. To follow up that sky-high hit, Cruise, inspired by Newman's love for the racetrack, faintly sketched the story for a film about a NASCAR driver. He would enlist the legendary screenwriter Robert Towne (*Chinatown*, 1974) to help him flesh out the screenplay, and reteam with Tony Scott and the producing partners Jerry Bruckheimer and Don Simpson. Kidman would audition in front of all five, plus a studio executive from Paramount. She was surprised to find that she was the only actress present, expecting a line out the door. The next morning, she was offered the part and the blockbuster team invited her to step into the dual American arenas of NASCAR driving and Hollywood excess. It was a coke-ravaged Simpson, in particular, who was responsible for blowing out a $40 million budget – already double what *Top Gun* was made with – to $70 million.[13] In the process, the literalist title *Daytona* became the metaphoric mess *Days of Thunder* (1990). Which days were thunderous, exactly?

Exactly to the letter, Kidman followed Peter Finch in making her Hollywood debut by signing on for what was earmarked as Paramount Picture's most expensive film of the year. There were similar scenes of chaos. The film was being rewritten throughout the shoot (to the point Towne was reading dialogue into Cruise's ear via radio headset as he raced around the track). Kidman's threadbare character, Dr Claire Lewicki, was reworked when she came on board, partly to pad out the romantic elements. Kidman was allowed to keep her accent in place (likely there was little time for effective vocal coaching) and her character's Australian-ness was hinted at when Cruise's character sends her a large novelty stuffed kangaroo, carefully placed in the middle of her apartment.

Watching it today, *Days of Thunder* retains some of its thrills and the romance between Kidman and Cruise leaves a camp residue. Scott's bombastic, overblown 80s aesthetics carry over to the early 90s – Tony Scott can't help being Tony Scott – and there is enjoyment to be found in its many indulgences. Audiences at the time agreed. *Days of Thunder* would earn back its bloated budget, and then some, but it carried an air of failure for not living up to its *Top Gun 2* tag. Real-life events had outrun it in the dramatic stakes too. Cruise had divorced his first wife of over two years during filming, and rumours began to spill that Cruise and Kidman were frequently found visiting one another on set. These were all but confirmed when Cruise took Kidman, alongside his mother, as his date to the 1990 Oscars Ceremony, where he was nominated for his performance in *Born on the Fourth of July* (1989). The makers of *Days of Thunder* capitalised on the relationship. To pump up the promotion of his product, producer Don Simpson grossly proffered: 'You'll see Tom and Nicole in all their hormonal glory'. An Australian journalist seemed to agree, reporting that the film was 'Less a movie than a 90-minute first date for Tom Cruise and Nicole Kidman.[14]

Days of Thunder continued the casting of Kidman in films centred on niche sports – windsurfing, bike riding, long distance running – but as she made her Hollywood debut, it looked as though the Americans might strip Kidman of her agency and order her to stand on the sidelines instead. It was a return to the backwardness of *Windrider*. 'I was cast back as the girlfriend', Kidman said, 'which I'd done when I was 16 in Australia.'[15] In the racing scenes of *Days of Thunder*, she is given a few cutaways to cheer on Cruise and little more. The conventional narrative then became that Kidman was the shipped-in novice to Cruise's wizened industry veteran. It was a wrongheaded interpretation; while Cruise is five years her senior, as the film historian David Thomson noted, by the time they met, Kidman had already featured in 18 movies or television miniseries and Cruise just 12.[16]

KIDMAN'S PROLIFIC OUTPUT IN HER TEENAGE YEARS before moving to Hollywood had certainly been enabled by the lawlessness of the 10BA era. Indeed, by the end of the 1980s, the Australian film industry was so overblown with its own excesses that it somewhat naturally began to parody itself, and Kidman co-starred in not one, but two films which took an inward aim. In *The Bit Part* (1987), featuring a hapless Chris Haywood as a late-in-life aspiring actor, an agent lets off a tirade about the state of the Australian film industry and that 'without all those juicy tax concessions, everybody is rushing off to sign up deals in the States'. Kidman played Haywood's tempting scene partner, a pairing which would be repeated in *Emerald City* (1988), a more extensive attack on the Australian film industry produced by those in the know, skewering the clash between art and commerce. The film focuses on a well-meaning but ultimately vain writer who is introduced to a social climber (Haywood), who come together to collaborate on a Kennedy Miller–like miniseries, which bombs in its prime-time slot. The hack sells out to the Americans and becomes a huge success, leaving behind the bitter literato, who turned down the overseas offers in order to keep his integrity intact. Some of the '10BA cowboys' who saw the film were affronted by their crass representation on screen.

One of *Emerald City*'s few fans was John Howard, leader of the Liberal Party, then sitting in opposition, who had been the federal treasurer when 10BA was introduced. Howard got great glee from watching the grilling of his own tax policy and excitedly attending the film's premiere at the State Theatre. He was so enthusiastic in his praise that a quote gleaned from him was included on a later movie poster ('"Great, very entertaining ... I laughed a lot" – John Howard, Leader of the Opposition'). Kidman didn't return the favour of an endorsement. In 1996, she dropped in an interview with the journalist Ray Martin that she was a Paul Keating supporter and that she still participated in Australian elections via postal voting, explaining, 'If I didn't my dad would kill me'.[17] Once Howard had come to power – defeating Keating and going on to become the second longest serving prime minister in the country's history – Kidman would co-sign an open letter opposing rumoured cuts to the arts expected within the new conservative government's first budget in 1997. The letter echoed the worries that had persisted in the Australian film industry across the decades:

> Inevitably, the cuts will lead to a rapid downturn in production and consequent unemployment, shake

investor confidence in Australia's audiovisual industries and lead to a brain drain of talent to Hollywood.[18]

There was concern among Australia's acting elite that Howard would put an end to the 10BA tax concessions, but in truth the winding back of that policy had started much earlier than his ascension. Bob Hawke, and his treasurer Keating, had been the ones to quietly defang the incentive – dropping the available deduction to 100 per cent in the 1988 budget – and Keating's establishment of the Film Finance Corporation was an attempt to make the industry move towards self-reliance (intending it to work as a 'bank-style portfolio management of Australia's screen industry', over its 20-year lifespan it invested over $1 billion, making just short of $275 million back).[19] Despite the financial challenges this walk-back presented, it was hard to argue against the fact that it gave the Australian film industry some breathing room and time to reflect on a decade's worth of glut. While such pruning might have had overall positive effects for aesthetic output, it put heavy constraints on an already precarious workforce. In 1991, Actors' Equity reported that 90 per cent of its membership were unemployed at any given time, up from 75 per cent in the 10BA era.[20] Film productions were effectively halved and the kind of miniseries that had launched Kidman's career were under threat on the commercial stations, looking for cost-cutting measures. There were notable gendered disparities: in the year of *Muriel's Wedding* (1994), out of the 32 films released, only five had female protagonists.

Kidman escaped such conditions, and while it was clear from a career perspective that Kidman was right not to stay in Australia, her work in America in those early years didn't exactly prove the point. Ensconced in Hollywood, Kidman cycled through a round of mostly forgotten films, including a literary adaption of the EL Doctorow novel *Billy Bathgate* (1991), a nasty erotic thriller named *Malice* (1993) and an unpalatable cancer weepie, *My Life* (1993). She reunited with Cruise on screen for *Far and Away* (1992), a lean boxing movie lost within the pomp of an Irish immigrant epic. The fact that she had reteamed with Cruise so soon after *Days of Thunder* did little to suppress misogynistic sentiment that she would never amount to anything more than 'Mrs Cruise'. Kidman did her best to cut off the blood to such a narrative: she set ground rules that she would not do side-by-side press with Cruise for the film, but it wouldn't kill the critical notices that she was being wasted in passive girlfriend roles.

DESTROYER (1995–1999)

Then almost a decade and a half into her acting career came the change she had been hoping for. In the middle of the 1990s, Kidman collaborated with two openly gay filmmakers – Gus Van Sant and Joel Schumacher, both graduates of east coast design schools – who not only saw her potential for playing electrified camp, and black comedy, but capitalised on her then, at least on screen, largely untapped capacity for conjuring up Old Hollywood. In doing so, Kidman became fuel for the twin engines of 90s cinema: the franchise blockbuster and the indie darling. So during the peak of the American movie season – summer – in flew *Batman Forever* (1995). The third film in the popular comic book adaptation series had served as a soft reworking of the superhero subject after Tim Burton steered the original films into bleak territory, which had pushed creative boundaries but mostly frightened off families. Joel Schumacher – a former production and costume designer – was perfectly fitted to retouch the series in a more pop palette. Kidman was one of his keys to this, playing Dr Chase Meridian. Potentially more secondary than her female predecessors – she was coming after Michelle Pfeiffer's unkillable Catwoman – she was at least more direct in expressing her desires for Batman as a curious sexual object, projecting the audience fantasies of the aberrant rubber-suited figure on to the big screen through flirtatious dialogue and fluttering eyelids.

Reviews compared Kidman's look in the film to that of yesteryear's Veronica Lake, making particular note of their shared get-up coming across as vampy (appropriate for a bat-themed film). Schumacher told multiple interviewers that this was his world, and in his world 'psychiatrists look like Nicole' (that is, also like Veronica Lake).[21] What was old was new again: *Batman Forever* would become the highest grossing film of 1995. Veronica Lake was not the only Old Hollywood talent Kidman resembled. Even without hair straightened and artificially blonded (via dye or wig), Kidman possessed more than a resemblance to the Swedish-born American singer and actor Ann-Margret.

Kidman's other film of 1995 called on the absolute chaos Ann-Margret wrought on screen as a teenage runaway turned hostage-taker in *Kitten With a Whip* (1964). Gus Van Sant's *To Die For* was a marriage between New Hollywood and what had come next, namely an ambitious Gen X. Adapted for the screen by the comedian Buck Henry, who had scripted *The Graduate* (1967) and *What's Up, Doc?* (1972), and who shared an agent with Van Sant, Meg Ryan had originally been courted for the title role, intending to play on her 'girl next door' goodness, but she turned it down. Kidman, on the other hand, wasn't going to let the role slip by her. She got Van Sant's home phone number and called him to lobby for the role.

Coveting a role such as Suzanne Stone was to get halfway to playing her convincingly, so Van Sant decided not to see anyone else. Kidman knew exactly what she could do with the scheming Suzanne Stone, who aspires to become that most revered form of the 1990s American: the daytime television personality. In Suzanne's case, the most direct route to her dream role is to first become a newsreader, via a stint as a weather person at the rickety local television station. There were clearly shared DNA strands between Suzanne Stone and Peter Finch's doomed Howard Beale. Her path to viral fame was more deliberate and plotting than Beale's spontaneous combustion on air – Beale had no idea the astronomical ratings his ranting and ravings would bring, but Stone had an inkling of the rewards her open season derangement would bring her.

To Die For and *Network* could be viewed as twin video tutorials on 'How to become an American'. Kidman's American accent, which could occasionally falter in other character work, is set in Stone. Like Finch studying the tapes of newsreaders to settle on the right voice, Kidman locked herself in a motel room in Santa Barbara, watching American television, for three days straight. Stone's newscaster smile came to her from watching Miss US pageants. Critics were clued in to her method. In a leery profile for *Esquire* written at the turn of the millennium, the magazine journalist Tom Junod hit on this aspect of Kidman's performance, noting that she: 'transformed herself not just into an American but into America itself: America as pure psychopathology, as an incarnation of pure wanting, infinitely corrupting and infinitely corruptible'.[22]

Many of the contemporaneous reviews for *To Die For* were written as if Kidman was being discovered for the first time. Queer subtext abounded. *LA Weekly* called it her 'coming-out party as a comedian'.[23] Australians, however, seemed comparatively conservative in their response. The *Sydney Morning Herald* reported a discrepancy in the local and international tag lines for *To Die For* running on the movie's posters and trailer. In Australia, the film was promoted with the anodyne line, 'She was prepared to go all the way ... for what she wanted'. In other markets, however, the film was promoted with: 'She knew what it took to get to the top ... a lot of heart and a little head'.

Suzanne Stone was a televisual product of her time. *To Die For* was released in cinemas the year before Rupert Murdoch, working alongside former Nixon media advisor Roger Ailes, launched the Fox News Channel. If Stone had survived the events of *To Die For* – spared from her icy demise – she may well have found a sympathetic home at the ultra-conservative broadcaster. Indeed, Stone might have gone on to become someone like Gretchen Carlson, the former *Fox & Friends* co-host, who blew the lid on sexual harassment at Fox News, and who Kidman would end up playing in the fictionalised exposé *Bombshell* (2019). In that film, echoing *To Die For*'s tagline, Carlson informs her lawyers that Ailes liked to joke, 'To get ahead, you gotta give a little head'.

KIDMAN'S MEGA-AGENT SAM COHN WAS OFTEN NOTED for his public derision of Los Angeles. *TIME* magazine had it down that he 'slags Hollywood at every opportunity' and the *New Yorker* dryly reported that 'Cohn does not think Los Angeles is a fun place'.[24] Kidman herself might have caught

Cohn's distaste for the City of Angels, as she never seemed to possess any particular attachment to Hollywood as a location. She once deadpanned to a reporter, 'If I had to live in Los Angeles for six months at a stretch it would drive me crazy.'[25] A month for meetings was all she said she needed. There was an aspiration instead that, with Cruise, she would be able to deliver a new model of the truly global film star, dividing each year between Sydney and New York, raising her children in her home country to give them a sense of Australian identity. Australians were entranced by the idea and by regular visits from Kidman and Cruise. A visit in 1990 was seen as an opportunity to 'meet the parents', but it might as well have been billed as a chance to 'meet the country'. Australians were ready to welcome Cruise into the family fold. A 1993 interview with a prime-time tabloid journalist was given the subtitle 'Australia's Favourite Son-in-Law'.

Sydney reported on where the couple would eat, drink, exercise and – the most Sydney activity of all – attend real estate inspections. There were almost as many reports for events they didn't attend as those they did, the status-obsessed city wishing to know what they snubbed. Had the couple found themselves in a trap of their own design? Paparazzi, after all, is partly an invention of film itself. The term was drawn from the name of a character – the seemingly omnipresent photographer named Paparazzo – in Fellini's *La Dolce Vita* (1960). With the increase of interest in what the paparazzi were selling, there seemed to be a concurrent growing indifference to the films themselves, as the celebrities they produced became the preferred form of entertainment. Within the tracking and tracing of Kidman and Cruise's Sydney movements, there would be little reporting, for instance, of creative meetings. There was, however, one notice

THE INTERPRETER: NICOLE KIDMAN

of a lunch between Kidman and the director Jane Campion at the popular Bayswater Brasserie, a Sydney 'social scene' restaurant.

In the years after she had seen a teenaged Kidman perform in *Spring Awakening*, Campion had graduated from the Australian Film Television School, made a number of striking feature films – including her full-throated song of suburban eccentricities *Sweetie* (1989) – and experienced immense international success with *The Piano* (1993), winning the Academy Award for Best Screenplay and becoming only the second woman to be nominated for Best Director. Kidman and Campion circling back to each other felt like a natural conclusion. It was announced that the director had decided to adapt a book that both women had adored since their youth, Henry James's austere *The Portrait of a Lady*. Kidman had read the novel at just 14. Campion, however, unable to see how to adapt the novel for a film, had originally intended the adaptation as a stage play in Sydney, returning Kidman to the theatre of her home city. Never one to hold back an opinion, Campion had been forthright in telling the *Sydney Morning Herald* that Kidman was 'looking for something with a lot more depth than what she's found so far in Hollywood.'[26]

Campion eventually came around to the idea that the material would work for a film – despite word that Merchant Ivory, those lofty executors of literary taste on film, were planning their own production – but Campion suffered a personal loss when her newborn son died just 12 days old, stalling the project indefinitely. When she finally did return, somewhere along the line, however, the director had watched Kidman's early American filmography and was spooked by what she saw. Her opinion of the actor, and her capabilities, soured. Campion called it a 'crisis of confidence', later frankly admitting: 'In the time that Nicole was in Hollywood, she made quite a few films I didn't think suited her and I don't think she felt suited her either. I started to feel unconfident about it.'

The role was no longer automatically Kidman's – if at all. Campion called Kidman to let her down gently. Kidman was distressed. Tom Cruise was reportedly furious with Campion – calling the decision 'upsetting' and 'very unpleasant' – and saying that 'Jane was wrong about it'.[27] Campion sent the message that she now wanted Kidman to audition for the part afresh and Cruise told Kidman to persist. There would be two days' worth of workshops – readings and improvisations – in Los Angeles. Campion and Kidman would also go out clubbing one night to see if they could simply get along given how closely they would be working together. Kidman met Campion's standards and their professional relationship was reaffirmed. The film went ahead with its original design in place.

The Portrait of a Lady (1996) was not, however, met with the same rapturous embrace that *The Piano* had received. A common complaint was that the film was 'cold' and critics were split when it came to Kidman's interpretation of the main character. Barbara Hershey playing the scheming Madame Serena Merle pulled the attention away from both Kidman and Campion with a sharp, showy performance, locking in the film's only other Academy Award nomination outside of the expected recognition for the corset-heavy costumes.

The 'cold' criticism of *The Portrait of a Lady* was a harbinger of the public view of Kidman to come. Kidman's personal likeability more than her acting talents, and more than most movie stars, seemed to be under scrutiny. This debate was tied to a particular pejorative phrase which has stuck to

THE INTERPRETER: NICOLE KIDMAN

her for decades. Kidman has long been called some variation of 'The Ice Queen' or 'The Ice Princess'. In researching, I found that 'The Ice Princess' tag was first used for Kidman's appearance as the high school bully in *Flirting* (1991), and she graduated to 'The Ice Queen' in descriptions of Suzanne Stone in *To Die For* (the fact that Stone is buried under a layer of ice at the end of the film surely put the term at the front of critics' minds). Isabel Archer is again referred to as an Ice Queen with complaints that the film was 'too cold'.[28] In the years since, the epithet seemed to stick to the character's real-life creator. When gothic horror *The Others* (2001) launched in cinemas, one critic wrote, 'If Hitchcock were alive today, Kidman would be his new ice queen'.[29] A *Miami Herald* reporter got particularly stuck on the terminology, writing of a screening at the Miami Film Festival that the film had failed due to the 'overhyped Ice Queen Nicole Kidman', while complaining that Kidman's 'consummate, onscreen iciness didn't help cool the 5000-plus crowd'[30] forcing them to go searching for drinks instead.*

---

* The countering of this for Kidman came in the fact that over the years she has, indisputably, become a queer icon. The internet has helped this along – a set of photographs allegedly of her taken on the afternoon of her divorce with Cruise, where she outstretches her arms, embracing her own freedom, are regularly shared on the internet. As is a cinema advertisement from 2021, promoting the AMC cinema chains in the US, in which Kidman rhapsodically speaks of her love of watching a movie in a theatre (lovingly lampooned by drag queens). Memes of Kidman at the Oscars are routinely shared with great affection. I bought a Kidman t-shirt that I have regularly worn to queer party nights as a signifier. For a friend who attended a house party in Sydney called 1001 Nights of Nicole – where attendees dressed as different characters from her long career – 'her earnest devotion to the craft means that people do struggle to engage with her' but 'for the queers, this earnestness is high camp'.

CAST MATES

KIDMAN BRIEFLY RETURNED TO THE MORE ANONYMOUS practices of studio filmmaking. The one interesting note was the gender switch of directors working outside of their typically designated genres; she collaborated with Mimi Leder on the George Clooney–starring nuclear holocaust thriller *The Peacemaker* (1997), a rare 90s action film led by a woman, and Griffin Dunne on *Practical Magic* (1998), as an unlikely choice to head the sisterly coven comedy. During this time Kidman's agency had been receiving requests for videotapes of her work from a director with an immeasurable mystique surrounding him. The sense of mystery was only compounded when Kidman received instructions to stay at home at a certain time to be present to receive a personalised letter and a screenplay. The sender was Stanley Kubrick, the New York–born director, who had an unparalleled standing in the film world, but was seen by many to be a reclusive figure – aloof and out-of-reach. Partly, this was geographical. Kubrick had moved to England in the mid-1960s and stayed there throughout the rest of his life. Based on most first-hand accounts, however, he was a deeply social creature. George Miller had struck up a relationship with Kubrick conducted exclusively on the telephone – sometimes talking for hours at night. The journalist Michael Herr – who co-wrote *Full Metal Jacket* (1987) – explained that Kubrick 'viewed the telephone the way Mao viewed warfare, as the instrument of a protracted offensive where control of the ground was critical and timing crucial.'[31] These conversations are lost to time (to the best of our knowledge there were no Nixonian tapes whirring away in a nearby desk). Miller was on the blower because he was deep in the process of trying to figure out how to make the movie *Babe* viable – it wouldn't work if they couldn't get the animals to talk realistically. Kubrick had been facing similar questions when it came to bringing a robotic boy to life for his much-cherished *AI* project. The two met in the middle with these technological problems in mind.

Outside of the telephone, Kubrick was a great fan of the fax machine. He had been sending faxes to Tom Cruise, following the release of Cruise's legal thriller *The Firm* (1993). The pair mostly discussed aeroplanes and cameras,[32] but Kubrick also had a potential project in mind. He was unpredictable when it came to what he was going to work on next – what material a film would be about, or, indeed, when it would be made. Kubrick had long been preparing a film based on Arthur Schnitzler's 1926 novella *Traumnovelle* (*Dream Story*). Warner Bros had announced the film as early as 1971. Production had come close to starting over the years since, and Kubrick had – according to a notebook left behind from the 1980s – considered Alan Alda, Albert Brooks and Bill Murray as potential leading men, suggesting the comic direction he was intending.[33] Instead, he decided to go with the straight-faced Cruise. At the same time, Kubrick had been watching the delivered videotapes of Kidman (she later said it was unlikely that *BMX Bandits* was part of the library he was given).

Kubrick wanted a couple married in real life to play the married couple in the film, to establish a lived-in intimacy immediately. Cruise and Kidman were naturally enticed and, ultimately, upended their careers and domestic lives to take on the roles. Kidman was kept on call throughout the filming, even when she wasn't needed. Kubrick made her personally decorate the room her character lived in, and on many nights she slept in the bed on the set. She was to sleep as a fictional character, indirectly instructed to dream fictional dreams. Was this a form of total, immersive acting, or unnecessary? It would turn out to be the longest shoot in film history – taking up 16 months in total – and, after that, would take another year of editing together the excessive amounts of footage.

There had been very little enthusiasm for reteaming Cruise and Kidman on screen based on their appearances together in *Days of Thunder* and *Far and Away* (Kidman later dismissed the latter as a 'kids' film'). Instead, the hype for *Eyes Wide Shut* came from the long absence of Kubrick on cinema screens and the erotic promise of an early, iconic teaser soundtracked to Chris Isaak's 'Baby Did a Bad Bad Thing' (which Kidman was said to have introduced to Kubrick). The legendary director was overly protective of his copy of the film – showing it with extreme reluctance – but Kidman and Cruise had to see it to sign nudity releases. They watched themselves in a cut of the film before its release with Warner Bros executives in New York. Kubrick died just six days later. Kidman had missed a call from Kubrick the night before he died; he'd left a message saying he wanted to speak with her. A final mystery descended. The film would open in July, during the summer blockbuster season. Reviews were divided. The public flocked to the film at first, intrigued by the celebrity couple and titillated at the idea of scenes of sexual orgy at its centre, but they did not return.*

---

* In Australia, perhaps uncomfortable with the overt sexuality, the results were played for laughs in the mockumentary-style sitcom *Kath and Kim*: when suburban mother Kath loses her sexual drive, her de facto partner Kel hires the movie on DVD hoping to rekindle their romance. The parody borrowed from the middle Australian, suburban reaction to the film – that it had the chance to be misread as a broad erotic thriller. Kath remembers the movie being 'funny' and on her rewatch deems it not to be 'as funny as she remembered'. But *Eyes Wide Shut* most certainly *is* funny, and intentionally so. It plays with farce and travesty as genres, worlds Kidman would comfortably live within. Kidman would be invoked in *Kath and Kim* again, when Kath and Kel co-star in a musical adaptation of *The Hours* (2002).

THE INTERPRETER: NICOLE KIDMAN

Tom Junod's classic piece of middlebrow journalism, profiling the actor for the 'menswear magazine' *Esquire*, was written to promote *Eyes Wide Shut*, in the hope audiences would turn out for the film. Mid-piece, Kidman and the journalist ascend the Sydney Harbour Bridge, on the commercial walking tour over the famous coathanger arch, which had started operations in 1998. Junod, under the impression that Australians presented themselves as anti-authoritarians, questioned why the country's parks featured statues of figures like Captain Bligh, rather than Fletcher Christian. The tour guide interrupts, 'That's because of our respect for authority':

> 'Really?' Nicole said. 'Do you really think that we
> respect authority? I always thought it was just the
> opposite.'
> 'That's what we're supposed to think', the tour
> guide replied.

Junod reported that the tour guide's observation left Kidman in a daze, and that she kept thinking about what he said. In Junod's reading the interaction recontextualised her thoughts about her relationship with Kubrick. She would do anything – go anywhere – he told her to. It's a realisation many Australians come to at some point; that our love of compliance and obedience are baked into the national character, via its penal colony foundations, but one in which we have mistakenly romanticised the figures of the captors. The tour guide put it simply when he noted that: 'We love authority figures. We're so laid-back, we let them get away with murder.'

Kidman had encountered her share of Australian authority figures in her youth. She was brought up with the influences of Catholicism through her household, coming from her father's devotion. After working with Kidman on *Dead Calm*, George Miller told a *Sydney Morning Herald* journalist he had a working theory about actors: the Catholic theory of acting. Miller believed that 'all the serious actors, the real actors – those people who cannot do anything but act – are Catholic ... certainly it's the case in America and Australia – Nicole's Catholic'. Miller went on to list Mel Gibson, Jack Nicholson, William Hurt, Robert De Niro and Judy Davis as having come from similar backgrounds.[34] Susan Sarandon, herself a lapsed Catholic, and who worked with Miller on his *The Witches of Eastwick* (1987), his big foray into the Hollywood system, as well as his later medical miracle drama *Lorenzo's Oil* (1992), pointed out to the director that the pageantry of the church and, specifically, the notion of transfiguration – you become something else and avoid the guilt – proved that his hypothesis was correct. Miller continued, 'But this is what really floored me: she said there is the masochism of the life. There is no more masochistic life than that of an actor. You present yourself – not only the body but the soul, because great acting bares the soul – out there for anyone to take a shot at.'

In her marriage to Cruise, Kidman would encounter another outsized religion, one with a growing reputation of being as brutal as any in history. The sinister cinematic operations of the orgiastic sex cult at the centre of *Eyes Wide Shut* were nothing compared to the workings of Scientology. Cruise's first wife had been the one to introduce him to it. Kidman had married into the religion and humoured the idea of practising it, at one point agreeing to study its teachings at the church's monumental San Jacinto headquarters, in a former Inland Empire spa resort. Kidman went along with it willingly. In Sydney to promote *Far and Away*, she confirmed to a press pool, sitting around in an Irish pub, that she had converted, but refused to give a reason beyond the fact that it was 'interesting' and that 'it works for me'. A *Sydney Morning Herald* journalist in the room noted the muted tenor of her remarks, writing that her 'explanation of the religion's appeal was not about to win any converts'.[35]

Kidman, however, would soon be perceived by the organisation as 'the greatest threat to Scientology's greatest asset'.[36] The church did themselves few favours. The 'Potential Trouble Source/Suppressive Person' course was always going to present to Kidman as a red flag, because it derided her father's profession; one of Scientology's key tenets is an opposition to psychiatry and psychology. Kidman would privately leave the religion, as the church was going against her family. This awakening coincided with a wider growing public consciousness as revelations in the American press began to unfurl the extent of Scientology's intimidating behaviour and the amount of money they solicited from people. *TIME* magazine featured a cover story calling the religion a 'Cult of Greed'. A 90-minute *Nightline* exposé followed. Cruise, alongside John Travolta, was named at the front of most pieces about the religion, to contextualise its hold on celebrities in particular. The negative press couldn't be escaped and Kidman had to counter it. She persuaded Cruise to distance himself from the church and its teachings.

Whether Kidman had been aware of Scientology before meeting Cruise is unclear. It had had a long, complicated history in Australia and had been suppressed in the country for a time. The organisation had planted roots in the country in the 1950s, and its founder L Ron Hubbard had seen potential, naming it the world's first 'clear continent'. In one of his redeeming moments, Rupert Murdoch was an early adversary of the religion, regularly referring to it as a cult in his newspapers in the 1960s, leading to what effectively amounted to a ban on it across Victoria, South Australia and Western Australia.

CAST MATE: CATE BLANCHETT

An oral history of the orgy scene of *Eyes Wide Shut*, published in *Vulture* magazine in 2019,[37] detailed the production's need to find an American actor to dub the voice of the 'Mystery Woman' who gives Cruise a tour of the playhouse mansion, as she had been played in the film by a British model, Abigail Good. Kubrick's assistant revealed that Cruise and Kidman had recommended Cate Blanchett to the production. Approval was given in Kubrick's untimely absence, and Blanchett showed up to Pinewood Studios to record the lines, and, despite her Australian-ness, was ready to offer her best American accent.

It was a rare intersection between the two actors, who have had largely separate careers despite some shared biographical notes. Both were born with American citizenship – Blanchett's Texan father died when she was ten – so entry into that country was easy. Their closeness with two leading women in the Australian film industry helped create a clear distinction: where Kidman had the close partnership with Jane Campion, Blanchett was aligned with Gillian Armstrong, starring in Armstrong's literary adaptations of Peter Carey's tricksy *Oscar and Lucinda* (1997) and the spy romance *Charlotte Gray* (2001). With only two years between them, however, it was natural Blanchett and Kidman would walk some crossing paths in their careers. Blanchett was nominated

THE INTERPRETER: NICOLE KIDMAN

for an Oscar for her portrayal as the ascending 'Virgin Queen' in *Elizabeth* (1998), a role that Kidman had originally been sought for.

Both actors certainly went chasing after the ghost of Vivien Leigh. Kidman would evoke the playful hardheadedness of Scarlett O'Hara in her spin on a Civil War epic, *Cold Mountain* (2003). Blanchett was far more direct, inhabiting the frequently cracking façade of Blanche DuBois for a revival of Tennessee Williams' famed *A Streetcar Named Desire* at the Sydney Theatre Company, which was later toured in America in 2009. 'Blanchett as Blanche' was feared by some to be a fatal tic and a dead end for her acting, but she more than recovered in the years after. The pair also stalked Katharine Hepburn. Kidman was rumoured to be playing Hepburn in what would become Martin Scorsese's *The Aviator* (2004). Blanchett took the role instead and won an Oscar for it. Kidman had long cited Hepburn as the key influence on her career and work, having expressed a desire to develop her own biopic before Scorsese let cameras roll on Hepburn's relationship with the reclusive director Howard Hughes, thinking poetically but realistically that she'd 'love to make a movie as an ode to her. I just need to find someone good enough to write it.'[38]

It may well have been that, as a child actor prodigy, Kidman had heard tell that Hepburn had shuttled across to her side of the Harbour Bridge, swinging by North Sydney, up to the northern beaches, setting up an easel to paint the Barrenjoey Lighthouse when she was on tour in Australia in 1955 with the Old Vic. Later in life, Kidman remembered that she'd bought a vintage photograph of Hepburn and asked her to sign it, but the elderly actress flatly refused.

If there is a great divergence between Blachett and Kidman, it might be that Blanchett more committedly balanced work on screen with work on the stage. In 2008, alongside her husband, Andrew Upton, she became the artistic director of the Sydney Theatre Company (STC) – whose 1989 production of *A Midsummer Night's Dream* Kidman had dropped out of to appear in *Days of Thunder*. Running a not-for-profit cultural institution meant that Blanchett was accountable and answerable to a very different set of stakeholders – a more demanding crowd than general cinemagoers, who pay their money and leave without any face-to-face interaction, no great right of reply. It also pushed her into political arenas cinema stars usually distance themselves from. In the same year that Blanchett took over the STC, the newly elected prime minister Kevin Rudd hosted the Australia 2020 Summit, a working group intended to strategise and project policy forward into the next decade, over two days. Blanchett was assigned as co-chair of the Creative Australia Stream. She had a vested interest in national arts funding given her responsibility for the theatre company.

In 2014, after her reign at STC had ended, Blanchett was featured in the speaker line-up for Gough Whitlam's funeral, delivering a eulogy touching on how she had benefited from his tertiary education policies. Whitlam had abolished university fees in 1974 and the policy had remained in place until 1988, ultimately dumped by fellow Labor leader Bob Hawke. Blanchett credited her ability to explore acting with Whitlam's policy. Another former prime minister, John Howard, was sitting among the mourners that day, and would pettily call Blanchett's largely innocuous speech 'outrageous', suggesting there had been selective scholarships, like his own, before 1974, meaning that free education predated Whitlam.[39]

Howard's damnation of Blanchett's eulogy as 'outrageous' felt a part of the usual conservative catchcry that people don't want celebrities to be political (the usual stress is on their celebrity status, rather than their central positions within the creative industries worth billions of dollars to the economy). Movie culture is inherently political. The hesitancy to admit as much makes sense when the backlash from conservative media can be severe. Blanchett came under particular fire from columnists in Murdoch's newspapers in 2011 for appearing in a series of advertisements pushing support for a carbon tax.

Kidman had supported a less controversial green movement effort a decade earlier when she stood side-by-side with Tom Cruise to record a straight-to-camera address to the International Olympic Committee, singing the praises of Sydney hosting the Olympic Games. The couple looked as if they were beaming in from a Country Road ad – standing in front of handsome horses on some mythic Californian ranch – and spoke vaguely of the environmental initiatives that Sydney was baking into its bid. Kidman smiled broadly, and offered, 'I grew up in Sydney and it would be wonderful if my hometown could provide an environmental role model for the world'.

It was only one part of a giant machine that worked to secure Sydney the right to host the Olympic Games for the year 2000, but it indicated that Kidman's ascendance in Hollywood had long been entwined with Sydney's growing confidence on the world stage and that both would meet, head on, at the end of one millennium and the beginning of another.

THE BEGUILED (2000–2005)

No history of Australian cinema in this century – or of Kidman's career – could be written without contending with

Bazmark Luhrmann. The indefatigable Luhrmann ripped through Australian cinema like *Looney Tunes*' terrifying tornado of perpetual motion, the Tasmanian Devil, sucking up everything in his path. Baz, for short, sits alongside George Miller in his tan leather jacket, as the most publicly visible Australian-born auteur. If you can make them both sit still for long enough, it is useful to study them side-by-side. They share a similar kinetic energy. Both grew up in sparsely populated rural towns, almost exactly the same distance from their nearest major cities. They are both productive but don't have huge filmographies despite their standing in the industry, and for strikingly similar reasons: they spend years developing projects, often to let design and technology catch up to their visions. There is the ongoing negotiation to make films outside of Hollywood, but using Hollywood money, which often can cause further delays. They are both the rare directors who frequently appear in Sydney's real estate pages. They are both married to women who they collaborate with – Margaret Sixel and Catherine Martin – who have collected Oscars for films they have directed, for which they were not personally awarded. They are also, of course, both mainstays in Kidman's career and central to her professional tethering to Australia. If Miller was instrumental in her early working life and getting her to America, Luhrmann was integral in bringing her back, and setting her up for the tallest peak of her career. You have to understand Luhrmann to understand Kidman's prime.

Luhrmann was born in Sydney but grew up nearly a four-hour drive away, in the minuscule township of Herons Creek, on the mid north coast of New South Wales. His parents owned a fuel station. The man who sold his parents petrol for the pumps also owned a quaint local cinema – the

THE INTERPRETER: NICOLE KIDMAN

Plaza Theatre in nearby lakeside Laurieton – and, after he died, Luhrmann's father took over its operations, working as a projectionist. The romantic image of a young Luhrmann watching old movie musicals and becoming film-struck took hold in that regional theatre. As a teenager, Luhrmann fled to Sydney after his parents' divorce, attending a school on the northern beaches of Sydney, and went on to study at NIDA as an acting student, with some success. He was in a small supporting role alongside Judy Davis in the sex worker romance *Winter of Our Dreams* (1981). In that early film, Luhrmann was just as jumpy and nervy as his public persona would be for decades to come. The often stern Davis, an alumni of the acting school, warned him to 'watch out, hang on to yourself' before he walked through NIDA's doors. He was an intense student and was found often acting out rather than just acting.[40] In a class on improvisation in which the students were asked to show anger, Luhrmann stalked around the room before putting his fist through a nearby window, shattering the glass and cutting his hand. The relative niceties and romanticisms of Luhrmann's film output might hide this 'angry young man' of his early student life.

Luhrmann's debut feature *Strictly Ballroom* (1992) began its life as a 30-minute play developed as a second-year student project (Kidman would recall seeing this early version of the play when she drove with her mother to Brisbane to attend the World Expo 88 – the centrepiece event of Australia's garish bicentennial celebrations – where Luhrmann's play was featured). The plot of *Strictly Ballroom* – following Scott Hastings, the son of ballroom dancers, who is creatively frustrated with the rigidity of the steps he is expected to follow in the conservative world of competitive ballroom dancing – can be read as thinly veiled autobiography of an actor rejecting the traditional teachings of an institution like NIDA. It is also, however, impossible to ignore that it is the direct product of that institution too. Luhrmann's success story was the result, in fact, of many Sydney-based and Australia-wide cultural institutions, as the prime minister, Paul Keating, made clear at his speech at the Sydney premiere of *Strictly Ballroom* at the Museum of Contemporary Art on Circular Quay (having already seen the movie a week earlier) listing off a number of organisations including NIDA, the Sydney Dance Company, the Sydney Theatre Company, the Film Finance Corporation, the Australian Film Institute, and the NSW Film and Television Office, who, in Keating's mind, could all take varying degrees of credit (and sitting above them all was, of course, their benevolent benefactor, Keating himself).

At the time he was slamming Paul Hogan in the press for taking the country backwards, Keating was openly embracing Luhrmann, and Luhrmann returned the love. Keating himself had studied ballroom dancing (he considered himself a 'refugee from the dance halls') as both his mother and father were dancers, taking part in competitions at locations across Sydney, including the art deco dance hall The Trocadero (which would eventually transform into the George Street cinemas). Even without such close biographical connections, *Strictly Ballroom* was *the* movie of the Keating era; highlighting the capacity for flourish and theatricality in the Australian character, simultaneously embracing modernism and tradition. *Strictly Ballroom* tells a story of progress and reform. At the core of its plot is the rejection of 'The Federation' in the hope of a republic and self-expression. In an issue of *Vogue* guest edited by Luhrmann, the director acknowledged Keating as one of his 'Leading Men' and the 'first person I had heard talk about the republic which is something I've

THE INTERPRETER: NICOLE KIDMAN

always wanted, even as a child.'[41] It was a passion he shared with Kidman: novelist Thomas Keneally, who was one of the leaders of the movement, furnished her with a pro-republic sticker, which she brandished on the back of her car.

Political precociousness might have explained Luhrmann's enthusiasm for working alongside Keating. It was unclear who approached whom; according to Keating's biographer and former speechwriter Don Watson, the young director agreed to give Keating 'instruction in speech delivery' but would take a more central role soon after, signing on to stage-manage Keating and the Australian Labor Party's 1992–93 election campaign.[42] The responsibilities seemed entirely aesthetic. Luhrmann, famous for grouping his first three films as the Red Curtain Trilogy, went with a blue curtain instead for Keating – having the incumbent leader stand in front of a cobalt-coloured drape, thinking it softened his look and, according to Watson, it 'took the "greens" out of the Prime Minister's Spanish colouring'. Luhrmann went even further, mixing blue into the Max Factor make-up that Keating carried around with him. Later, in the final film of the Red Curtain Trilogy, *Moulin Rouge!*, Luhrmann illuminated Kidman's skin with blue light to give her character a deathlike pallor.[43] It was clear then that Paul Keating had served as a make-up test subject for Kidman's first Oscar-nominated performance.

MOVIES WOULD BE BACK ON KEATING'S MIND IN LATE 1994 when he stood in front of an audience at the National Gallery of Australia in Canberra to announce his grand Creative Nation policy. Buried among the overarching announcement was a commitment to build a film studio in Sydney. Keating had long been in talks with Rupert Murdoch and his spokespeople about placing Fox Studios within the Sydney Showgrounds (the *Sydney Morning Herald* reported that Kidman was signed to a celebrity 'advisory board' for the studios, alongside Luhrmann and Gillian Armstrong, which the head of the Australian Directors Guild dismissed as smoke and mirrors, to give only an impression that the industry as a whole had been consulted and given approval).[44] Don Watson considered the agreement with Murdoch to be a 'secret plan' – snuck into cabinet by Keating without warning – and that it would prove to be 'the bombshell of the cultural statement'.[45] Murdoch was reported to have called the project 'Hollywood by the Harbour'.[46] Locals referred to it as 'Rupertworld'.[47]

Rupertworld had its origins in R&R, a production company Murdoch formed in 1980 with fellow Australian expat Robert Stigwood, the music producer best known for rolling out *Saturday Night Fever* (1977) as both movie and vinyl smash. The pair would back *Gallipoli* (1981), a revival work of national myth making, to be directed by Peter Weir, and which would have had personal mythic connections for Murdoch (his father, Keith, had served in the First World War and visited Gallipoli on tour). It would, however, be the one and only film R&R would ever produce. Murdoch didn't leave film production behind entirely, taking over 20th Century-Fox in 1985. This was a legacy-making purchase: 20th Century-Fox was forged in 1935 from the mythic merger between Fox Film Corporation and 20th Century Pictures. The company had had an uneasy start in the market, but by the 1940s it was one of the leading majors, sitting in the top three beside MGM and Paramount. From there, the company had a long and storied history with the usual peaks and troughs – creative and commercial – typical of film studios of its size. It experienced immense success with the *Star Wars* and *Alien* franchises in the

THE INTERPRETER: NICOLE KIDMAN

1970s and 1980s. Murdoch, however, ever the vulture, bought Fox after it had reported a monumental loss in the year prior. He would never be the hands-on studio head; it was only ever going to be an asset in a vast portfolio, not a passion project as R&R had been. According to one of his biographers, Murdoch doesn't watch television or movies.[48]

Fox would brand its logo on Sydney, just as it would make a distinct mark on Luhrmann's youthful career. Following the unexpected success of *Strictly Ballroom*, Luhrmann signed an exclusive 'first look' deal with 20th Century Fox, the company securing pre-emptive rights on whatever Luhrmann chose to work on next. He would pitch a contemporary adaptation of *Romeo and Juliet* to the studio. The heads were not convinced but they did, however, give him money to bring Leonard DiCaprio – flying economy – to Sydney to film proof-of-concept footage. *William Shakespeare's Romeo + Juliet*, as styled by Luhrmann, became an unexpected sleeper hit when it reached cinemas in 1996. The film had a difficult shoot in Mexico City – where the chief hairstylist was kidnapped – and there were complications in completing post-production when teams were split between Los Angeles and Melbourne. This all helped Luhrmann decide that he wanted to be based entirely out of Sydney for future projects. In 1997, Luhrmann leased the heritage-listed Darlinghurst estate Iona – an icon of Sydney – eventually buying it outright in 2006 for $10 million. He and his wife, Catherine Martin, turned their home into a makeshift space for rehearsals, including a recording studio and writers' room. In an interview with the BBC, Luhrmann likened the residence to Francis Ford Coppola's Zoetrope and George Lucas's Skywalker Ranch, again echoing George Miller in finding that Sydney had a sisterly bond in San Francisco and Northern California's satellite relationship to Hollywood.

It was stationed in Iona that Luhrmann – with collaborator, confidante and former Kidman co-star Craig Pearce – would write a movie for Nicole. The actor and director had first met in 1994, for a photoshoot for Luhrmann's guest edition of *Vogue*. He cast Kidman in a series of photographs where she took on the guise of early Hollywood stars. It was inevitable that at a certain point Old Hollywood would become a cultural commodity of a different kind: a reference library. New stars could evoke old stars as shorthand for glamour and prestige. Kidman was particularly good at evoking old ghosts. Luhrmann had her dress up to look like an early silent star, a talkies glamour icon, and a broad musical comedian in full colour.*

Their eventual film collaboration would attempt to revive the movie musical.† *Moulin Rouge!* (2001) would be one of the first productions to be mounted on the new Fox Studio sound stages, with filming beginning in late 1999, and Nicole Kidman and Ewan McGregor taking the leads. For Kidman, swinging from the cold austerity of Stanley Kubrick to the frenzied lunacy of Baz Luhrmann must have been a hell of a trip. She was at least back in her home city, with her family in tow (Cruise would be based in town for the protracted filming of the much-anticipated *Mission Impossible* sequel,

---

* Luhrmann exaggerated Kidman's naturally red hair to dress her up to look like Lucille Ball, a premonition given that nearly 30 years later Kidman would be playing the comic in a biopic, *Being the Ricardos* (2021), for which she would receive her fifth nomination in an acting category at the Academy Awards.

† I re-watched the movie while working on this book in a hotel room with Baz Luhrmann's picture hanging on the wall beside the bed. The Fantauzzo Hotel was mostly soulless concrete and littered with framed reprints of works by its namesake, the artist Vincent Fantauzzo, known for his photorealist paintings, including his uncharacteristically tortured portrait of Luhrmann called *Off Screen*.

THE INTERPRETER: NICOLE KIDMAN

which proved to be another difficult shoot). There were echoes between Luhrmann's and Kubrick's demanding projects. The script would not be settled by the time cameras began to roll, and would be rewritten throughout the months-long shoot. It wasn't a good sign. Omens abounded: Luhrmann's father died on the first day of filming. Kidman broke ribs during rehearsals. Rumours flew around that the production was in trouble. The shoot went on so long that the team were kicked out of Fox Studios as the *Star Wars* sequel was bumped in (Ewan McGregor would, of course, stay on to reprise his role of Obi-Wan Kenobi). Production would be picked up in Spain where Kidman was working on the Cruise-produced haunted house horror *The Others* (2001). In the end there were 192 days of filming.

Despite being kicked out of its home city, *Moulin Rouge!* is as much about Sydney celebrating itself in 1999, at the turn of the new millennium, as it is about Paris in 1899. The central plot is, after all, about putting on a show, working with deadlines and one too many stakeholders, right as Sydney was planning its own party in the background, designing and developing the opening and closing ceremonies of the 2000 Olympics. The party atmosphere must have been soaked into Luhrmann's bloodstream. For the Sydney premiere of the finished film, Luhrmann booked out all 11 cinemas at the Fox Studio complex, allowing 3000 people to attend. The domination of the space and Sydney's cinematic imagination was, more or less, complete. To celebrate the turn of the millennium – and Sydney being one of the first places of the world to see the clock turn over – Luhrmann had a merchant navy vessel refitted by his set designers. Floating on the harbour, the guest list included Kidman, Cruise, Russell Crowe, and the billionaire heirs Lachlan Murdoch and James Packer.

CAST MATES

The party had to end eventually: at the start of 2001, after the glow of the Sydney Olympics began to dim, it was announced that Cruise and Kidman would be divorcing; a marriage which had defined celebrity culture for much of the 1990s was coming to a close. It soon became clear that Cruise had been lured back into the Scientology fold. Cruise was rumoured to be back recruiting for Scientology himself, and to have come close to ensnaring Packer. Prior to the divorce, his former brethren were allegedly undermining his relationship with Kidman to gain greater control over him, and had attained considerable ground. In his history of Scientologists in Australia, *Fair Game*, the journalist Steve Cannane gives voice to several sources who allege Cruise requested Scientologists tap Kidman's phones prior to their divorce, adding paranoia to existing strain. Kidman paid surveillance experts to come and sweep their Los Angeles mansion, but one suggested the tap was coming from the main phone company.

KIDMAN ENTERED 2001 NEWLY SINGLE, WITH TWO FILMS that would become major hits for her – *Moulin Rouge!* and *The Others* – that should have made the year a lasting winner, but both were released in the months before the September 11 attacks. Just as the attacks destabilised the real world, so too Hollywood. Film critic J. Hoberman asked, looking back on a terrorist event that produced footage beyond anything Hollywood could imagine: 'Did the history-changing shock of this cinematic event plunge the nascent twenty-first century into an alternative universe, one in which motion picture fairy tales actually did come true? Or was it rather a red pill that parted the veil on a new reality that already existed?'[49]

Hoberman reminded readers that the studios had leaked

to the press that they had been informed by the FBI they could be the next target, which sent Los Angeles into a panic. An anonymous source at 20th Century Fox said the 'studio could be expected to restrict access to its lot, increase the number of its security officers and install barricades at the lot entrance. About 3500 people work on the Fox lot'.[50]

Others in Hollywood felt culpable, leading the director Robert Altman to cop to reporters: 'Nobody would have thought to commit an atrocity like that unless they'd seen it in a movie. We created the atmosphere and taught them how to do it'.[51]

Few would have thought to ask if Osama bin Laden had been watching *Gladiator*. But earlier in 2001, Russell Crowe had arrived in Los Angeles and was unpacking in his hotel room when the FBI entered and explained to him that he was part of a 'cultural destabilisation plan' plotted not by Hollywood but by Al-Qaeda. The terrorist group was hoping to seize American actors in a high-profile, A-list attack (Crowe was amused that Al-Qaeda mistook him for American). Crowe was given a security detail comprising FBI agents, who shadowed him – not inconspicuously – at awards ceremonies in the months before September 11. The FBI would be by his side for the next two years, undercover on the sets of his movies, a plot point more outrageous than anything depicted within the scenes he was acting in.[52]

Crowe had direct experience with the hysterical reality of the years following the September 11 attacks – attending an awards ceremony with tight security detail – before Hollywood would have to contend with it *en masse*. In the aftermath of September 11, many understandably questioned the suitability of hosting major events. The president of the academy, however, promised to forge ahead, writing an editorial saying that if the Oscars were not held in early 2002 'the terrorists have won the war'. Kidman was nominated for the Academy Award for Best Actress that year and though she would not win, her loss set her up for success in the following year, where she was nominated again, this time for playing Virginia Woolf in *The Hours* – a movie seemingly designed in a genetic laboratory to win Oscars.

The events of September 11 continued to reverberate that year. The 75th Academy Awards were held only days after America and Australia, alongside other 'allied nations', launched the war in Iraq. The red carpet for the awards show was cancelled out of what organisers labelled 'respect'. Cate Blanchett dropped out of her scheduled presenting duties. The mood on the evening was a strange mix of sombre reflection and the usual celebratory excess. The convergence eventually got ugly. Documentarian Michael Moore punctured the sense of ceremony with his speech calling out the war and George W Bush, which was drowned out by a mix of applause, boos and music coming up from the orchestra pit trying to play him off the stage.

Kidman was all but a lock to win that night for her performance as Woolf. Heavy-handed Harvey Weinstein had been out on the hustings, promoting her for the win. When her name was finally announced, Kidman took to the stage and in her winner's speech offered little more than a polite, political-in-an-apolitical-way nod to the exterior turmoil in the wider world:

> Why do you come to the Academy Awards when the world is in such turmoil ... because art is important ... because you believe in what you do, and you want to honour that, and it is a tradition that needs to be upheld

THE INTERPRETER: NICOLE KIDMAN

and at the same time you see there are a lot of problems in the world. Since 9/11, there's been a lot of pain in terms of families losing people and now with the war families losing people, and ... God bless them.

It was an unenviable task to take the stage that night, particularly in the electric atmosphere following Moore's speech. Kidman could have gone to Woolf's repeated refrain in *Three Guineas*, 'How in your opinion are we to prevent war?' Instead, on that night, there was no real opinion to offer. She had reached the height of a form of celebrity through centrist appeal – offend no one, please as many as possible, garner the highest number of votes. There is a reason Oscar season has become one of 'campaigns'. Awards can be lost due to poor politicking.

Yet Kidman was far more daring in the artistic decisions she made and was willing to risk upsetting the masses. Going off her films alone, cinema in the first decade of the 2000s looked deranged. *Birth* (2004) – possibly Kidman's best film – flirts dangerously closely with showing paedophilia onscreen. Indeed, *The Hours* has aged into one of Kidman's least interesting films, best remembered both then and now for the actor's jutting prosthetic nose. Her real nose, and nous, led her in more interesting directions. *Dogville* – her follow-up to *The Hours* – made its premiere at Cannes in 2003, just weeks after George W Bush landed on the USS *Abraham Lincoln* to announce with a printed banner that the war in Iraq was a 'Mission Accomplished'. Bush's production design was stagier than anything Lars von Trier put forward in his parable of American corruption. J. Hoberman noted that American film critics responded to *Dogville* 'as a personal attack ... with a defensive bitterness verging on panic'. The feeling was that they should have saved the moral outrage for the war that was being fought in their name. It was being fought in Australia's name too.

'AUSTRALIA' (2006–2022)

At the end of the first decade of the 21st century, Kidman featured in a small role in the overcrowded *Nine* (2009) a strained Broadway musical spin on Federico Fellini's *8½* (1963). Disney-friendly director Rob Marshall was coming off the back of his Oscar-winning Best Picture *Chicago* (2002), and was all too happy to cash in on his cultural capital to help the Weinstein Brothers go forth and Americanise the classics of Italian Neorealist cinema. In *Nine*, Daniel Day-Lewis plays director Guido Contini – a Fellini stand-in – who is feeling like an artistic imposter, despite all the adoration and fame surrounding him. Kidman plays Contini's constant muse Claudia Jenssen – partly drawn from Anita Ekberg, star of Fellini's *La Dolce Vita* (1960) – who is growing tired of waiting for Contini to begin his next production. Contini is struggling to force himself to work on an overly ambitious film he had the temerity to call *Italia*.

Naming a film after an entire country ultimately proved too much for Contini to handle. It did little to wear down the unflagging Baz Luhrmann at first. Indeed, the bouncy director was happy to name his movie after an entire continent. Luhrmann started out on what would eventually become his *Australia* in the mid-2000s after he drew his Red Curtain Trilogy – *Strictly Ballroom, William Shakespeare's Romeo + Juliet* and *Moulin Rouge!* – to a close. His intention was to begin on another trilogy, a set of films focused on reviving the cinematic

THE INTERPRETER: NICOLE KIDMAN

'epic'. He had David Lean's *Lawrence of Arabia* (1962) in front of mind – and his experience of seeing it as a boy – but more for its formal scope (Overtures! Intermissions!) rather than its subject matter. It seemed unwise to start with a genre rather than a story. Luhrmann and his creative team decided they would mount a biopic of Alexander the Great – Kidman was recruited to star as Olympias, mother to Leonardo DiCaprio's Alexander – but the project collapsed when news arrived that Oliver Stone was working on a competing project. Luhrmann had already put in a request to use the Australian army for the film – calling in the cavalry, quite literally – and the NSW government lobbied the federal government on his behalf to make it so. Admitting defeat, Luhrmann simply swapped out the story of one colonising empire for another. There is, after all, no place like home.

How to go about trying to represent Australia on the big screen? Luhrmann started with the casting of Nicole Kidman and Russell Crowe. Luhrmann had a range of Australian A-listers to choose from to sell his product. Through the 1990s and early 2000s, Australian actors had dominated in America in packs, strong-arming many an American out of a role. If anything *Australia* seemed, in part, designed to celebrate the country's international cultural success since the advent of the Australian New Wave. Crowe was announced to be appearing opposite Kidman as her romantic interest, The Drover. Kidman and Crowe, long friends, had already lost the chance to star together in *Eucalyptus* after Crowe's demands for a rewrite of the screenplay. Crowe would similarly depart *Australia*, citing the usual industry smokescreen term, 'creative differences' (the pair would finally unite in the conversion therapy biopic *Boy Erased* in 2018). Hugh Jackman took Crowe's spot. It wasn't the first

251

time the pair switched places. Jackman's career-making turn as the hirsute Wolverine, in the *X-Men* comic book movie series, came about after Crowe turned down that role but recommended Jackman on his way out.

Until that point Jackman was best known internationally, if at all, for appearing in the Rodgers and Hammerstein musical *Oklahoma!* in London. Crowe's reference resulted in Jackman becoming a strange hybrid of gruff action star and goofball songster – both the Übermensch and the Nice Guy.* It also made him come across like a movie star from yesteryear retrofitted for 21st-century cinema screens. The film critic Dana Stevens questioned, for instance, whether Jackman played 'like a throwback to an earlier age of entertainment, a man who could plausibly appear on *The Ed Sullivan Show* or squire Claudette Colbert to the Brown Derby?'[53]

Jackman and Luhrmann were an ideal fit for a project designed to be a return to a bygone era of filmmaking. Story-wise, Luhrmann had started his research by reading generalised Australian history for six months.[54] He briefly

---

* Jackman's female equivalent might be Kidman's close friend Naomi Watts, who, like Jackman, was capable of reviving the gold and silver ages of Hollywood. It took Watts longer than her immediate Australian contemporaries to break into Hollywood (her first appearance was weirdly in an advertisement where she gave up going on a date with Tom Cruise to have a roast lamb dinner at home). But in a very minor, early role, in Joe Dante's *Matinee* (1993) she briefly appears in a movie-within-the-movie, a 1950s *Herbie*-style groaner about a sentient shopping trolley, and plays the wide-eyed ingénue perfectly. Her breakthrough role would see her expand that wide-eyed 1950s sensibility, as she walked out of LAX as an aspiring actress, Betty Elms, in David Lynch's *Mulholland Drive* (2001). A question lingers watching Watts becoming one of Lynch's go-to blondes (she would reappear in a rabbit mask in 2006's *Inland Empire* and the 2017 return of *Twin Peaks*): what would David Lynch do with the inner eeriness of Nicole Kidman?

considered, and abandoned, setting the film during the arrival of the First Fleet, though he knew he wanted to explore Australia's relationship to England. Luhrmann stuck with his usual bowerbird approach when it came to pulling together his references. The film featured a practical constellation of other Australian actors, cast from across the decades. It works almost as an Australian New Wave answer to the Marvel Cinematic Universe. Bryan Brown, Bill Hunter, Jack Thompson and David Gulpilil all made the call sheet. The film referenced Australia's screen history as much as its stars. The opening shot of the film featured Gulpilil framed against the backdrop of a dramatic sunset, purple night sky bleeding into orange light at the horizon, immediately evoking an iconic poster of *Walkabout*.

Luhrmann could have made more room for Australian cinema. American cinema was *Australia*'s main reference point. The action opened in 1939 seemingly only to invoke two of the film's biggest influences, which were both released that year: *Gone With the Wind* and *The Wizard of Oz*. The timing dragged out the plot. The bombing of Darwin – which was supposed to be the centrepiece of the film – didn't take place until 1942, giving *Australia* a multi-year arc (though Luhrmann was, of course, going for the 'epic'). Luhrmann was forced, however, to look at more obscure work when he came to references to Australian cinema – all Australian cinema in the first half of the 20th century, as I hope this book has sadly proven, had become obscure by the 21st. In its first half, *Australia* borrows from *The Overlanders*, taking its cattle droving plot. The film did little, however, to send contemporary audiences in the direction of the titles it was harking back to. It would have been worth pointing out, for instance, that *The Overlanders* was released two years ahead of

Howard Hawks' John Wayne–starring mustering movie *Red River* (many American critics pointed to the latter, but likely would not have known about the former). The collage artist cuts and pastes, but when it comes to a frantic collagist like Luhrmann, you're more likely to see the residue of the glue than where the source material originated.

One of *Australia*'s critical design flaws was that it was built to work as a cultural event as much as a satisfying finished film. Luhrmann might have lost track of what was personal cinema and what was gig-for-hire. During the lengthy intermissions between making films, Luhrmann had not been idle. Filling his time were advertising campaigns, fashion shows, a vodka branding exercise, a holiday store window to dress, a hit spoken word single ('Everybody's Free (to Wear Sunscreen)'), Met Galas, and the interior decoration of a Miami hotel. Most famously, he would obsess for over a year on a short film designed to advertise Chanel No. 5, with Kidman playing its glamorous lead; the rare advertisement to be deemed worthy of its own review in the *New York Times*. Was it any wonder then that *Australia* became part advertorial too? The product placement was in the title itself. Luhrmann, and his co-conspirators, were clearly hoping for a revival of the success of both Paul Hogan's *Crocodile Dundee* and the 'Come and Say G'day' campaign. Why not merge the two, bringing film and tourism campaign together in one package? The film came with a pair of ads directed by Luhrmann – one set in New York, the other in Shanghai – where stressed-out office workers were enticed by the film's youngest star, Brandon Walters, to 'Come walkabout' and forget their worries. The Western Australia tourism board put in $1 million. Tourism Australia ran a campaign pleading 'See the Movie, See the Country', as if they were one and the same.

Leaden *Australia* – weighed down by the outsized expectations of the Australian public, whether betting on its success or failure – would land in local cinemas after the arch-conservative John Howard had been ousted by his successor, Kevin Rudd. The year of its release – 2008 – would open with Rudd delivering an apology to the Stolen Generations, after more than a decade in which Howard had pointedly refused to do so. *Australia*, opening ten months after the apology, would acknowledge Rudd's apology in its *Gone With the Wind*–style end credit title cards. If the history lesson summary felt hasty, Luhrmann at least seemed wise to the fact that the national mood was changing and that while he had started making the film under Howard, the prime minister who refused to say sorry for Australia's past crimes would not be around for its release. *Australia* was, indeed, in tune with Rudd's populist appeal, and though both were well meaning, their attempts to appeal to as many people as possible would spell their end.

American critics largely recused themselves from talking about the racial politics of the film. They ignored the response of the film from First Nations audiences back in Australia. Yiman and Bidjara woman Professor Marcia Langton wrote a short, spirited appreciation of the 'fabulous, hyperbolic' film in the *Sydney Morning Herald*. Langton was, in fact, credited as having assisted with research and 'cultural clarification' for Luhrmann on the film (Gulpilil was credited with character development and cultural authenticity).[55] Germaine Greer, writing from the UK for the *Guardian*, quickly countered Langton, suggesting that the film was a 'fake epic'[56] and using broad generalisations that, according to Langton, would have made the denialists of the 'History Wars' happy.[57] It was unsurprising, perhaps, that a film designed as a cultural event would have its coverage move from the pages reserved for film criticism and into those for opinionated editorial.

Greer thought she was landing a finishing blow when she wrote: 'The only history Luhrmann seems to care about is the history of movies'. But what film director doesn't see history partly reflected through a referential library of films? Greer also ignored one of the most unique aspects of Luhrmann's careful film history, which Langton, writing in her appraisal, had pointed out: 'In his imagined cinema of the 1940s, the spatial and social shape of racism is reconstructed with such exact detail, I felt I had been transported back to my own childhood'. Langton was referencing the fact that Luhrmann – working particularly with his production design team – had carefully recreated the history of Australia's First Nations people as active and enthusiastic moviegoers, despite private and governmental attempts at restricting their access to cinema.

In her landmark book-length essay '*Well, I heard it on the radio and I saw it on the television ...*' Langton quoted the *Guess Who's Coming to Dinner in Arnhem Land?* report, stressing their finding that First Nations audiences have always been 'extremely film literate: from the fifties even very remote communities, reserves and missions commonly had up to three film nights a week in the open or in halls'.[58] This, of course, perfectly describes the conditions that allowed for Gulpilil's early cinephilia at school in Maningrida.

In white-owned cinemas, with paying attendance, however, the experience of cinemagoing could be extremely discomforting and unpleasant. This was 'back-aching and neck-craning territory' according to Dr Maria Nugent in her powerful essay outlining Luhrmann's approach to documenting the racial segregation of Australia's cinemas.[59] This segregation was not directly lifted from America's well-known practices. In fact, the separation was spatially flipped between the two countries – typically the balcony was cordoned off for African Americans, whereas that space was reserved for white families in Australia. First Nations audience members in Australia were given the most uncomfortable chairs at the front of the cinema. It was an important reminder that the spaces we watch movies in are just as political as the movies themselves.

Released in a politically charged world, in the year of the Great Recession, *Australia* performed well at the box office in Australia, but was seen as a disappointment in the US. The year 2008 also marked the coming of the superheroes who would dominate cinema screens throughout the 2010s, threatening the sort of smaller independent films Kidman had been used to making. *Australia* wouldn't be able to compete with *The Dark Knight* (2008). In January of that year, its 28-year-old star, Heath Ledger, Australia's most promising actor in Hollywood since Kidman and Blanchett – and who had been rumoured to replace Crowe as The Drover before Jackman came on board – had died in his New York loft, cutting short a career with decades of work ahead of it. He would appear as a spectral figure, face painted ghostly white, in cinemas later that year, in the new *Batman* film, which would drain the colour out of Kidman's effort in the series.

Moving on from such an ambitious movie seemed an awkward process. Luhrmann later claimed that *Australia* 'nearly killed' him. Kidman was reportedly embarrassed by her performance in the film, 'squirming' through the premiere in Sydney. 'I can't look at this movie and be proud of what I've done.'[60] Luhrmann would go chasing after the American myth instead – unable to wring a wholly convincing one out of his home country – making his own version of American

CAST MATES

foundational text *The Great Gatsby* (2013) and the life and times of *Elvis* (2022), even if, in fact, both were filmed in Australia, using largely Australian casts and crew. Kidman retreated to Nashville with her Australian country and western singing husband and began a new family.

It was a time of broken embraces. *Australia* marked the end of Luhrmann's relationship with 20th Century Fox. A decade later, Rupert Murdoch would be done with the company too. In 2019, after more than a year of negotiations, Disney bought the famous studio for $71.3 billion, sucking an incredible film library and legacy into its corporate black hole. Murdoch himself had become an increasingly toxic commodity. The 2011 phone-tapping scandal put him on the wrong side of a number of celebrities. The year before, however, Kidman and Hugh Jackman had become the godparents to Rupert Murdoch's youngest children, attending their christening at the River Jordan. The pair were invited on a three-day tour of Jordan in the days following, accompanied by Ivanka Trump (Kidman would land in hot water after the election of Ivanka's father as president of the United States, when she appealed to voters to come together behind Trump to support the idea of the presidency, no matter who is in office).*

The age of the movie star was coming to an end too, although few of them would be out of work. You could either enlist as a superhero – where your character traits and names would have more immediate recall than your own name – or

---

* What would Murdoch have made of Kidman starring in *Bombshell*, the fictional exposé of the sexual harassment claims within Fox News, and against its CEO Roger Ailes? Murdoch appears at the end of that movie, played by Malcolm McDowell. The casting of McDowell is appropriate enough given that one of McDowell's lasting images in cinema is of a viewer, eyes forcibly opened, being forced to watch images of degradation and violence.

you could downsize to the small screen. With the transition to online video-on-demand from video rental service Netflix in 2007 – and its launch of original programming in 2013 – the rise of streaming platforms has seen an almost unsustainable growth in productions in Hollywood and around the world. It turned films and television series into 'content' for vast, competitive libraries. Former movie stars became television players. Kidman was, perhaps, out of all of her contemporaries, uniquely primed to do so because of her history of making miniseries with Kennedy Miller. The distance between a show like *Bangkok Hilton* and a show like *Big Little Lies* (2017) is not so great. *Big Little Lies*, as an adaptation of Liane Moriarty's pulpy novel set on the fictional shores of the northern beaches, was a homecoming for Kidman, both to television screens and the psychic space of northern Sydney (although the setting was changed in the series to Monterey on the coast of California, proving crazy rich white people can work in either country).

Kidman would become a figurehead of the miniseries revival of the late 2010s, reuniting with Jane Campion for a six-episode sequel to Campion's crime procedural *Top of the Lake* (2017), returning to Moriarty-land with a second, unloved season of *Big Little Lies* (2019) and an adaptation of her *Nine Perfect Strangers* (2021), while dropping a further six-episode order with *The Undoing* (2020). This commitment to longer shoots – more scenes, more dialogue, more close-ups – embodied Kidman's devotion to her chosen career.

Kidman, like Baz Luhrmann, is a maximalist, defying the widely accepted idea of the Australian character being a retiring and reticent type. Kidman and Luhrmann perhaps didn't quite speak for Australia though; instead they manifested Sydney in the 1980s and early 2000s: the port city, facing outwards, thriving under market deregulation and unexpected international attention. Was it any surprise that they were trained to want more of everything? Kidman and Luhrmann, via their frontier myth making, had proved if Australia and America shared anything in common it was a taste for the expansionist. Indeed, if Luhrmann ever circles back around to his Alexander the Great biography, he should sincerely consider casting Nicole Kidman as his Alexander. There has never been a film star so ready to set forth and conquer. She will only weep on seeing there are no more movies to make.

EPILOGUE
WESTWARD EXPANSION

At the end of 2020, a fatigued year if ever there was one, I drove west, to Blacktown, to visit the set of a movie co-scripted by my oldest friend, Bina Bhattacharya, alongside seven other young writers – Nisrine Amine, Matias Bolla, Claire Cao, Arka Das, Dee Dogan, Vonne Patiag and Tien Tran. The production had started its life as a developmental arts project, designed to support young filmmakers from across Western Sydney, bringing them together to workshop a short, spirited screenplay each. The idea had originally been to make a low-budget web series – no one ever wants a 'web series' except funding body executives who don't want to properly invest in emerging filmmakers – but the talent of those involved saw the project balloon into a proper feature.

Here Out West (2021), as it was eventually titled, merged those eight short films into one intersecting, Robert Altman–style anthology and went into production with a modest budget in the midst of the Covid-19 pandemic, shooting under closely supervised conditions. Given the global conditions it was astounding that the film had even made it to production. For my part, it felt radical to even be allowed to drive across the span of a city (Melbourne had only recently emerged from its historic 111-day lockdown).

I thought it might be useful, in writing about the lives and careers of actors, to get an up-close look at how films were made, but due to the careful restrictions in place, only a limited number of people were permitted on set, and Bina wasn't allowed to take her seven-month-old daughter with her, so I pulled up into a small cul-de-sac, cordoned off with tape and orange witches' hats, ready to offer my babysitting services instead. The baby and I slipped away as Bina entered into the dream space she had long imagined. Together we walked through the suburban back streets while production rolled. The high noon sun turned it into a steamy stroll.

Meanwhile, closer to the coastline, Hollywood was cooling itself off by the harbour. Because of Australia's relative isolation from the rest of the world, the country had remained largely free of the novel coronavirus for long stretches and, in doing so, had become a desirable destination to many. It was in Australia that film productions of a reasonable scale – and so steady work too – could go on. Distance was no longer tyrannical. The household names began their descent. Tom Hanks was already expected pre-Covid, arriving early in March 2020 to film Baz Luhrmann's ambitious *Elvis* biography on the Gold Coast, but, in catching the emergent virus, he became the first big celebrity in the world to do so. The trade publication *Deadline*, who had the scoop, saw the story become their most read ever and it was almost as if Hanks's own infection was part of a public health campaign. The *NYT* noted his diagnosis made him 'the face of an outbreak that has cascaded around the globe.'[1] Production on *Elvis* was shut down as a result and would not resume until September that year.

WESTWARD EXPANSION

Natalie Portman – who had been in Australia before to film the divisive *Star Wars* prequels as a teenager – arrived to get to work on another blockbuster series, and seemed to integrate with the city better than most, perhaps through these historical connections. Portman was a portent of the parade of celebrities to come, all of whom would prove a welcome distraction from the grim realities of that first year of the pandemic and a reminder of Australia's relative good fortune. With cinemas frequently shuttered, and the opening dates of major movies pushed back by nervous studios, stories of films being made became the entertainment itself, placeholders for the real product. We looked at photographs of the celebrities instead of seeing them on the screen. A paparazzi shot of Portman pushing a trolley filled with green reusable shopping bags down the escalators of a 'Woolies' shopping centre went viral online, making her look like an ordinary eastern suburbs parent.* It felt, for a moment, as if this would be a permanent vacation for some. Zac Efron and Dev Patel both had Australian girlfriends, and were seen deglamourised and hanging around Adelaide. Matt Damon was looking into putting money down on a historic Sydney pub, the aptly named Hollywood Hotel (around the corner from the former Paramount Pictures colonial outpost). Portman had signed to stay on in Sydney for an HBO adaptation of an Elena Ferrante novel. But Portman abandoned *Days of Abandonment* days before cameras were set to roll, returning to America and breaking the reverie.

---

* I attended a revival screening of *Twin Peaks: Fire Walk with Me* (1992), as part of a David Lynch retrospective at the historic Randwick Ritz cinema in the city's east, when buzzy whispers started passing around that Portman had entered the cinema late and had made her way down to the front.

A decade earlier, the amiable sci-fi adventure picture *Thor* (2011) had introduced the world to the Melbourne-born Chris Hemsworth, who could be seen either as a new style of Australian star or simply a revived Errol Flynn with added muscle and better business sense. *Thor* was but a small cog in the mechanical wheeling-out of the so-called Marvel Cinematic Universe. Like the comic book series' Celestial Ego – a villainous conquering-mad planet – Disney had expanded to subsume Marvel Studios in 2015 and two years later would announce its intention to make a grab for 20th Century Fox. After its successful takeover, Disney dropped the Fox name from 20th Century Fox in 2020 – rebranding as the now anachronistic 20th Century Studios – perhaps in the hope of cleansing itself of Murdoch's sticking mud. It would take another two years before Fox Studios in Sydney was renamed, when a new Labor federal arts minister announced with extraordinarily little fanfare that it would host a tenth film in the *Planet of the Apes* series (has anyone actually noticed it's now Disney Studios?).

For fans of old and new Hollywood alike it was a downgrade. Disney was no longer interested in the sorts of independent, non-franchise films 20th Century Fox once made. The studio might have abandoned tending to the history of cinema for the sake of preserving film culture, but they were active in returning to the old ways of producing to cut costs and better control their product. Sound stages were preferred over location shoots. What was 'green screen' if not a modern form of rear projection? Looking across the filmography of someone like Chris Hemsworth, it is no stretch to suggest that Marvel have reanimated the long-dead 'star system'. Hemsworth has been a devoted contract player, appearing in nine Marvel films as Thor at the time of writing.

WESTWARD EXPANSION

Errol Flynn once wrote a note to Hollywood gossip columnist Hedda Hopper, stating firmly that he would never appear as 'Superman, Flash Gordon, Popeye, or Mamaduke the Magician [sic – he meant Mandrake, but who was Flynn to pay attention to detail?]'. In reality, if Jack Warner had deemed it so any time after 1935, he too would have had to don a cape.[2]

Like his antecedent Flynn, Hemsworth debuted in Hollywood at the age of 26, without having had much to do with the Australian film industry. Unlike Flynn, Hemsworth was known as an Australian from the outset and would pose a threat for being so. The leading light of 80s and 90s erotic thrillers and son of Hollywood royalty Michael Douglas complained that there was something wrong with the younger generation of American actors and that Australians had what they were lacking, namely masculinity. Douglas believed that Hollywood's problem was this 'relatively asexual … area' but Douglas was on the speaking circuit because he too had just been sucked into the vortex of the Marvel universe and did not seem to notice that in Marvel's world, as one powerful essay put it, 'Everyone is beautiful and no one is horny'.[3] Paul Verhoeven and Pedro Almodóvar – two of the most important filmmakers to nurture eroticism on screen – would come out and condemn the Marvel films as 'sexless'. Almodóvar was blunt in calling the series 'neutered'.

Yet Hemsworth and Hollywood wanted to send us back to a time when this wasn't the case. Graduating straight from the schools of *Neighbours* and *Home & Away* to a spot in JJ Abrams' glossy blockbuster reboot of *Star Trek* (2009), as Captain Kirk's doomed father, Hemsworth was to have been introduced in a lead role in the unasked-for remake of the Reagan era-defining *Red Dawn* (1984). The new *Red Dawn* (2012) was originally scheduled for a September 2010 release but was shelved for two years. The original film, written and directed by John Milius, centred on a group of teenagers, in their modest Colorado town, fighting off Russian, Cuban and Nicaraguan invaders. It was one of the great right-wing fantasias of the 1980s. The remake had been pulled from its release date by its studio MGM, because this new *Red Dawn* was to focus on China as the invading nation state. The financially struggling studio backed out after bad press. The invading nation was recast as North Korea.

Australia, of course, had its own bookish version of *Red Dawn* in *Tomorrow, When the War Began*, a popular young adult series, as nativist as anything in Milius's work. The first book in the series was made into a feature film in the same year that the *Red Dawn* remake was due in cinemas. It would be easy to imagine Hemsworth in the cast's line-up, had he not been signed on to its American equivalent. Hemsworth's absence only served as another reminder that, as a symbol of the new star order, with its ever-porous borders, he never made a film in Australia before his steep American ascent. The other big-name Australian star of this unwieldy new era, Margot Robbie, had at least made a couple of micro-budget throwaways before landing in Scorsese's *The Wolf of Wall Street* (2013) and being subsumed into the DC comic adaptations – for three chaotic films as Joker's gangster girlfriend Harley Quinn – competing with Marvel and Hemsworth for superheroic supremacy.

As the 100th anniversary of the Royal Commission on the Moving Picture Industry in Australia fast approaches, the careers of Hemsworth and Robbie only serve as reminders of how little has changed for both the trade and its players. The concerns aired within the report – that Australia wouldn't be

WESTWARD EXPANSION

able to afford to entice expatriates to return home to support the industry – have largely held true a century later.

And yet Hemsworth partly turned this equation on its head, at least returning to Australia to live on a permanent basis. He settled on the country's easternmost point, Byron Bay, building a sprawling mansion – which vocal locals derided as an eyesore looking like a shopping mall, a car park or a regional airport – as a space where he would host Hollywood mates. Hemsworth would use his power to pull not only his Hollywood friendship circle into his personal orbit, but Hollywood itself – insisting productions shoot in Australia or face his withdrawal. He was explicit about this being the case in an interview with the *Sydney Morning Herald*, telling them that the 'last three or four films I've done were supposed to shoot in Atlanta or the UK' and that he told producers, 'I'm not doing it unless it shoots here.'[4]

Despite Hemsworth's success in securing such concessions – a seeming win for Australia over Hollywood – he wasn't particularly interested in telling stories about Australia. He was, however, very visibly public in pushing the government for more investment. Political interventionism in Australian cinema remains a necessity. Hemsworth was on call for stage-managed photoshoots with Australian neo- and hard conservative leaders – call them the T(h)ories – announcing unprecedented levels of subsidies to major Hollywood productions, which Hemsworth's blockbuster productions benefit from, often over smaller independent productions or, indeed, other art forms. In the same year that the Australia Council for the Arts was brutally gutted of $104.7 million by the chaotic Tony Abbott government, $47.25 million was directed to underwrite the making of *Thor 3* and *Alien 5*. The

Abbott government proudly trumpeted that the investment would 'bring more than $300m AUD in offshore investment to Australia's economy [and] provide over 3000 jobs'. Never mind, however, that the wages for many of those jobs had stagnated for ten years, with union officials accusing the Hollywood producers of 'double dipping' by negotiating low wages after tax concessions from the government were already agreed to.*

In 2017, then foreign minister Julie Bishop was grilled at a Senate Committee hearing over $1.2 million in expenses, with a particular focus on her attendance at the premiere of *Thor 3*. The ministerial code of conduct was called into question, particularly the edict to 'refrain from wasteful and extravagant spend of public money'. The Attorney-General stepped in to defend the minister, suggesting:

---

* Hemsworth would be back at it during the height of the pandemic in 2021. In announcing the funding for the *Mad Max: Fury Road* prequel *Furiosa*, Hemsworth stood alongside conservatives from both the state and federal governments, including a candid selfie with the NSW Premier Gladys Berejiklian taken in the back of a golf buggy as they whisked through the Fox Studios lot. Berejiklian announced that *Furiosa* was 'expected to support more than 850 local jobs and bring in around $350 million into the NSW economy'. She would be gone from office six months later, under investigation by the state's Independent Commission Against Corruption to determine whether she had encouraged the corrupt behaviour of her former partner. *Furiosa*, meanwhile, will be Hemsworth's first film that could reasonably be designated 'Australian', and yet, tellingly, is part of another proven franchise, this one with a nearly 50-year history. It's hard to blame him for taking sure bets. Hemsworth's most complex and original film is almost certainly Michael Mann's forward-thinking global tech thriller *Blackhat* (2015), which made just $4 million on opening weekend against its $70 million budget and, in doing so, became one of the most notable box office bombs of the 2010s.

It may be the case that she attended this particular event in the role she assumed as foreign minister in advocating for Australia's interests including … the promotion, particularly in the United States, of the Australian cinema and film industry.[5]

It was true that executives of Marvel and Disney were at the event and Bishop may well have made a beeline for them, but it was extremely difficult to imagine her pleading a case for 'Australian cinema', unless Thor and his Norse mythology were now, by proxy, considered foundational folklore of the Australian state.

Bishop was, above all, in the Hemsworth business – Australian stars had taken priority over the promotion of cinema itself. Consorting with Bishop, Hemsworth had become the voice of Tourism Australia, working a busy room in New York with her to try and sell the country. The pair were attempting to revive Paul Hogan's 'Come and Say G'day' campaign (Hemsworth had bought Hogan's Malibu home from the comedian in 2013). The *New York Times*, however, suggested that Hemsworth 'had come to bury that campaign, not to praise it'. Hemsworth called it a 'hangover' (he would, however, happily go on to appear in the 2018 Tourism Australia prank, *Dundee: The Son of a Legend Returns Home*).[6]

It was easy to imagine Hemsworth calling the Australian film industry a 'hangover' in need of curing too. Was the reason Hemsworth had never appeared in a film that told a uniquely Australian story because he was embarrassed by the tired conditions of his home country's cinema? He would not have been alone. Australians themselves were often reported to be aghast at the quality of the movies produced in their own country. Common complaints included that the films themselves were dark, depressing and substandard. Familiar headlines asked, 'What's Wrong with Australian Cinema?' and 'Why Won't We Watch Australian Films?' throughout the 2010s.[7] When the actor Josh Lawson – who had played a Rupert Murdoch spoof in *Anchorman 2* (2013) and Murdoch's actual son James in *Bombshell* (2019) – was out hyping his directorial debut, he told audiences to see his film because, like them, he 'doesn't like Australian films'.*

The attempts at self-diagnosis – more chronic than any underlying malady – were nothing new. In his speech announcing his ambitious Creative Nation policy in 1994, in which he revealed his government's agreement with 20th Century Fox to 'establish a movie studio in Australia to produce major international feature-length films', Keating outlined the tug-of-war that had occurred throughout Australia's waning 20th century:

> These arguments run right through our history in this century. At the extremes it was 'evening dress and the opera' versus the 'wattle and bottle'. Anglophilia and

---

* When Hemsworth did, finally, shoot in Australia, playing an Australian (himself), it was for a six-part National Geographic documentary series – *Limitless* (2022) – produced for the Disney+ streaming service, which detailed his quest for longevity through health. It was an extension of his desire for us to be able to attain his supposedly attainable body through Centr, a fitness training app he launched in 2019. The app's daily workout routines also came with meal plans and guided meditations. When Jane Fonda's *Workout* became the highest selling VHS of all time, she used its success to fund her political advocacy, funnelling all profits into her Campaign for Economic Democracy, a New Left organisation designed to promote environmental causes, labour rights and rent control. I downloaded the Centr app, and did a single day of workout, but couldn't go on because it made walking the next day nearly impossible. It did, however, make me think of Hemsworth's politics: was he *Centr*-left or *Centr*-right?

WESTWARD EXPANSION

Anglophobia. The debate tended to lurch between the cultural cringe and cultural swagger ... the two extremes don't make much sense.[8]

Keating was directly referencing AA Phillips' ubiquitous essay on the 'Cultural Cringe', first published in 1950. Keating was strategically positioning the Cringe as the likely outcome of John Howard's election as prime minister. It was a warning to the country that Howard would set a path, just as Doc Brown does for Marty McFly in *Back to the Future*, to send them hurtling back to the 1950s. It was no mistake that this was the exact era in which Australia had no cinema, denied opportunities for both creative self-expression and historical documentation through film. To Howard, the 1950s were a 'Golden Age'; to Keating, a 'Nothingland'. Australians voted for a return to the Cringe.

As perhaps foreseen by Keating, the transition from the Hawke–Keating government to that of Howard would see a significant drop in the performance of Australian films at the domestic box office. The average share of Australian films in a count of ticket sales nationally was 8.6 per cent from 1983 to 1995. (Under Hawke, the first two *Crocodile Dundee* movies helped Australian films account for almost a quarter of the local box office in their years of release; Keating had helpful boosts due to the confident storytelling of *Muriel's Wedding*, *Strictly Ballroom* and *The Adventures of Priscilla, Queen of the Desert*). During Howard's tenure, however, the average almost halved to 4.75 per cent and reached a post–New Wave nadir of 1.3 per cent in 2004. For all the nationalistic rhetoric of conservative politicians, their jingoism would appear to drive away audiences, and a lack of committed investment resulted in underwhelming product.

271

The push for Australia to become a republic was a chance to wrest the nation free from the likes of Howard and Menzies. Baz Luhrmann's lust for such independence surely signified his own desire for greater national confidence. In the exact same month that cameras started rolling on *Moulin Rouge!* – November 1999 – the director placed an editorial piece with the Fairfax newspapers, to be published on the eve of the referendum vote for Australia to become a republic. Luhrmann was making his impassioned case for the 'Yes' vote and, naively, he was advocating for the presidential role to sit 'above party politics':

> To my mind, a president should be like the artistic director of a theatre company, with the prime minister as a general-manager figure, attending to day-to-day business and leaving the artistic director free to synthesise the vision of the company into articulate and practical sense. Good artistic directors, in my experience, know more than the play, its author, and who the actors should be and where they should be standing.[9]

The specificity of Luhrmann's artistic director analogy made his opinion piece read, in part, like a cover letter. Did Luhrmann see himself graduating from Keating's make-up man to 'leading man' status himself? It would be no surprise, as self-interest abounded in the leadership of the pro-republic vote. The movement's proxy head Malcolm Turnbull would, after all, go on to become prime minister in 2015, rolling Australia's chief monarchist Tony Abbott. America, however, had proved Luhrmann's thesis wrong. It wasn't artistic directors or general managers who went on to become presidents in nascent republics. It was actors. The ones to lead the country were

WESTWARD EXPANSION

Ronald Reagan and the Donald Trump of *Home Alone 2: Lost in New York* (1992) – whose parade of cameos as 'himself' were performances nonetheless, auditions for his eventual rise. The retail side of politics came easily to them – they were trained to sell slogans, aiming to convert those into attendance (whether at the box office or the voting booth).*

DESPITE A CENTURY OF TIDES BOTH HIGH AND LOW, THE state of the industry looked much stronger than what had come before. Production in the country was now of a size that Sydney alone could not house it. The Queensland state government had strategically invested in studios themselves, overtaking Sydney as the biggest landlords of cinema productions in the country. Luhrmann saw the future in the Gold Coast, producing *Elvis* from start to finish in a city he would call home for two years.[10] Russell Crowe wanted in on the action too. In 2021, he announced plans to open a studio complex in Coffs Harbour, designating the site of a luxury resort for the $400 million development; according to one journalist this, like the Gold Coast, was 'another town built, LA-like, around a highway'. A recent report suggested the resort would stay open, allowing cast and crew to use it as lodgings, and that the ambitious plans for the site included a 'branch of the national film school and office' and a

---

* Baz Luhrmann's first true leading man, Paul Mercurio, who in *Strictly Ballroom* played a character named Scott Hastings, won the *seat* of Hastings in the 2022 State Election of Victoria. Hastings out on the hustings for Hastings, proved that as Australia made small moves towards a second referendum on a republic – sequelised – more than 20 years after the last, it seemed just as likely that we would end up with a President Hemsworth as a President Baz.

film museum (would Crowe try to buy back some of his memorabilia sold at Sotheby's for the collection?).[11]

In the same year as Crowe's announcement it was revealed that a new film studio would be built in Penrith in Sydney's west, with an aim to open ten sound stages on the 96-acre (39-hectare) site. The team behind the development suggested it was a direct response to Marvel productions constantly taking up the Disney Studio lot in the city. Indeed, Luhrmann was only working on the Gold Coast because his former home city was all booked out. It was an industrial competition worthy of its own war movie.

The filmmakers behind *Here Out West* were not in need of a Hollywood-sized studio hangar to accommodate their shoot. The film's modest scale meant that it could be released a year after it wrapped, securing the coveted opening-night spot at the Sydney Film Festival. The film's publicity was engaged in the questions of locality it seemed designed to garner. The Sydney-based cultural journalist Jared Richards, on seeing the finished film, reflected on the 'opening overhead shots of the interweaving highways – an image that equates Western Sydney's multiplicious nature to that of Los Angeles, whose highways have been ingrained in cinema as a signifier of sprawl'.[12]

The psychic gangway, at last, had a concrete foundation in my mind. Had a version of Los Angeles long been sneakily embedded inside Sydney's broad boundaries, unnoticed because of its lack of representation on screen? For the majority of my career working in the arts, it seemed as if Western Sydney had been artistically outperforming the rest of Sydney, in literature in particular. A 2018 report into the state of the arts in Western Sydney, presented to the NSW government, found that despite the fact that film had 'been identified in consultation sessions as a particular strength of the Western Sydney arts and cultural landscape' there was a distinct lack of infrastructure to support filmmaking and exhibition in Western Sydney.[13] The expensive nature of producing film meant that it was off limits for many young, aspiring artists.

The enthusiastic response to *Here Out West* proved what was possible if the right level of resources were handed over. Talent could be retained. The high-energy Arka Das – who both co-wrote and acted in the film – came to the project with his own Hollywood credentials, having already appeared in Disney's live-action remake *Mulan* (2020), which had filmed in New Zealand and China. Das would return to work with Disney for Taika Waititi's terminally unfunny *Thor 4* – eventually released in cinemas with the bombastic, plastic subtitle *Love and Thunder* – as the 'Sycophant God'. The role, perhaps, promised to be bigger than it actually was. A week after the film was released in cinemas the young actor tweeted, 'Apparently I made it into #ThorLoveandThunder! About to find out for myself lol'. Das did make the final cut but only as a featured extra. He was visible to those familiar with him in the background of a scene where a gilded Russell Crowe as Zeus faces off with a digitally denuded Hemsworth as Thor. If Das had once recorded lines of dialogue for Marvel they had been left on the cutting-room floor.

It was a shame because Das, as an actor and writer, possesses just as much organic charm as the young Chris Hemsworth. Yet the billing and opportunities would not be equal. In 2019, the *New York Times* reporter Isabella Kwai profiled the Asian-Australian cast of the global box office hit *Crazy Rich Asians*, discussing the fact that they had to leave home to find opportunities overseas. Kwai met some of the castmates for 'beers and cigarettes' on a Melbourne rooftop bar to vent about the industry. Chris Pang, the tall supporting actor in the film, mapped out his trajectory from voice-over work for a dub of a Jackie Chan film to being overlooked for opportunities in Australia, after debuting in *Tomorrow, When the War Began*. Like so many before him, a move to Los Angeles was credited with a reversal in his career's fortunes.[14]

Debbie Zhou, writing in the *Guardian*, pointedly expanded on Kwai's reporting, highlighting Australia's possessiveness over its white talent – often deploying 'our' to denote a patriotic ownership – countered by a distinct and noticeable lack of corresponding pride when it came to actors of colour:

> So why *doesn't* the media want to celebrate these actors' Australianness? The media regularly, proudly crowns 'our' Cate, 'our' Baz and 'our' Nicole (who, for the record, was born in Hawaii). Is it another symptom of our under-resourced outlets? Is it because their audiences tend not to identify non-white immigrant Australians as our 'own'? Or is it the fault of primarily white media institutions that overlook them, consciously or otherwise?[15]

Zhou was damning of a media who failed to take note of the particular talents of Geraldine Viswanathan, who had appeared alongside Arka Das in a short film directed by Catherine Kelleher in 2015, before breaking through in the unexpectedly incisive teenage 'raunch' film *Blockers* (2018) and taking down Hugh Jackman's smarmy school superintendent in *Bad Education* (2019). Like Das, Viswanathan runs the electric current that powers a 'star' with great ease and Zhou was quick to point out that in the face of Viswanathan's snub from

WESTWARD EXPANSION

mainstream media, it was regional newspapers that stepped in to cover her success story. For the steel city of Newcastle, Viswanathan was a hometown success story, having attended the Hunter School of Performing Arts (another unexpectedly close-to-home Hollywood connection for me as well – my sister had briefly attended the same school and I had forgotten until recently that I had successfully auditioned for the school too, though I declined the offer, choosing to stick with the mostly unambitious Gorokan High).

Hyper-locality was one pathway for the future of Australian cinema. After the experience of *Here Out West*, Bina decided to go deeper into the specificities of the western suburbs, writing her own full-length film set in Campbelltown, in the city's south-west, to be called *From All Sides*. Given the film's story would, in part, focus on male bisexuality, a topic underrepresented on screen and without many precedents, I recommended she watch *Sunday Bloody Sunday* for Peter Finch's sensitive performance. She finished her original screenplay in record time and decided to forge ahead with the project. The fact that some said the 'project was too ambitious to get up off the ground as a first feature' – particularly without a white producer attached, something Bina absolutely refused – only seemed to add to her drive. I could feel echoes of Brian Syron's frustrations with the country's funding bodies' lack of foresight when the usual suspects of risk-averse governmental sources were approached and, despite the unique nature of the project, declined to offer their support. Like Syron, Bina decided to move ahead without the funding bodies, putting her own money into the project, in the hope of eventually receiving post-production funding. The story of Australian cinema has always been one about who exactly gets to make movies. Would history repeat itself and Australia extinguish another attempt to broaden the scope of what is allowed on screen?

Shooting over four weeks in November and December 2022, at a time when Covid-19 restrictions had significantly eased, I could walk freely onto Bina's own film set and see the work in progress for myself. Wanting to contribute somehow, I offered to cook and deliver catering every Thursday. Never having made food for more than 30 before, it was trial and error with mass quantities of potato salad, grilled vegetables and buffalo chicken wings. On a Wednesday night, before I was due to take my catering into the film set, I received a message from Bina: 'We gots no white ppl'. She needed extras for a scene in which her main character is surrounded in an office in Fairfield by well-meaning consultants from an employment agency. I was asked to step in and play 'Paul', a neo-conservative social welfare fixer, a figure known to many people who have been out of work. I had little preparation, although I knew men like Paul, and had had to answer to their checks in exchange for welfare in my twenties.

Playing Paul made me a featured extra – no lines of dialogue but I would be prominent in the background and visible in the finished film. I was given my own 'mark' – an X on the ground where I was supposed to stand – on which I fixed my feet, nodding in silent, conspiratorial agreement, while a fast-talking actor from *Neighbours* recited one of Bina's wordy monologues over and over again in front of me. In that moment, I could feel myself transform into a subject of my own writing about film.

Towards the end of the afternoon, I was asked to stand back on my mark to film a series of close-ups to be used for potential reaction shots. Staring directly into a film camera myself for the first time I was shocked by the black void. The

WESTWARD EXPANSION

lens was a porthole looking out into the dead of space. It was easy to be intimidated. Such small yet imposing machines had captured the 100 years or so of cinema I had been busy watching. They had captured lives and history through miracle manoeuvres.

In the office boardroom, under artificial light, which magically turned late afternoon to mid-morning, there was no sense of anyone else staring back at me, no sense of history to the proceedings. The camera forces you to be in the moment and in the moment alone. I had spent years by now thinking about actors and their abilities to shape cultural and national identity, but had not given quite so much thought as to whether they themselves were aware of this subject position. Was it possible for an actor to think as they worked a scene, when their job is to inhabit someone else, about what they might soon be projecting to a nation and a world at large? That actors are both active and passive in the filmmaking process, lending their talents to the service of writers' and directors' visions, might recuse them from this bigger picture thinking. Yet, through sheer public ubiquity and the amounts of capital they can amass at an elite level, they can find themselves closer to centres of power than any other artist.

For me – standing there as 'Paul', acting as an invented representative of Australia's corrupt white-collar class – there was the camera and its unnerving void. Behind the machine was that which it was making and would one day be projected: the 'shared fantasy', the 'common illusion', a new collective memory, a screening of both what had been and what was yet to come.

ACKNOWLEDGMENTS

First and foremost, thank you Jida Gulpilil for reading the chapter on your father. Your response to what I had written was incredibly generous. I hope that writing about your father and his important work continues on – through many stories – for a long time to come, and that my small contribution has properly paid respect to his powerful legacy.

Thank you to my nan, Dot Twyford, who kindly passed on a copy of Brian Syron's *Kicking Down the Doors* to the Syron members of our extended family, providing a meaningful personal remembrance. Hopefully, this book will direct readers to Brian Syron's monumental film history and his debut feature, *Jindalee Lady*, and point to the potential for a revival of both.

Thank you also to my parents for tracking down a VHS tape, feared lost, so that I could properly quote our home movie. What a relief the footage survived the floodwaters.

This book had its origins in walking down to see 'The Art of Divorce' – Russell Crowe's Sotheby's auction – in 2018 at Carriageworks, where my grandfather once worked as a rail yard apprentice. Alan Vaarwerk responded to a tweet I sent asking if anyone would let me write about the collection on display. The piece was eventually published in that sharp little

ACKNOWLEDGMENTS

journal *Kill Your Darlings* under Alan's careful eye. Thank you, Alan.

Thank you too to Sarah Farquharson at *The Monthly* who published an extract about Gulpilil as documented in *Walkabout to Hollywood*, which helped strengthen some of my thinking in relation to this project. Sarah has indulged me in writing about many cultural curios since and it has always been an immense pleasure. Valerie Ng and Debbie Zhou similarly published out-of-the-box longform profiles of Hugh Jackman and Matthew McConaughey in their film journal *Rough Cut*, which again helped push me along and get this book across the line.

Parts of each of these previously published pieces reappear here in newly adapted forms, and I thank each of their original editors for their work on them and express a sincere hope that spaces for cultural journalism continue to thrive in Australia to allow writers to test the durability of ideas.

When it came time to see if the idea driving these pieces could really go the distance of a book, *Cast Mates* found its ideal publisher in Harriet McInerney. It has been a pleasure to work with Harriet at the start of her publishing career, and I look forward to reading many brilliant books she publishes in the years to come. The incisive, close copy-edit the book received was by Jocelyn Hungerford. Paul O'Beirne skillfully shepherded the project in its final stages. Given all were involved with my last book, working with the combination of Harriet, Jocelyn and Paul felt like getting the old team back together in a heist movie montage for just one more 'job'. I couldn't have asked for a better crew – including everyone behind the scenes at NewSouth, who continue to lead the way in supporting nonfiction writing.

New to this NewSouth line up is Katherine Rajwar, who I'm proud to count as a friend, and who has brought so many terrific ideas about how to get this book into the hands of its ideal readers.

The book's brilliant cover design was by Reg Abos. The cover image is of the Palais Theatre, which stands as an iconic music venue in Melbourne today, but with a hidden history as a 'picture palace' in the 1910s, started by three brothers from Spokane, Washington, and so is a perfect emblem of the contents of this book. Thank you to Reg for bringing this history to life.

The writing and research of this book was supported by a Create NSW grant. The core research was conducted in the early years of Covid-19 when libraries and archives were locked down due to the pandemic. When they finally reopened, I discovered how impossible it had been to make any headway without them. My sincere thank you to the staff of the State Library of NSW, the National Library of Australia (NLA) and the National Film and Sound Archive (NFSA) in both Canberra and Sydney. Special thanks to Simon Drake at the NFSA's Pyrmont office for his enthusiastic assistance in helping me navigate and access the collection.

So much detail in this book wouldn't have been uncovered without the genius digital architecture of the NLA's Trove archive – like many writers and researchers, I was happy to see the federal government commit to its future funding, right as this book went to print. I hope funding for all the institutions I visited remains secure and prosperous.

Thank you to my friends, particularly Toby Hemmings for sharing his impassioned thoughts on Nicole Kidman – his thoughts on her 'high camp' are quoted within her chapter – and to Bina Bhattacharya for doing the same. Bina also gave

ACKNOWLEDGMENTS

the book its dramatic and most satisfying conclusion, giving me a taste of the nerve needed to be an actor.

Going to the cinema alone is an underrated pleasure, but if I had to have someone sitting beside me, I am glad it was you, Bridie. Thank you for sharing my enthusiasm for letting the big screen take up so much room in our life together.

NOTES

Abbreviations

LAT = Los Angeles Times
NYT = New York Times
SMH = Sydney Morning Herald
DT = Daily Telegraph

Prologue: Sydney to Los Angeles and back again

1   J. Hoberman, *The Dream Life*, The New Press, 2003, p. xvii.
2   Monica Tan, 'Russell Crowe claims twice denied Australian citizenship', the *Guardian*, 25 March 2015.
3   *Age* staff, 'The Fall of a Film', *The Age*, 19 February 2005 and Sharon Waxman, 'The Unravelling of 'Eucalyptus'', *NYT*, 23 February 2005.
4   Jocelyn Moorhouse, *Unconditional Love*, Text Publishing, 2019, p. 231.
5   The Formosa was earmarked for demolition in 1991 to make way for a parking lot to be named after Warner Bros but the restaurant was saved by LA history advocates, including *L.A. Confidential* director Curtis Hanson, who was on the advisory council for the Los Angeles Conservancy group. This detail is in Martin Howden, *Russell Crowe: The Biography*, Wilkinson Publishing, 2010.
6   J. Hoberman, '"A Bright, Guilty World": Daylight Ghosts and Sunshine Noir', *Artforum*, February 2007.
7   Clive James, *Flying Visits*, Jonathan Cape, 1984, p. 82.
8   Delia Falconer, *Sydney*, NewSouth Publishing, 2010, pp. 3–5.
9   The other two cities were, inexplicably, Miami and Honolulu (what did they do to him?). The great novelist would find more to like in San Francisco: 'fascinating, beautiful, peaceful'. Words most Australians wouldn't associate with Los Angeles. This detail is in David Marr, *Patrick White: A Life*, Vintage, 1991, p. 183.
10   Helen Garner, 'Hit Me', *The Monthly*, October 2005.
11   Jack Marx, 'I Was Russell Crowe's Stooge', *SMH*, 7 June 2006.

NOTES

12   Diane Collins, *Hollywood Down Under: Australians at the Movies 1896 to the Present Day*, Angus and Robertson, 1987.

1   The Perfect Specimen: Errol Flynn

1   Ross Melnick, *Hollywood's Embassies: How Movie Theaters Projected American Power Around the World*, Columbia University Press, 2022, p. 93.

2   Truman Capote, *Music for Chameleons*, New American Library, 1980, p. 234.

3   David Niven, *Bring on the Empty Horses*, Hamish Hamilton, 1975, p. 112.

4   James Wolcott, 'In Like Flynn', *New York Review of Books*, 15 May 1980.

5   Robert de Young, 'Errol Flynn: A Life at Sea', *Senses of Cinema*, Issue 65, November 2012.

6   Ian Hancock, *John Gorton: He Did It His Way*, Hodder, 2002.

7   The accounting for films Flynn watched is from John Hammond Moore's *The Young Errol Before Hollywood*, Trafford Publishing, 2011. One of the films Flynn saw in Hobart – *Dick Turpin* – co-starred the hearty Alan Hale, who would later become Flynn's frequent onscreen side-kick, most famously as Little John in *The Adventures of Robin Hood*. The pair co-starred in 13 films together, and one has to wonder if, when they first met, Flynn mentioned to Hale he had seen him on screen in *Dick Turpin* on the other side of the world.

8   Earl Conrad, *Errol Flynn: A Memoir*, Dodd, Mead & Company, 1978, p. 31.

9   Don Whitington, 'Errol Flynn – Adventurer', *SMH*, 31 March 1936.

10   Hays quoted as an epigraph in Erich Schwartzel's *Red Carpet: Hollywood, China and the Global Battle for Cultural Supremacy*, Penguin, 2022.

11   Graham Shirley and Brian Adams, *Australian Cinema, The First Eighty Years*, Currency Press, 1989, p. 77.

12   Jill Julius Matthews, *Dance Hall & Picture Palace: Sydney's Romance with Modernity*, Currency Press, 2005, p. 232.

13   *Report of the Royal Commission on the Moving Picture Industry in Australia*, Government Printer, 1928.

14   *Mercury* staff, 'A Visit to Hollywood: Tasmanian's Success', the *Mercury*, 4 May 1935.

15   Stuart Cunningham, *Featuring Australia: The Cinema of Charles Chauvel*, Allen & Unwin, 1991, p. 19.

16   Susanne Chauvel Carlsson, *Charles and Elsa Chauvel: Movie Pioneers*, University of Queensland Press, 2003. On Chauvel and Flynn see also: Elsa Chauvel, *My Life with Charles Chauvel*, Arcadia edition, 2019.

17   John Tulloch, *Legends on the Screen: The Narrative Film in Australia 1919–1929*, Currency Press, 1981, p. 271.

18   Lloyd Pantages, 'I Cover Hollywood', the *San Francisco Examiner*, 22 December 1934.

19   Alan K Rode, *Michael Curtiz: A Life in Film*, University Press of Kentucky, 2017.

20 Manny Farber, *Farber on Film: The Complete Film Writings of Manny Farber*, the Library of America, 2009, p. 700.

21 Isaac Butler, *The Method: How the Twentieth Century Learned to Act*, Bloomsbury, 2022, p. 198.

22 Bryony Cosgrove, 'The Stuff of Silent Legend', *SMH*, 3 March 2012.

23 Thomas Schatz, *The Genius of the System: Hollywood Filmmaking in the Studio Era*, Pantheon, 1988, p. 302.

24 Errol Flynn, *My Wicked, Wicked Ways*, Aurum Press, 2005, p. 290.

25 Read Kendall, 'Around and About Hollywood', *LAT*, 24 November 1934.

26 *SMH* staff, 'Now A Hollywood Star', *SMH*, 13 September 1938.

27 Rosalind Shaffer, 'Meet Merle Oberon, Film Find of the Year', *Chicago Tribune*, 31 March 1935.

28 Nicholas Shakespeare, *In Tasmania*, The Overlook Press, 2006, p. 297.

29 Grace Wilcox, 'The Meaning of "Glamour"', *Detroit Free Press*, 19 May 1935.

30 Maree Delofski (dir.), *The Trouble with Merle*, 2002.

31 Bette Davis with Michael Herskowitz, *This 'N That*, G. P. Putnam's Sons, 1987, p. 198.

32 Jennifer Schuessler, 'The Long Battle Over "Gone with the Wind"', *NYT*, 14 June 2020.

33 Alan K Rode, *Michael Curtiz: A Life in Film*, University Press of Kentucky, 2017, p. 277.

34 Bosley Crowther, 'The Screen', *NYT*, 21 December 1940.

35 Stephen Vaughn, *Ronald Reagan in Hollywood: Movies and Politics*, Cambridge University Press, 1994.

36 George Frazier, *The One with the Moustache Is Costello*, Random House, 1947, pp. 153–154.

37 Tony Thomas, *The Spy Who Never Was*, A Citadel Press Book, 1990, pp. 137–138.

38 David Thomson, *Warner Bros: The Making of an American Movie Studio*, Yale University Press, 2017, p. 150.

39 Raoul Walsh, *Each Man in His Time*, Farrar, Straus and Giroux, 1974, p. 317.

40 *LAT* staff, 'Jury Frees Errol Flynn in Girls Case', *LAT*, 7 February 1943.

41 *Daily Telegraph* staff, 'Errol Flynn Not Guilty of Rape', *Daily Telegraph*, 8 February 1943.

42 Patricia O'Brien, 'Wild Colonial Boy: Errol Flynn's Rape Trial, Pacific Pasts and the Making of Hollywood', *Australian Historical Studies*, vol. 52, no. 4, 2021.

43 *LAT* staff, 'Anzacs Mass Forces for War Relief', *LAT*, 22 January 1941.

44 Desley Deacon, *Judith Anderson*, Kerr Publishing, 2019, p. 153.

45 Sheilah Graham, 'In Hollywood', *Chattanooga Daily Times*, 30 September 1939.

46 David Burke, 'Alfred Hitchcock Has Found It ... A Better Use for the Gap', *SMH*, 8 May 1960.

NOTES

47 Art Buchwald, 'The Great Feud of Mr Hemingway and Mr Zanuck', *LAT*, 29 November 1957.

48 Jeffrey Meyers, *Inherited Risk: Errol and Sean Flynn in Hollywood and Vietnam*, Simon & Schuster, 2002, p. 263.

49 Errol Flynn (edited by Tony Thomas), *From a Life of Adventure: The Writings of Errol Flynn*, Citadel Press, 1980.

50 Eric Hoyt, 'Hollywood and the Income Tax, 1929–1955', *Film History*, vol. 22, no. 1, 2010, pp. 5–21.

51 Frank Clune, 'The Debunking of Errol Flynn', the *Bulletin*, 13 April 1938.

52 Nora Eddington Flynn Haymes with Cy Rice, *Errol and Me*, Signet, 1960.

53 Charles Higham, *Errol Flynn: The Untold Story*, Granada Publishing, 1980. Higham's fictitious nonfiction about Flynn at least held value as fiction, provably so when the Flynn-as-Nazi-spy gambit became a gripping plot in *The Rocketeer* (1991), in which Timothy Dalton plays a scheming, Nazified version of Flynn, chasing down technology, which could win the war. The filmmakers went so far as to recreate the set of *The Adventures of Robin Hood* to get their point across.

54 *SMH* staff, 'Errol Flynn Honour Goes to The Dogs', *SMH*, 16 June 2003.

2 The Forgotten Elite: Peter Finch

1 Trader Faulkner, *Peter Finch: A Biography*, Angus & Robertson, 1979.

2 Hal Boyle, 'Life to Peter Finch is Phfft, Marvelous', *Associated Press*, 10 August 1968.

3 *ABC Weekly* staff, 'Peter Finch: Much Travelled Actor is ABC Contract Artist', *ABC Weekly*, 24 February 1940.

4 Elaine Dundy, *Finch, Bloody Finch*, Holt, Rinehart and Winston, 1980.

5 Ken G Hall, *Australian Film: The Inside Story*, Summit Books, 1980.

6 Ruth Park, *Fishing in the Styx*, Text Publishing, 2019, p. 67.

7 Bosley Crowther, 'The Screen: Four Films Have Premieres Here', *NYT*, 24 May 1951.

8 Garry O'Connor, *Darlings of the Gods: One Year in the Lives of Laurence Olivier and Vivien Leigh*, Hodder and Stoughton, 1984.

9 George Johnston, 'Stairway to Stardom', the *Sun-Herald*, 22 August 1954.

10 Garry Kinnane, *George Johnston: A Biography*, Nelson, 1986.

11 George Johnston, *Clean Straw for Nothing*, Collins, 1969, p. 163.

12 William Hall, 'Mel and Gillian, Together Again', *LAT*, 22 September 1985.

13 *Variety* staff, 'Train of Events', *Variety*, 31 December 1948.

14 Simon Callow, *Orson Welles: One Man Band*, Jonathan Cape, 2015, pp. 112–118.

15 David Thomson, *Rosebud: The Story of Orson Welles*, First Vintage Books Edition, 1997, p. 313.

16 Thomas Wiseman, 'Focus on Finch', *Evening Standard*, 30 November 1954.

17 Philip Ziegler, *Olivier*, MacLehose Press, 2013, p. 246.

18 Alan Strachan, *Dark Star: A Biography of Vivien Leigh*, Bloomsbury Academic, 2020, pp. 188–196.

19 Laurence Olivier, *Confessions of an Actor*, Coronet edition, 1983, pp. 168–179.

20 Bosley Crowther, 'The Screen in Review: "Elephant Walk" Opens at Astor Theatre', *NYT*, 22 April 1954.

21 Yolande Finch, *Finchy*, Wyndham Books, 1981.

22 François Truffaut, *Hitchcock*, Martin Secker & Warburg, 1968, p. 100.

23 Quentin Falk, *The Golden Gong: Fifty Years of the Rank Organisation, Its Films and Its Stars*, Columbus Books, 1987 p. 73.

24 Mary Blume, 'Peter Finch an Eloquent Underplayer', *LAT*, 19 March 1972.

25 Diane Cilento, *My Nine Lives*, Penguin, 2006, p. 238.

26 Errol Flynn, *My Wicked, Wicked Ways*, Aurum Press, 2005, p. 256.

27 Andrew Pike and Ross Cooper, *Australian Film 1900-1977*, Oxford University Press, 1990, p. 201.

28 Lon Jones, '"Kangaroo" Story Again Changed', the *Advertiser*, 21 October 1950.

29 *LAT* staff, 'Star System Finished, Says British Player', *LAT*, 13 August 1962.

30 Renata Adler, 'Screen: Legendary Star: Kim Novak and Finch in "Lylah Clare"', *NYT*, 23 August 1968.

31 Edwin T Arnold and Eugene L Miller (eds), *Robert Aldrich Interviews*, University Press of Mississippi, 2004, p. 76.

32 Kevin Thomas, 'Why "Madding Crowd" is Haunting Peter Finch', *LAT*, 19 October 1967.

33 Brian McFarlane, *An Autobiography of British Cinema*, Methuen, 1997.

34 William J Mann, *Edge of Midnight: The Life of John Schlesinger*, Billboard Books, 2015.

35 Nick Pinkerton, 'We Love This Dirty Town', *Bookforum*, March/April/May 2021.

36 Dave Itzkoff, *Mad as Hell: The Making of* Network *and The Fateful Vision of the Angriest Man in Movies*, Henry Holt and Company, 2014, p. 87.

37 Shaun Considine, *Mad as Hell: The Life and Work of Paddy Chayefsky*, Random House, 1994.

38 Nancy Buirski (dir.), *American Masters: By Sidney Lumet*, PBS, 2015.

39 Trader Faulkner, *Inside Trader*, Quartet, 2012.

3 The Right Stuff: David Gulpilil AM

1 Reg Cribb with David Gulpilil, *Tales Tall & True*, Currency Press, 2011.

2 Darlene Johnson (dir.), *Gulpilil: One Red Blood*, Jotz Productions, 2002.

3 Marcia Langton, 'Vale Dalaithngu, who charmed Australia and the world', *SMH*, 30 November 2021.

4 Lucienne Fontannaz, 'David Gulpilil and Maningrida school's class of 1967-68', *Art and Australia*, vol. 48, no. 4, December 2011.

5 *SMH* staff, '"*Walkabout*" Good for Tourism', *SMH*, 25 April 1971.

6 Mary Murphy, 'Aborigine Prefers Freedom to Stardom', *LAT*, 31 August 1971.

NOTES

7   Sylvia Lawson, 'The Sight of Green Galahs', *Nation: The Life of an Independent Journal of Opinion 1958–1972* (ed. K S Inglis), 1989, p. 113.

8   Ina Bertrand and Diane Collins, *Government and Film in Australia*, Currency Press, 1981.

9   Jenny Hocking, *Gough Whitlam: His Time*, The Miegunyah Press, 2013, p. 44.

10   Lenore Nicklin, 'Hot Reception for US Film Chief', *SMH*, 2 February 1973.

11   Mark Rozzo, *Everybody Thought We Were Crazy*, Ecco, 2022, p. 23.

12   Jake Wilson, 'What Happened to Billy?: David Gulpilil on *Mad Dog Morgan*', *Senses of Cinema*, July 2015.

13   Maryrose Casey and Liza-Mare Syron, 'The Challenges of Benevolence: the role of Indigenous Actors', *Journal of Australian Studies*, vol. 29, no. 85, 2005.

14   Peter Travers, 'A Few Nuggets Amongst the Clinkers', the *Daily Argus*, 25 February 1979.

15   Paul Hogan, *The Tap-Dancing Knife Thrower*, HarperCollins, 2020.

16   Roderick Mann, 'The Man from Down Under's on His Way Up', *LAT*, 20 September 1986.

17   Euny Hong, *The Birth of Korean Cool*, Simon & Schuster, 2014.

18   J. Hoberman, *Make My Day: Movie Culture in the Age of Reagan*, The New Press, 2019, p. 149.

19   Robert Hawke, 'Speech by the Prime Minister of Australia' at the Economic Club Luncheon, Chicago, 20 June 1988.

20   Andrew Main, 'Murphy Gives Croc the Axel', *SMH*, 9 December 1992.

21   Richard Eder, 'New Faces: A Guide to Fresh Talent in the City Now', *NYT*, 5 January 1979.

22   Tiriki Onus and Alec Morgan (dirs), *Ablaze*, Umbrella Entertainment, 2021.

23   Philippa Day Benson, 'Dreamtime in Connecticut', the *Australian Women's Weekly*, 4 September 1974.

24   Susan Taylor, 'Gulpilil Asks $1m for Sequel to *Dundee*', *SMH*, 7 June 1987.

25   Jake Wilson, 'What Happened to Billy?', 2015. See also the book, which inspired Wilson to track down Gulpilil: Jake Wilson, *Mad Dog Morgan*, Currency Press, 2015.

26   Rolf de Heer, 'A Toxic Mix', *Griffith Review*, May 2007.

27   Chips Mackinolty and Michael Duffy, *Guess Who's Coming to Dinner in Arnhem Land?*, Northern Land Council, 1987.

28   *SMH* staff, 'Kakadu: Hoges pays out $200 000', *SMH*, 13 September 1987.

29   Chris Seage, 'Dundee's done deal with the ATO', *Eureka Street*, 1 May 2012.

30   Simon Black, '"Mad as Hell" Actor Paul Hogan Compares Australian Tax Office to the Taliban', *DT*, 9 March 2011.

31   Richard Guilliatt, 'The Double Life of David Gulpilil', *SMH*, 7 December 2002.

32   Ronn Ronck, 'Walkabout Turns Into a Long Run', the *Honolulu Advertiser*, 30 January 1979.

CAST MATES

33 Don Riseborough, 'Gumpilil [sic] is a Star', *SMH*, 29 May 1971.

34 Brian Syron and briann kearney, *Kicking Down the Doors: A History of First Nation Films 1968–1993*, Lulu Inc., 2015.

35 Derek Rielly, *Gulpilil*, Pan Macmillan, 2019, p. 139.

36 Dr Gary Foley, 'Brian Syron – Forgotten Aboriginal Hero of Theatre', *Tracker Magazine*, July 2013.

37 Philippa Day Benson, 'Dreamtime in Connecticut', the *Australian Women's Weekly*, 4 September 1974.

38 *SMH* staff, 'First Lady of the US Theatre Arrives Soon', *SMH*, 24 May 1974.

39 David Stratton, *The Avocado Plantation: Boom and Bust in the Australian Film Industry*, Pan Macmillan, 1990, p. 12.

40 Tony Hewett, 'Australia Loses Film As Finance Is Refused', *SMH*, 21 March 1991.

41 Marc Horton, 'A Different View of Aboriginal Life', *Edmonton Journal*, 22 September 1992.

42 Rosalie Higson and Ashleigh Wilson, 'Gulpilil's Two Worlds Still a Painful Divide', the *Australian*, 4 May 2007.

43 Victoria Laurie, 'Indigenous talent "needs an agency"', the *Australian*, 26 January 2009.

44 Therese Davis, 'Darlene Johnson on Making Films in Arnhem Land', *Screening the Past*, 2011.

45 Stanley Kauffmann, 'Transmutations', *The New Republic*, 9 February 2004.

46 Robert Warshow, *The Immediate Experience*, Harvard University Press, 2002.

47 Susan King, 'Their Turf, Their Tongue', *LAT*, 19 July 2007.

4   The Interpreter: Nicole Kidman

1 Rachel Syme, 'The McConaissance', *The New Yorker*, 16 January 2014.

2 Matthew McConaughey, *Greenlights*, Headline Publishing Group, 2020, p. 80.

3 Tom Keneally, 'Nicole Kidman, From Down Under to "Far and Away"', *NYT*, 24 May 1992.

4 Tim Ewbank and Stafford Hildred, *Nicole Kidman: The Biography*, Headline Book Publishing, 2002, p. 49.

5 Ingo Petzke, *Phillip Noyce: Backroads to Hollywood*, Pan Macmillan, 2004, p. 123.

6 Dale Pollock, 'Hot Wheels: His Road to Success', *LAT*, 24 March 1982.

7 James Robert Douglas, *The Kennedy Miller Method: A Half-Century of Australian Screen Production*, Doctor of Philosophy thesis submitted to RMIT University, October 2019, p. 133.

8 Lucy Ellis and Bryony Sutherland, *Nicole Kidman: The Biography*, Aurum Press, 2002, p. 64.

9 Petzke, *Phillip Noyce*, pp. 22 and 36.

NOTES

10   Petzke, p. 149.

11   Kurt Anderson, 'Requiem for a Heavyweight', *TIME*, 6 September 1993.

12   Jacqueline Lee Lewes, 'Antennae', *SMH*, 16 October 1989.

13   Charles Fleming, *High Concept: Don Simpson and the Hollywood Culture of Excess*, Bloomsbury Publishing, 1998, pp. 142–143.

14   James Cockington (ed.), 'Today's People', *SMH*, 25 March 1991.

15   Anne Summers, 'Nicole Kidman's 1997 bombshell: "I wouldn't classify myself as a Scientologist, but my husband is"', *SMH*, 16 September 2016.

16   David Thomson, *Nicole Kidman*, Bloomsbury Publishing, 2006.

17   Andrew Main (ed.), 'Rear Window', *Australian Financial Review*, 14 February 1996.

18   *LAT* staff, 'Movies: Angry Aussies', *LAT*, 22 April 1997.

19   Alex Burns and Ben Eltham, 'Boom and Bust in Australian Screen Policy: 10BA, the Film Finance Corporation, and Hollywood's "Race to the Bottom"', *Media International Australia*, 2010.

20   Karen McGuinness, 'I Want to Be in the Movies!', *SMH*, 9 February 1991.

21   Rebecca Ascher-Walsh, 'Sneak peak [sic] at "Batman Forever"', *Entertainment Weekly*, 10 March 1995.

22   Tom Junod, 'A Bridge, a Bed, a Bar, and A Real Ozzie Gull', *Esquire*, vol. 132, no. 2, 1 August 1999. Junod overegged it when he went with the non-sequitur: 'There was nothing Nicole Kidman wouldn't do in *To Die For*, and that, according to my theory, is not only what made her "American" performances sexier than her "Australian" ones but also what makes America a much sexier country than Australia, despite the Australian advantage in marsupials'.

23   Ella Taylor, 'To Die For', *LA Weekly*, 12 October 1995.

24   Mark Singer, 'Dealmaker', the *New Yorker*, 11 January 1982.

25   Phillip McCarthy, 'Cruising Solo', *SMH*, 27 November 1993.

26   Lynden Barber, 'Playing it Low-Key', *SMH*, 3 August 1993.

27   Brett Thomas, 'Kidman Role Crisis', *SMH*, 13 October 1996.

28   Charles Britton, '"Portrait" Nice to Look at but Proves Uninvolving', the *News-Pilot*, 24 December 1996.

29   Katherine Monk, 'A Year in Film', the *Vancouver Sun*, 28 December 2001.

30   Lesley Abravanel, 'No Time for Glamour in Miami', the *Miami Herald*, 1 February 2002. Abravanel seemed to particularly have it out for Kidman, using the ice queen tag at least four times from 2002 to 2004.

31   Michael Herr, *Kubrick*, Grove Press, 2000, p. 3.

32   Robert P Kolker and Nathan Abrams, *Eyes Wide Shut: Stanley Kubrick and the Making of His Final Film*, Oxford University Press, 2019, p. 68.

33   David Mikics, *Stanley Kubrick*, Yale University Press, 2020, pp. 188–189.

34   Tony Squires, 'Picture of Calm', *SMH*, 19 May 1989.

35   Lynden Barber, 'Romance with More Than a Touch of the Blarney', *SMH*, 2 June 1992.

36   Steve Cannane, *Fair Game: The Incredible Untold Story of Scientology in Australia*, HarperCollins, 2016, p. 175.

37 Bilge Ebiri, 'An Oral History of an Orgy', *Vulture*, 27 June 2019.

38 Lucy Ellis and Bryony Sutherland, *Nicole Kidman: The Biography*, p. 275.

39 *SMH* staff, 'John Howard dubs Cate Blanchett's celebrated Gough Whitlam speech "outrageous"', *SMH*, 8 December 2014.

40 Tony Squires, 'Strictly Baz', *SMH*, 27 June 1992.

41 Baz Luhrmann, 'Leading Men', *Vogue Australia*, January 1994.

42 Don Watson, *Recollections of a Bleeding Heart*, Vintage Books, 2002, p. 431.

43 Pam Cook, *Nicole Kidman*, Palgrave Macmillan/British Film Institute, 2012, p. 106.

44 Paolo Totaro and Malcolm Knox, 'Stars Enlisted by Fox', *SMH*, 10 November 2022.

45 Don Watson, *Recollections of a Bleeding Heart*, p. 708.

46 Frank Walker and John Synnott, 'Stage Set for Epic Fight', *SMH*, 20 November 1994.

47 Margie Blok, 'The Road to Rupertworld', *SMH*, 20 July 2000.

48 Claude Brodesser-Akner, 'Rupert Murdoch, "the Man Who Owns the News" ... and a Lot of Hollywood', *KCRW*, 23 February 2009.

49 J. Hoberman, *Film After Film: Or, What Became of 21st Century Cinema?*, Verso, 2012, p. 28.

50 Seth Schiesel, 'A Nation Challenged: FBI warning; Movie Studios Possible Target of Terrorists', *NYT*, 21 September 2001.

51 J. Hoberman, *Film After Film: Or, What Became of 21st Century Cinema?*, Verso, 2012, p. 29.

52 Bernard O'Riordan, 'How Bin Laden Put the Word Out: Get Russell Crowe', the *Guardian*, 9 March 2005.

53 Dana Stevens, 'We Need More Weird Movie Stars', *Slate*, 19 February 2009.

54 Baz Luhrmann, 'How We Made the Epic Oz', the *Guardian*, 2 November 2008.

55 Marcia Langton, 'Faraway Downs Fantasy Resonates Close to Home', *SMH*, 23 November 2008.

56 Germaine Greer, 'Once Upon a Time in a Land Far, Far Away', the *Guardian*, 16 December 2008.

57 Marcia Langton, 'Why Greer Is Wrong on *Australia*', *SMH*, 23 December 2008.

58 Marcia Langton, '*Well, I heard it on the radio and saw it on the television ...*' *An Essay for the Australian Film Commission on the Politics and Aesthetics of Filmmaking by and About Aboriginal People and Things*, Australian Film Commission, 1993.

59 Maria Nugent, '"Every Right to Be There": Cinema Spaces and Racial Politics in Baz Luhrmann's "Australia"', *Australian Humanities Review*, iss. 51, November 2011.

60 Lori Fradkin, 'Nicole Kidman on *Australia*: "I Can't Look at This Movie and Be Proud"', *Vulture*, 9 January 2009.

NOTES

Epilogue: Westward Expansion

1   Nicole Sperling, 'Tom Hanks Says He Has Coronavirus', *NYT*, 12 March 2020.

2   Hedda Hopper, 'Hedda Hopper's Hollywood', *LAT*, 9 October 1942.

3   RS Benedict, 'Everyone Is Beautiful and No One Is Horny', *Blood Knife*, 14 February 2021.

4   Robert Moran, '"I'm not doing it unless it shoots here": Chris Hemsworth Brings Hollywood Home', *SMH*, 16 June 2022.

5   Staff writers and AAP, 'Julie Bishop's $1.2m Expenses Questioned Including a Trip to the *Thor: Ragnarok* Australian Premiere', the *West Australian*, 23 October 2017.

6   Ben Widdicombe, 'Chris Hemsworth Is the New Face of Australia', *NYT*, 27 January 2016.

7   Steve Dow, 'What's wrong with Australian cinema?', the *Guardian*, 26 October 2014 and Karl Quinn, 'Why won't we watch Australian films?', *SMH*, (also) 26 October 2014.

8   Paul Keating, 'Commonwealth Cultural Policy Launch' speech, 18 October 1994.

9   Baz Luhrmann, 'If This Was a Movie, There'd Be No Oscar', *SMH*, 5 November 1999.

10   Brook Turner, 'How Baz Luhrmann aims to make Australia the new Hollywood', *Australian Financial Review*, 19 August 2021.

11   Claudia Jambor, 'Russell Crowe's plans for major Coffs Harbour film studio taking shape in regional NSW', *ABC News*, 6 March 2023.

12   Jared Richards, '*Here Out West* Is Redefining the Australian Story', *Junkee*, 4 November 2021.

13   SGS Economics & Planning, 'Mapping Arts and Culture in Western Sydney', May 2018.

14   Isabella Kwai, 'Asian-Australian Actors, Overlooked at Home, Flourish in Hollywood', *NYT*, 9 January 2019.

15   Debbie Zhou, 'These actors are doing huge things in Hollywood. So why isn't Australia celebrating them?', the *Guardian*, 7 February 2019.

SELECT FILMOGRAPHY

In writing this book, I assigned myself the task of watching every film which starred an actor I was profiling. This meant more than 50 films for Errol Flynn and close to 60 for Nicole Kidman, who, as of writing, shows no signs of slowing down. This also led to some increasingly compulsive viewing behaviour during the years of research (according to the Letterboxd app – an incredibly useful tool for researching this book – I watched 325 films in 2020, 433 in 2021, then 473 in 2022).

It made sense then to offer up a select filmography, one in which I have picked a handful of films for each actor. Please note that these selections do not necessarily indicate the actor's best work – quite the opposite in a few cases – but rather, they seem to me to be the best representation of their careers and lives, as I have written about them, and might make reading this group biography richer having watched them.

Note: if you're averse to watching one of my favourite genres of film – the 'bad yet interesting' movie – I've put an asterisk against the ones to avoid. Double asterisks denotes 'bad yet interesting yet could be facist agitprop', meaning they are of note, watchable, but doubly avoidable.

SELECT FILMOGRAPHY

Russell Crowe
L.A. Confidential, directed by Curtis Hanson, 1997

Errol Flynn
In the Wake of the Bounty, directed by Charles Chauvel, 1933*
Captain Blood, directed by Michael Curtiz, 1935
The Adventures of Robin Hood, directed by Michael Curtiz, 1938
Dodge City, directed by Michael Curtiz, 1939
Santa Fe Trail, directed by Michael Curtiz, 1940**
They Died with Their Boots On, directed by Raoul Walsh, 1941
Gentleman Jim, directed by Raoul Walsh, 1942

Judith Anderson
Rebecca, directed by Alfred Hitchcock, 1940
Edge of Darkness, directed by Lewis Milestone, 1943
Pursued, directed by Raoul Walsh, 1947
The Furies, directed by Anthony Mann, 1950

George Beranger (alias André de Beranger)
The Birth of a Nation, directed by DW Griffith, 1915**
So This Is Paris, directed by Ernst Lubitsch, 1926

Peter Finch
Indonesia Calling, directed by Joris Ivens, 1946
Elephant Walk, directed by William Dieterle, 1954*
Passage Home, directed by Roy Ward Baker, 1955
The Shiralee, directed by Leslie Norman, 1957
The Legend of Lylah Clare, directed by Robert Aldrich, 1968*
Sunday Bloody Sunday, directed by John Schlesinger, 1971
Network, directed by Sidney Lumet, 1976

CAST MATES

Diane Cilento
Hombre, directed by Martin Ritt, 1967
The Wicker Man, directed by Robin Hardy, 1973

David Gulpilil AM
Walkabout, directed by Nicolas Roeg, 1971
Mad Dog Morgan, directed by Philippe Mora, 1976
The Right Stuff, directed by Philip Kaufman, 1983
Until the End of the World, directed by Wim Wenders, 1991
Gulpilil: One Red Blood, directed by Darlene Johnson, 2002
The Tracker, directed by Rolf de Heer, 2002
Crocodile Dreaming, directed by Darlene Johnson, 2007
Charlie's Country, directed by Rolf de Heer, 2013

Paul Hogan
Crocodile Dundee, directed by Peter Faiman, 1986*

Brian Syron
Backlash, directed by Bill Bennett, 1986*
Jindalee Lady, directed by Brian Syron, 1992

Nicole Kidman
Dead Calm, directed Phillip Noyce, 1989
Days of Thunder, directed by Tony Scott, 1990
To Die For, directed by Gus Van Sant, 1995
The Portrait of a Lady, directed by Jane Campion, 1996
Eyes Wide Shut, directed by Stanley Kubrick, 1999
Moulin Rouge!, directed by Baz Luhrmann, 2001
Birth, directed by Jonathan Glazer, 2004
Australia, directed by Baz Luhrmann, 2008
Stoker, directed by Park Chan-wook, 2013

SELECT FILMOGRAPHY

Cate Blanchett
The Aviator, directed by Martin Scorsese, 2004
I'm Not There, directed by Todd Haynes, 2007

Chris Hemsworth
Red Dawn, directed by Dan Bradley, 2012**
Blackhat, directed by Michael Mann, 2015

Geraldine Viswanathan
Big Bad World, directed by Catherine Kelleher, 2015
Blockers, directed by Kay Cannon, 2018
Bad Education, directed by Cory Finley, 2019

Arka Das
Here Out West, directed by Leah Purcell, Ana Kokkinos,
　　Fadia Abboud, Julie Kalceff and Lucy Gaffy, 2021

INDEX

20th Century-Fox (20th Century Fox after 1985, 20th Century Studios after 2020) 16, 60, 86, 86, 117, 124, 143–44, 146, 242–43, 247, 258, 264, 270
20th Century Pictures 20, 64, 242
3.10 to Yuma 6

A Girl's Own Story 204
A Midsummer Night's Dream 236
A Streetcar Named Desire 103–104, 235
A Time to Kill 200
A Town Like Alice 118–19, 123, 206
Aadland, Beverly 70, 72, 115
Abbott, Tony 267–68, 272
Abrams, JJ 265
Academy Awards *see also* Oscars 7, 42, 58, 61, 67, 76, 85, 94, 110, 113, 136, 225, 226, 244, 248
Adler, Stella 182, 185
Adventures of Don Juan 13, 18
Agee, James 55–56
Ailes, Roger 223, 258
Albanese, Anthony 9
Aldrich, Robert 115, 125
Almost an Angel 166
Altman, Robert 214, 247, 261
Anderson, Judith **57–62**, 118
Ann-Margret 221
Apocalypse Now 2

Armstrong, Gillian 97, 162, 178, 208, 234, 242
Asher, Irving 29, 102
Australia 250–58
Australian Labor Party 21, 90, 148, 161–62, 202, 236, 241, 264

Babe 228
Back to the Future 271
Backlash 187
Bail, Murray 4
Bana, Eric 166
Bandilil, Dick 141–44, 184
Bangkok Hilton 211, 259
Barrymore, Diana 66
Barrymore, Drew 66
Barrymore, John 65–66, 100
Barrymore, John Jnr 285
Barrymore, Lionel 35
Batman Forever 220–21
Baumbach, Noah 77
Baz Luhrmann 237–45, 250–60
Beatty, Warren 9, 131, 136, 182
Bennett, Bill 187
Beranger, George 35–36
Beresford, Bruce 148, 162, 208
Besant, Annie 78, 80
Bhattacharya, Bina 261–62, 277–78
Big Little Lies 259
Billy Bathgate 220
Billy West and Lightning Thunderboy 177–80, 191, 197

INDEX

bin Laden, Osama 247
Birth 249
Bishop, Julie 268–69
Bitter Springs 152
Blanchett, Cate **234–37**, 248, 257
Blockers 276
Blood Money 60–61
BMX Bandits 206–208, 229
Bogart, Humphrey 43–44, 59
Bogdanovich, Peter 73, 120, 182, 184
Bombshell 223, 258, 270
Bonnie and Clyde 131
Born on the Fourth of July 216
Bowie, David 141
Boy Erased 251
Boyd, Russell 158
Brando, Marlon 1–2, 9, 17, 92, 102, 105–106, 124–25, 144
Brown, Bryan 253
Bush Christmas 91, 206
Bush, George W 248–49

Campion, Jane 204–205, 225–26, 234, 259
Capote, Truman 17–18
Captain Blood 31, 35–36, 42, 71
Carey, Peter 169, 234
Carlson, Gretchen 223
Casey, Maryrose 152, 170
Castro, Fidel 67–69
Cave, Nick 195
Charlotte Gray 234
Chauvel, Charles 22, 26–28, 30, 69–70, 83, 87, 117, 168, 191, 212
Chayefsky, Paddy 131–33, 135
Christian, Fletcher 22–23, 31, 124, 231
Christie, Julie 127–28, 136
Cilento, Diane **107–114**, 120
Cinderella Man 5
Clean Straw for Nothing 96–97
Cleopatra 124–25
Clift, Charmian 96–97

Clooney, George 228
Clune, Frank 72, 74
Cohn, Harry 89–90
Cohn, Sam 214, 223–24
Colbert, Claudette 252
Cold Mountain 235
Collins, Diane 11
Columbia Pictures 87, 89
Come and Say G'day tourism campaign 157, 161, 165, 254, 269
Connery, Sean 110–114, 120
Coppola, Francis Ford 2, 210, 243
Cornell, John 161
Crocodile Dreaming 193–94
Crocodile Dundee 154–58, 160–63, 166–67, 169, 171–73, 177, 179, 181, 193, 214, 254, 271
Crocodile Dundee II 161, 163, 165, 175
Crocodile Dundee in Los Angeles 165
Crowe, Russell **1–13**, 17–19, 165, 245, 247, 251–52, 257, 273–75
Crowther, Bosley 47, 87, 105
Cruise, Tom 214–17, 220, 224, 226–27, 229–30, 232–34, 237, 244–46, 252
Cuban Rebel Girls 69–70
Curtiz, Michael 32, 36–37, 42, 46, 52

Dad and Dave Come to Town 84
Dallas Buyers Club 200
Damita, Lili 30–31, 40, 42, 70
Damon, Matt 263
Daniels, Lee 204
Dark Age 153
Darling 128–29
Das, Arka 261, 275–76
Davis, Bette 44–45, 65
Davis, Jack 187
Davis, Judy 205, 232, 239
Davis, Miles 195
Day-Lewis, Daniel 250
Days of Abandonment 263

CAST MATES

Days of Thunder 215–17, 220, 230, 236
de Havilland, Olivia 17, 45, 47, 61
de Heer, Rolf 172, 194–98
De Niro, Robert 182, 194, 232
Deacon, Desley 60, 62
Dead Calm 212, 214, 232
Dean, James 92, 150
Deane, Sydney 35
DeMille, Cecil B 35, 59
Desperate Journey 51, 54–56
DiCaprio, Leonardo 2, 243, 251
Dingo 195
Dingo, Ernie 170
Disney Studios 14, 115, 258, 264, 269, 274–75
Disney, Walt 168
Dive Bomber 52
Djigirr, Peter 197
Djulibing, Frances 194
Dodd, Steve 152
Dodge City 37, 52, 150
Dog Day Afternoon 134
Dogville 249
Don't Bet on Blondes 35–36
Donat, Robert 31
Douglas, Michael 265
Dr No 110
Dunaway, Faye 131, 135–37
Dundy, Elaine 83, 134
Dunne, Griffin 228

Ealing Studios 116, 119, 125
Eastwood, Clint 166, 195
Easy Rider 150
Eddington, Nora 70, 72–74
Eder, Richard 167
Edge of Darkness 36, 118
Efron, Zac 204, 263
Ekberg, Anita 250
Elephant Walk 102–107, 115, 124
Elizabeth 235
Elvis 258, 262, 273
Emerald City 217

Eureka Stockade 116–17
Eyes Wide Shut 204, 230–32, 234

Faiman, Peter 158
Fairbanks, Douglas 28
Falconer, Delia 7
Fantastic Four 147
Fantastic Four: Rise of the Silver Surfer 147
Far and Away 220, 230, 232
Far From the Madding Crowd 127
Farber, Manny 33
Faulkner, Trader 134
Fellini, Federico 224, 250
Finch, Eletha 77, 128
Finch, George Ingle 78, 120
Finch, Laura 78–80
Finch, Peter 12, **76–137**, 138, 142, 202, 206, 215
First Blood 209
Flirting 227
Flynn, Errol 12–13, **14–75**, 81, 102, 110, 114–15, 118, 150, 264–65
Foley, Gary 139, 182
Fonda, Henry 132
Fonda, Jane 126, 270
Ford, Harrison 208
Ford, John 61, 154
Forty Little Mothers 60
Fraser, Malcolm 122
From Sand to Celluloid 193
Full Metal Jacket 228

Gallipoli 162, 242
Gentleman Jim 33
Ghost 166, 214
Gibson, Mel 97, 205, 208, 232
Gladiator 6–8, 13, 247
Goldstone 193
Gone With the Wind 45, 61, 94, 102, 253, 255
Gorton, John 20, 42, 147–48
Gray, Eve 29
Greenberg 77

300

INDEX

Greer, Germaine 255–56
Griffith, DW 32, 35
Guess Who's Coming to Dinner in Arnhem Land? 174–75, 256
Gulpilil, David 12, **138–198**, 206, 253, 255, 256
Gulpilil: One Red Blood 193

Hackman, Gene 130
Hall, Ken G 23, 83–87, 117, 168, 211
Hamlet 94
Hanks, Tom 262
Hansen, Betty 54–57
Hanson, Curtis 5
Hawke, Bob 161–64, 175, 188, 219, 236, 271
Hawks, Howard 197, 254
Haywood, Chris 217–18
Hearst, William Randolph 54, 67, 143
Heat 194
Heaven Can Wait 136
Hemingway, Ernest 64
Hemsworth, Chris 264–270, 273, 275
Hepburn, Audrey 123
Hepburn, Katharine 74, 235
Here Out West 261, 274–77
Higham, Charles 73–74
Hitchcock, Alfred 61–62, 88, 111, 113, 194, 227
Hoberman, J. 1, 6, 10–11, 246–249
Hoffman, Dustin 129
Hogan, Paul 153, **154–68**, 169–72, 174–75, 180, 214, 240, 254, 269
Hollywood Down Under 11
Holt, Harold 147
Hombre 111
Home & Away 265
Home Alone 2: Lost in New York 273
Hong, Euny 160
Hoover, J Edgar 52
Hopper, Dennis 150–51

Hopper, Hedda 265
Howard, John 218–19, 236, 255, 271–72
Hubbard, L Ron 233
Hughes, Billy 83, 90
Hughes, Howard 235
Hunter, Bill 253

I Thank a Fool 113
In Like Flynn 50
In the Cool of the Day 126, 134
In the Wake of the Bounty 22, 40, 70
Indonesia Calling 86

Jackman, Hugh 165, 251–52, 257–58
Jagger, Mick 141, 150
James, Clive 7
Jedda 26, 152, 191
Jindalee Lady 187–92
Johnson, Darlene 193–95
Johnston, George 96–97
Jungle Patrol 86
Junod, Tom 222, 231

Kangaroo 117–18
Kauffmann, Stanley 195
Kaufman, Philip 153, 176
Kay, Sydney John 91–95
Keating, Paul 164, 188, 218–19, 240–42, 270–71
Keaton, Diane 208
Kellaway, Cecil 84
Kelleher, Catherine 276
Keneally, Thomas 202, 241
Kennedy Miller 209–213, 218, 259
Kicking Down the Doors: A History of First Nations Films 1968–1993 180, 185, 187, 192
Kidman, Nicole 12, **199–260**
Kokoda Front Line! 85
Korda, Alexander 40, 109
Kotcheff, Ted 145, 209
Kubrick, Stanley 70, 228–31, 234, 244–45

CAST MATES

Kunoth-Monks, Rosalie 152
Kwai, Isabella 275

L.A. Confidential 5–6, 50
La Dolce Vita 224, 250
Lady for a Day 58
Lake, Veronica 221
Langton, Marcia 140, 255–56
Lanthimos, Yorgos 204
Lawrence of Arabia 251
Lawson, Sylvia 145
Lean, David 98, 251
Leder, Mimi 228
Ledger, Heath 77, 257
Legend 215
Leigh, Vivien 93–95, 102–106, 115, 124, 235
Leimbach, Bill 176–80
Lewis, Tom E 194
Lightning Jack 180
Lilacs in the Spring 110
Lolita 70
Looney Tunes 238
Lorenzo's Oil 232
Lost Horizon 130
Lubitsch, Ernst 35
Lucas, George 210, 243
Lumet, Sidney 76, 112, 133–35, 214

Mad As Hell 135
Mad Dog Morgan 149–51, 170–71
Mad Max 37, 209, 268
Mad Max 2 209
Malice 220
Man of Steel 1
Mann, Michael 194, 268
Marnie 111
Martin, Catherine 238, 243
Marvel 16, 253, 264–66, 269, 274–75
Marx, Jack 8–9
Massey, Raymond 47
McConaughey, Matthew 200–202
McGregor, Ewan 244–45

McKenzie, Catriona 193
McClelland, Doug 149
McMahon, Billy 147
McMahon, Julian 147
Menzies, Robert 116, 272
Merritt, Robert J 184
MGM 22, 30, 40, 63, 86, 133, 242, 266
Midnight Cowboy 129
Milestone, Lewis 57, 118
Milius, John 266
Miller, George 37, 209–213, 228, 232, 238, 243
Mission Impossible 2 15, 244
Moffatt, Tracey 188, 191
Monroe, Marilyn 16–18, 194
Montana 51
Moore, Michael 248–49
Moore, Roger 106
Moorhouse, Jocelyn 4
Mora, Philippe 150–51, 171
Moulin Rouge (1952) 109
Moulin Rouge! 244–46, 250, 272
Mr Chedworth Steps Out 84
Mrs Soffel 208
Mulan 275
Murder at Monte Carlo 28–29, 102
Murdoch, Henry 152
Murdoch, James 270
Murdoch, Lachlan 245
Murdoch, Rupert 15–17, 211, 223, 233, 237, 241–43, 258, 264, 270
Muriel's Wedding 219, 271
Murphy, Eddie 165
My Brilliant Career 148, 162, 208
My Forgotten Man 50
My Life 220
My Name is Gulpilil 198
My Wicked, Wicked Ways 37, 75
Mystery Road 192–93
Mystery, Alaska 5

Naked Under Capricorn 186
Ned Kelly 150

INDEX

Neighbours 265, 278
Neill, Sam 213
Netflix 259
Network 76, 123, 131–37, 222
Never Say Goodbye 43
Newman, Paul 111, 132, 215
Newsfront 211
Night Cries 191
Niland, D'Arcy 119–20
Nine 250
Nine Perfect Strangers 259
Niven, David 18, 25, 30, 104
Nixon, Richard 161, 223
Northern Pursuit 36
Noyce, Phillip 178, 195, 209–14
Nugent, Dr Maria 256

Oberon, Merle 39–41, 40
Objective, Burma! 53
Oliver, John 5
Olivier, Laurence 45, 61, 93–104, 115
On Our Selection 83–84
Onus, Bill 168
Oscar and Lucinda 234
Oscars *see also* Academy Awards 85, 94, 128, 216, 238, 248
Othello 99–102

Pacino, Al 134, 194
Packer, James 245–46
Packer, Kerry 161
Page, Stephen 192
Pang, Chris 276
Paper Moon 120
Paramount Pictures 15–16, 102–107, 159, 165, 214–16, 242, 263
Park, Ruth 84, 120
Passage Home 108–109, 114
Patel, Dev 263
Pearce, Craig 244
Pearce, Guy 6, 50
Penn, Arthur 131
Performance 141

Perkins, Charles 183
Pfeiffer, Michelle 221
Phillips, AA 271
Picnic at Hanging Rock 148, 152
Poitier, Sidney 174
Portman, Natalie 263
Powell, Michael and Pressburger, Emeric 98, 127
Practical Magic 228
Proof 4–5
Psycho 63

Rabbit-Proof Fence 178, 195
Raid on Entebbe 136
Randell, Ron 88–89
Rank Organisation 107–108, 127, 138, 206
Reagan, Ronald 45–48, 51, 54, 59, 162–63, 215, 265, 273
Rebecca 60–62
Red Curtain Trilogy 241, 250
Red Dawn 265–66
Red River 154, 197, 254
Reeves, Keanu 15
Risky Business 215
River of No Return 194
RKO Pictures 84
Robbery Under Arms 121–22, 206
Robbie, Margot 165, 266
Robin Hood (2010) 6, 8
Robson, May 58
Rocky 76
Roeg, Nicolas 138, 141–42, 145–46
Romeo and Juliet 102, 243
Romper Stomper 4
Roosevelt, Franklin D 42, 52
Rudd, Kevin 236, 255

Santa Fe Trail 46–48
Satellite Boy 193
Satterlee, Peggy 54–57
Saturday Night Fever 242
Schlesinger, John 127–130, 134
Schumacher, Joel 200, 220–21

CAST MATES

Scorsese, Martin 76, 235, 266
Scott, Ridley 6, 8, 215
Scott, Tony 215–16
Selznick, David O 44, 46, 61
Sen, Ivan 192–93
Simpson, Don 215–16
Sixel, Margaret 238
Smithy 88–90, 117
So This is Paris 35
Spencer, Danielle 2
Spielberg, Steven 53, 163, 166
Spring Awakening 203, 225
Stallone, Sylvester 76
Stanislavski, Konstantin 92, 182–83
Star Trek 265
Star Wars 242, 245, 263
Stevens, Dana 252
Stewart, Jimmy 132
Stigwood, Robert 242
Stolen Generations 193
Storm Boy 152–53, 206
Strasberg, Lee 151, 182
Stratton, David 188
Streisand, Barbra 184
Strictly Ballroom 239–40, 243, 250, 271, 273
Sunday Bloody Sunday 123, 129, 142, 277
Sunset Boulevard 36, 136
Superman 1, 265
Syme, Rachel 200
Syron, Brian 153, **180–192**, 277
Syron, Liza-Mare 152, 170

Taxi Driver 76
Taylor, Elizabeth 104–105, 124
Ten Canoes 197
Tender Mercies 162, 208
That Forsyte Woman 63
The Adventures of Priscilla, Queen of the Desert 271
The Adventures of Robin Hood 17, 43
The Aviator 235
The Battle of the River Plate 127

The Big Boodle 67
The Birth of a Nation 35, 48
The Bit Part 217
The Blue Lightning 187
The Cake Man 184
The Case of the Curious Bride 32
The Chant of Jimmie Blacksmith 194
The Color of Money 215
The Dark Avenger 114–15
The Dark Knight 257
The Deep 212
The Dream Life 1, 10
The Firm 229
The Flight of the Phoenix 125, 129–30
The French Connection 130
The Graduate 221
The Grapes of Wrath 61
The Great Gatsby 258
The Hill 112
The Hours 230, 248
The Island of Dr. Moreau 2
The Kangaroo Kid 117
The Last Movie 150
The Last of Robin Hood 50
The Last Wave 152–53, 167, 176, 186
The Legend of Lylah Clare 125
The Lincoln Lawyer 200
The Man From Snowy River 162, 173, 207
The Man Who Fell to Earth 141
The Matrix 15
The Mosquito Coast 208
The Moth of Moonbi 26
The Mutiny on the Bounty 22
The Nun's Story 122–23
The Others 227, 245–46
The Overlanders 116–17, 152, 168, 253
The Paperboy 204
The Paul Hogan Show 156, 158, 161
The Peacemaker 228
The Perfect Specimen 58
The Portrait of a Lady 225–26

INDEX

The Private Life of Henry VIII 40
The Private Lives of Elizabeth and Essex 44–45
The Proposition 195
The Rats of Tobruk 87
The Red Tent 113, 130
The Right Stuff 153, 176
The Roots of Heaven 66
The Sheik 20
The Shiralee 119–20
The Siege of Pinchgut 125
The Simpsons 159, 164
The Sins of Rachel Cade 106, 123
The Sisters 44, 65
The Spoilers 20
The Story of the Kelly Gang 10
The Strange Love of Martha Ivers 62
The Sun Also Rises 64–65, 67
The Sundowners 145–46
The Thief of Baghdad 28
The Tonight Show Starring Johnny Carson 77
The Tracker 195–98
The Trials of Oscar Wilde 123
The Undoing 259
The Wicker Man 113
The Witches of Eastwick 232
The Wizard of Oz 53, 253
The Wolf of Wall Street 266
The Wooden Horse 119
They Died with Their Boots On 46, 55
Thompson, Jack 253
Thomson, David 53, 217
Thor series 264, 268–69, 275
Thornton, Warwick 193
Three Men and a Baby 166
Tildesley, Beatrice 24
Titanic 15–16
To Die For 221–23, 227
Tom Jones 110, 113
Tomorrow, When the War Began 266, 276
Too Much, Too Soon 66–67

Top Gun 159, 215–16
Top of the Lake 259
Train of Events 98, 107
Travers, Peter 153
Travolta, John 176, 233
Trenchard-Smith, Brian 206
True Detective 200
Trump, Donald 273
Trump, Ivanka 258
Tudawali, Robert 152
Turkey Shoot 206
Turnbull, Malcolm 272
Turner, Yolande 122

Ullmann, Liv 76
Uncertain Glory 36
Under Capricorn 62
Unforgiven 195
Universal Pictures 15, 30, 35
Until the End of the World 169–70

Valenti, Jack 149
Valentino, Rudolph 20
Van Sant, Gus 220–22
Vertigo 63, 88, 125
Vietnam 211, 213
Virginia City 43
Virtuosity 5
Viswanathan, Geraldine 276–77
von Trier, Lars 204, 259

Wake in Fright 145–46, 201, 209
Walkabout 138–146, 150, 167, 176–77, 186, 253
Walkabout to Hollywood 166, 176–79
Wallis, Hal 29
Walsh, Raoul 28, 32, 46, 53, 66
Walters, Brandon 254
Warner Bros 15, 17, 28–31, 38–40, 43–45, 47, 52, 54–55, 57, 59, 63, 66, 68, 102, 106, 145–46, 184, 213, 229–30
Warner, Jack 29, 33, 37, 75, 265
Warshow, Robert 196

CAST MATES

Washington, Denzel 5
Watson, Don 241–42
Watt, Harry 117, 168
Watts, Naomi 252
Wayne, John 20, 139, 154, 166, 196, 254
Weaving, Hugo 4
Weinstein, Harvey 55, 89, 248
Weir, Peter 149, 158, 186, 208, 242
Welles, Orson 73, 91, 95, 99–102, 115, 212
Wenders, Wim 169–70
What's Up, Doc? 184, 221
White, Patrick 8, 91, 122

Whitlam, Gough 147–49, 161–62, 184–85, 236
William Shakespeare's Romeo + Juliet 243, 250
Wilson, Jake 170
Windom's Way 122
Windrider 207–208, 217
Winter of Our Dreams 239
Woolf, Virginia 248–49

Zanuck, Darryl F 60, 64,
Zhou, Debbie 276
Zinnemann, Fred 122, 145